PERSONS AND MASKS OF THE LAW

John T. Noonan, Jr.

PERSONS
AND MASKS
OF THE LAW

Cardozo, Holmes,
Jefferson, and Wythe
as Makers of the Masks

Farrar, Straus and Giroux   *New York*

Copyright © 1976 by John T. Noonan, Jr.
All rights reserved
First printing, 1976
Printed in the United States of America
Published simultaneously in Canada by McGraw-Hill Ryerson Ltd., Toronto
Designed by Paula Wiener

Library of Congress Cataloging in Publication Data

Noonan, John Thomas.
  Persons and masks of the law.

  Includes index.
    1. Law—United States.   2. Jurisprudence.
  3. Lawyers—United States.   I. Title.
  KF380.N6   340.1   75-30991

To Mary Lee

Foreword

IN OCTOBER 1971 I was asked by Louis Jaffe on behalf of the faculty of the Harvard Law School to give the Oliver Wendell Holmes, Jr., Lectures in the spring of 1972. I had just completed a long study of the historical development of a legal institution, and it seemed to me that such an occasion, calling for a larger view of the law than that taken when immersed in examination of a particular subject, afforded opportunity for critical reflection on what I had been doing—to look at the relation of history to law. The lectures were given as "The Alliance of Law and History," a title accurately conveying my sense of the insecure but valuable bond between the two disciplines.

As I reached what seemed to me the heart of law's dependence on history, however, I became increasingly conscious of the central place of the human person in any account of law. I also became increasingly conscious of the neglect of the person by legal casebooks, legal histories, and treatises of jurisprudence. Only in the response of person to person, so it seemed to me, did history have a significance to law. Neglect of persons, it appeared, had led to the worst sins for which American lawyers were accountable.

My audience, appropriately for lectures focused on personal response, was composed mostly of friends; and their receptivity could have been attributed as fairly to personal benevolence as to critical conviction. Giles Constable did observe to me that "some of *them* (*scilicet,* law-school faculty) looked as though their feathers had been ruffled in unaccustomed ways," and circulating the text in the academic world, I found my readers divided. Humanists—historians, sociologists, and lawyers aware that law is not a closed system—reacted warmly to the central theme. Professionals—if the classification is not too harsh for those who accept the legal system on its own terms—replied with frigid politeness or clear indifference to my contentions. Plainly I had failed to convince the latter group of the seriousness of the suppression of persons in legal education, history, and philosophy.

The lectures were too long for an article, too short for the most presumptuous of short books; and it is, in any event, a grave mistake to suppose that words uttered orally to a particular audience are the right words in a different medium for a more general public (David Daube is the only exception to this rule). Hence, I undertook the revision of the lectures, with the view now that my principal subject was the place of the person in the understanding of law and with the purpose of bringing at least some "professionals" into the camp of the "humanists." In doing so, I have found myself carrying out—not as fully as I should like, but illustratively—the program I had called for in the lectures, relating the history of legal doctrine to the persons who shaped it. Lawyers such as Thomas Jefferson and Moorfield Storey, judges such as George Wythe and Benjamin Cardozo, litigants such as the American Banana Company and Helen Palsgraf have entered my story as they advocate legal rules, announce legal rules, or afford occasion for legal rules to be applied.

The persona of an author is different from the masks of the law. Yet there is one form of mask used in writing on jurisprudence as bad as any of the law's. I mean that adopted by professors who, attributing universality and cosmic rightness to their own views, put them forward as the teaching of

Science, History, or The Law. It would be agreeable to believe that such personification was merely modesty; but the vigor with which personal assertions are then said to be the teaching of the Personified Discipline makes modesty an unlikely motive. It would be comfortable to suppose that this style—''the Science of Law teaches'' style—was a mere defect of the German language or a harmless affectation of German academic discourse; but the failing is far more universal.

Here at any rate is not what Jurisprudence teaches but what a forty-eight-year-old American lawyer, with some experience in teaching law, serving bureaucracies, arguing cases, drafting legislation, and writing legal history, thinks to be true. For twenty years I have seen, I have touched, I have lived in the universe of rules and persons that I analyze.

I cannot understand those who write on law asking abstractly, ''What is law?'' How can that question be answered without asking another—''Why do you want to know?'' The definition of law depends on the purpose of the definer. Small wonder that jurisprudence is so neglected a subject in American law schools, when so many of those who write about jurisprudential matters analyze rules abstractly, without reference to their aim, and argue about each other's definitions. My purpose as I implicitly explore the question here is to determine the matter on which legal history, legal philosophy, and legal education should focus if lawyers are to act toward others as to themselves.

At least since twelfth-century Bologna, law has been taught by the presentations to students of imaginary situations, ''hypotheticals,'' in which imaginary characters get into the legal difficulties the teacher wants to explore—Gratian's *Harmony of Unharmonious Canons* is as rich as any modern teacher's notebook in such cases where depersonalized actors illustrate the issues. The method is an excellent one for exploring doctrinal alternatives with strict impartiality.

''Are you pro plaintiff,'' Austin Scott used to ask when I was a student in Procedure, ''or pro defendant?'' A *reductio ad absurdum*. Without knowing more, how could you favor the plaintiff or the defendant? Pressed to choose between them, you could only admit the choice to be indifferent. The excellence of the question was that it implied that there was no more to be known. You were in a legal universe whose rules were framed impartially for *P* and *D*, anonymous plaintiffs and defendants.

"Baby stuff," Warren Seavey would say, blowing out his cheeks, when a student in Torts answered a hypothetical by adding a further supposition to the description made by Seavey. When he had framed a question to raise an issue of doctrine, you were expected to discuss doctrine, not disturb the purity of the analysis by varying the facts. Being infinite, they could be invented by anyone. For the purposes of teaching law, the facts imagined by the professor sufficed. Entering the universe of the hypothetical, you were supposed to argue whether the rule was right or not, without rearranging the elements of the problem.

Seavey and Scott—masters of a method properly called Socratic. Like Gratian, they focused on the individual actor—"a certain man" in Gratian, *P* and *D* in their language; to that extent, their focus was on a person, but on a person illustrating a doctrine. By questioning they elicited the statement of the doctrine they themselves held for truth, and elicited it in such a way as to compel assent from their students, and elicited it as truth independent of the persons it affected. Their memory is with me as their pupil as I write on the law and reject their assumption that a neutral universe of *P*'s and *D*'s governed by rules exists.

As a law student, I saw, or thought I saw, the great advantage of legal education over the philosophical education I had just received—it dealt with cases. Seavey used to confess an inability to think if confronted by an abstract proposition—"Give me a case," he would demand. Through cases, generalizations were tested. Working with cases, I supposed, was a way of exercising and developing a sense of justice—a sense of what was due to particular individuals in a concrete situation. Law students and *a fortiori* lawyers, I imagined, had a better sense of justice than philosophers or, say, sociologists. Unlike such dealers in abstractions, the lawyers could never forget that their actions affected persons.

After twenty years' experience, I see that I was wrong. The cases are not concrete enough. The characters in them, turning into *A* or *B, P* or *D,* lose personal identity. The Prudent Man of tort law is as much an abstraction as the Steady Man of canon law. Gratian's "certain man" or "certain woman" became the Titus and Bertha of seventeenth-century moral theology—no improvement in moral education was effected. Seavey—I say it only partly in criticism—would have been a shining ornament of that golden age of casuistry. The cases must be rooted in the historical process to contribute to the moral education essential to the professional preparation of lawyers, who are to be formed less as social engineers than as the charitable creators of values.

My purpose, then, is not dissimilar from Scott's or Seavey's. Focusing on rules, they instilled in students a sense that the legal system was not the creature of individual caprice or the expression of raw power, but tradition constantly refined by reason: judges and lawmakers, professors and students were responsible for continuing that development. Their purpose, as is mine, was to increase the sense of responsibility of those who by their thought and action make the system exist. But, for me, the responsibility comes in the response to other persons; it is the greater the more one is conscious that he or she—not some imagined entity—is acting, and the more one is conscious that the action affects not a hypothetical *A* but a real Helen Palsgraf.

Legal history, legal philosophy, and legal education, or rather, the persons who are engaged in legal history, philosophy, and education, are or should be concerned with law not as a set of technical skills which may be put to any use but as a human activity affecting both those acting and those enduring their action. The analytic bent of most of those now so engaged leads them to reduce "person" to a congerie of "rights," with the highest ideal, if any is expressed, to do "justice" by enforcing the rights. Evading analytical reduction, the whole person escapes them. But it is necessary to insist that the person precedes analysis, and to seek to do justice in the narrow sense is no more a full human aspiration than such justice is the sum of human virtues.

The central problem, I think, of the legal enterprise is the relation of love to power. We can often apply force to those we do not see, but we cannot, I think, love them. Only in the response of person to person can Augustine's sublime fusion be achieved, in which justice is defined as "love serving only the one loved."

The structure of this book is simple—in the first chapter are set the themes and definitions which recur and are exemplified in concrete situations in chapters two, three, and four. The last chapter is not a summation but a reflection on the dependence of the legal enterprise on history and the focus on persons to which such dependence leads.

Throughout the composition of this work, I have been conscious of Holmes, not only because his filial piety to Harvard paid for the lectureship in his honor, or because he was the first of American legal historians, or even because I disagree with so much of what he said; but because as a man he transcends his paradoxes and Yankee epigrams. My book begins with a quotation from *The Common Law* and ends with a quotation from his extraordinary Memorial Day address, given in 1884 at Keene, New Hampshire. I trust I am not mistaken in responding to a person distinct from the masks I criticize.

I am grateful to Louis Jaffe for his committee's invitation, and to Dean Albert Sacks for his hospitality, and to O. Meredith Wilson of the Center for Advanced Studies in the Behavioral Sciences, which provided both the stimulation and the leisure for the completion of this book. I am greatly indebted for their reading of the manuscript in its present or earlier forms, and for their comments, to these friends: my associates at the Center, Martin Krieger, Robert K. Merton, and

Walter Ong, S.J.; my past colleagues at the University of Notre Dame, Joseph O'Meara, Jr., and Robert E. Rodes, Jr.; my present colleagues at the University of California, Robert N. Bellah, Natalie Davis, Sanford Kadish, Paul Mishkin, and Philip Selznick, all at Berkeley, Joe Feldman, Lester J. Mazor, and Walter O. Weyrauch, visitors at Berkeley, and George Fletcher at Los Angeles; my old law-review companion, Norman Dorsen, now at New York University; my law-school classmate Andrew L. Kaufman at Harvard Law School; and my father, John T. Noonan, who has not only read the manuscript but has for over fifty years in the practice of law in Boston given an example of justice in the sense of Augustine.

JOHN T. NOONAN, JR.

Berkeley, California
March 25, 1975

Contents

Foreword   vii

1   The Masks of the Participants   3

2   Virginian Liberators   29

3   The Overlord of American Law and the
    Sovereign of Costa Rica   65

4   The Passengers of *Palsgraf*   111

5   The Alliance of Law and History   152

Notes and References   171

Index   199

His office is dramatic no less than the office of an actor in theatrical exhibitions, they both represent others; and the object of both is to deceive. In this latter character however they differ thus: they use their art to persuade, one that he is, the other that he is not whom he personateth.

George Wythe, *Hinde v. Pendleton* (1799)

There is an element of theatre in the law, but this is not to say that it is all farce.

Mortimer R. and Sanford H. Kadish, *Discretion to Disobey* (1973)

Un des chapitres les plus instructifs d'une philosophie chrétienne de l'histoire concernerait ce qu'on peut appeler l'entrecroisement des masques et des rôles. Non seulement des rôles d'iniquité sont tenus par des masques ou des figures de justice, mais des rôles de justice sont tenus (et gâtés) par des masques d'iniquité.

Jacques Maritain, *Humanisme Intégral* (1937)

PERSONS AND MASKS OF THE LAW

The Masks of the Participants

"THE LIFE OF THE LAW," Holmes said in his most famous epigram, "has not been logic: it has been experience." With these words, written on page one of *The Common Law,* Holmes endowed impersonal rule with existence and memory, a power of assimilation, and the capacity to develop. Like a medieval lawyer transferring from the Virgin to his craft the appellation Our Lady, like a modern dean repeating to first-year students the old saw that law is a jealous mistress, Holmes made legal knowledge into an entity—an entity which acted "by the very necessity of its nature" to transmute moral standards into external or objective ones. So endowed with vitality, law was a personification.

Holmes himself supposed that "the personification of inanimate nature common to savages and children" was the reason why early law made forfeit as deodands the weapons by which death was caused. Holmes even saw the primitive attraction of personification as leading to lawyers' acceptance of feminine gender for a ship, and not only of gender but of personality, so that Chief Justice Marshall could write: "The vessel acts and speaks . . ." and a ship herself could be made the object of suit. Behind the "personifying language," he suggested, lay hidden grounds of policy which it was useful for the historian to bring into consciousness. Yet no less than savages or children, Holmes—all unconsciously it appears—imparted life to an inanimate concept. The law for him became a personification or, better said, an impersonation.

His mistake was double. By a form of misplaced concreteness, he attributed to an abstraction the action of living men and women. A scarecrow was given life. At the same time he overlooked the actual people in the process. The jar and motion of their experience was replaced by the imaginary adventures of the law.

Subjectively, Holmes as historian was plotting an evolutionary development of particular rules. He had a thesis to demonstrate on the relation of morals to the rules of law. By his personification he concealed that the synthesis reflecting the development was effected by himself. The law—rules or prediction, a mere set of statements if Holmes's own definition was attended to—was pictured as a mighty, majestic, irresistible entity, educating and transmuting itself. Holmes gave it a fictitious life.

No person itself, the law lives in persons. Rules of law are formed by human beings to shape the attitude and conduct of human beings and applied by human beings to human beings. The human beings are persons. The rules are communications uttered, comprehended, and responded to by persons. They affect attitude and conduct as communications from persons to persons. They exist as rules—not as words on paper—in the minds of persons.

The paradigm of law is trial before a court. For almost a century the chief business of American lawyers has been elsewhere. The image of the courtroom as the center of the legal process has remained. The principal participants in the paradigmatic form are the lawyers, the judge, and the litigants. Visually examined or subjectively experienced, the form emphasizes the role of persons. The speech and action of the advocates and the judge, and the testimony elicited from the witnesses, are the principal events.

Unlike the formulae of magic and of science, legal rules do not predetermine the trial's outcome. There is one exception: when all the participants have in advance agreed to the rules to be used, interpretation and application of the rules becomes a ritual, as in the standard action for divorce. The only "clear cases," where the single rule to be applied is evident, the facts undisputed, are uncontested ones—the parking-ticket or traffic-safety violation, conceded by the motorist and typically punished without trial by a forfeiture of bail at a clerk's window: no lawyer intervenes in the process.

In contested litigation, however, the rules are invoked, interpreted, invented by the professional participants. Use of the rules depends on the ability of attorneys. The better the advocate, the less likely he is to admit a disadvantageous application of a rule. If he cannot deny the existence of a rule, or if he cannot argue against its settled interpretation, he will discover the exception, or he will show how other rules converge to a different result.

The paradigm of the trial, it may be objected, supposes that the lawyers will be equal, canceling out the importance of individual ability and making the upshot turn on the true rule. The paradigm, however, sets no standard of equality between lawyers if they meet the minimum qualification of admission to the bar; still less does the paradigm require that opposing lawyers devote equal time and care to the preparation of a case. Operationally, the paradigmatic form gives an advantage to the lawyer who by his aggressiveness or his determination, his analysis of the facts or his presentation of the rules, his sense of timing or his skill in interrogation, is a better contestant than his adversary. The advantage which goes with the better advocate is bred into the marrow of the trial. The dominant place of a lawyer in a lawsuit dramatizes what is the general case. As a process, law depends on persons.

The strongest form of the paradigm is the criminal trial where the life of the defendant is at stake. Not only is it manifest there that the process depends on persons; justice is centered on giving what is due the accused. Standing alone before the court, the prisoner is the focus of our interest and our sympathy. It is no accident that in those trials which have been celebrated in literature and in the history of our consciousness—the trial of Socrates, the trial of Thomas More, the trial of Jesus—the rules were followed and yet the human judgment has always been that injustice was done, the person condemned to death was not given his due, the paradigm of justice was violated.

THE DOMINANCE OF RULES IN LEGAL STUDY

Rules, not persons, are the ordinary subject matter of legal study. Legal reasoning is by analogy or example, as the classic introduction of Edward Levi describes it; and the problem addressed is, "When will it be just to treat different cases as though they were the same?" But the cases are classified by the rules they exemplify, and judicial decisions come in the form of rules stated so as to be applicable to all similar situations. What atoms are to chemistry, such units of discourse are to the study of law. Rearrangements and permutations of them are the normal way of legal development and the normal center of legal scholarship. The cataloguing work of the digest-makers, encyclopedists, and annotators consists of their analysis and arrangement. The evaluating work of treatise writers and law reviews consists of their analysis and criticism.

Little or no attention is given to the persons in whose minds and in whose interaction the rules have lived—to the persons whose difficulties have occasioned the articulation of the rule, to the lawyers who have tried the case, to the judges who have decided it. No key reporting system is keyed to counsel. No encyclopedia is arranged in terms of judges. The prime teaching tools, the casebooks, have been composed to shed light on the life of a rule, not upon the parts of the participants in the process. Those in the classic mold, with snippets of appellate opinions arranged to display variations and contradictions of a principle, carry the indifference to the participants to the maximum.

The custom is still general, even in more modern casebooks, to give no space to the lawyers or firms who helped shape the decision. Their very names are pruned as irrelevant. Apart from Family Law, no great attention is given to the impact of the rule upon the individual lives of the litigants. Concerned with social policy, the modern casebooks reflect the play of social interests. To a very large degree, those interests are so many severed heads, detached from the persons who carried them. Such a way of study permits masks to be taken for persons.

The success of American law reviews has rested on this kind of abstract indifference. In what other learned discipline can students, one year after introduction to the methodology of the matter, evaluate successfully the work of expert practitioners? If the facts are taken as given, without respect to persons, agile minds without experience may dissect the rules by which the facts are ordered. A good law student can answer a law professor's dream of an examination question. The answer will be about *P* and *D*.

The historians of law have not provided a counterbalance to the analytical approach. They have been generally lawyers themselves, affected by professional education and outlook. Few in number, they have been isolated in schools devoted to training practitioners. They have written the life of doctrines. The best American work in legal history, that of James Willard Hurst, has been the careful investigation of the interplay between economic forces and the legal rules. Like the sociological jurisprudence of Roscoe Pound, it is by no means exclusively centered on rules: the interests of human beings are seen as affecting the results. But it is characteristic of Hurst's focus that in a book entitled *The Growth of American Law: The Law Makers,* he speaks of lawyers, legislators, and judges as "the principal agencies of law"; the individuals have become instruments. For the purpose of assessing the personal responsibility of the judges, legislators, and lawyers, this species of social history, like Pound's jurisprudence, is insufficiently attentive to persons. The classic model is still *The Common Law.*

"I shall use the history of our law," Holmes wrote on page two of his book, "so far as it is necessary to explain a conception or interpret a rule." Lawyers, litigants, and particular decision makers did not enter into his explanation or interpretation. Like "the law" in his opening metaphor, the principles had their own existence.

No litigant who had suffered an accident and no litigant who had caused one were mentioned in Holmes's account of the development of the true principle underlying the law of negligence. Holt was noticed as a Chief Justice who had affirmed as judge a rule he had argued for as counsel. With this single exception, no relation was signaled between the enunciation of a rule and the experience of the judge who enunciated it. With this single exception, counsel in the cases of trespass and negligence were unmentioned. Half a dozen English judges were named as deciding particular cases. Nothing followed from their being named. Holmes might as easily have said "the court." Of American judges, only Lemuel Shaw, Chief Justice of Massachusetts in Holmes's youth, was recognized by name. His decision in *Brown* v. *Kendall,* Holmes wrote, was not "politic" (i.e., political), for he was "a great judge" whose strength lay in "an accurate appreciation of the requirements of the community whose officer he was." Only in this instance did Holmes acknowledge that the quality of the judge affected the judge's articulation of a rule, and he did so to dispel any notion that partisan sentiments adventitious to the emergence of the true principle had determined the result.

The metaphor of the living law had the flavor of Darwinian biology. Holmes told "a story" which afforded "an instructive example of the mode in which the law has grown, without a break, from barbarism to civilization." An evolutionary model controlled his presentation of the material. Treating of torts, he sought "to *discover* whether there is any common ground at the bottom of all liability, and if so, what the ground is.'' His effort would, he said, if successful, *"reveal* the general principle of civil liability at common law.'' The italics are mine, the emphasis on revelation through history Holmes's. His principles marched to a triumphant epiphany. This false focus on the life of doctrines has scarcely changed in a century of legal history—Milsom's *Historical Founda-tions of the Common Law,* published in 1969, is witness.

THE DOMINANCE OF RULES
IN JURISPRUDENCE

Suppose a Conference on the Study and Improvement of Railroads. The first expert, a believer in fundamentals, de-clares that to understand railroads is to understand how the tracks are laid out and how they lead into each other; close study of track, section by section, as it is encountered, will lead to the perfection of the science of railroading. The sec-ond expert objects to the static emphasis of the first speaker and points out that railroading is an activity, a process. To understand it one must watch the movement of the locomo-tives; to master it is to be able to predict the direction and the time of arrival of the trains. A third sage interjects that railroads cannot be understood at all except in terms of their interconnections—to that extent, the first speaker was correct; but if Science is to proceed scientifically, one must imagine a hypothetical master plan in terms of which each real fragment of road may be comprehended and rationalized. A fourth ex-pert observes that railroads will not be properly planned in today's world unless one appreciates that railroads serve im-portant objectives of society; to plan them well one must take the stance not of a trainman but of a social engineer. A fifth, more detached speaker notes that running a railroad is essen-tially like playing croquet. There are a number of tunnels through which objects must be propelled at the direction of those who grasp the reciprocal relationship between the moving objects and the holes through which they move, so that it is of the highest importance to comprehend that a croquet ball without a wicket makes no more sense than a croquet wicket without a ball. So talking of tunnels and of track and of locomotives, and sometimes of social goods and intermittently of games and occasionally of engineers, the participants might greet with surprised stares a passenger who rose to ask if the persons riding on the trains are not to be considered within the province of railroading.

The cataclysms which have overtaken railroads neglectful of passengers are omens of what awaits the law after it has been studied in the terms proposed by John Austin and Oliver Wendell Holmes, Jr., and Hans Kelsen and Roscoe Pound, and Herbert L. A. Hart. The principal defect with the analogy is that persons are far more integrally part of the law than passengers are of railroads. The major writers on jurisprudence of the last hundred years, by and large—Jerome Frank and Lon Fuller are the preeminent exceptions—have not acknowledged that truth.

Their indifference, influencing and responding in turn to the indifference to persons in legal history and legal study, is most dramatically illustrated by their unconcern for a major function of Anglo-American law for three centuries, the creation and maintenance of a system in which human beings were regularly sold, bred, and distributed like beasts. Collective amnesia is the most benign description possible for this cruel neglect. The cases making these distributions of human beings as property are in the Reporters in which the fundamentals of Anglo-American common law are set out. The system in use today is continuous with that system of precedents, fictions, and ways of argument. In *The Common Law,* for example, Holmes calmly uses an Alabama case where Lewis, a slave, chased a white girl on a country road, stopped the chase, and was indicted for attempted rape, an offense punishable by death, as a routine illustration of the rule on criminal attempts. That the case depends on the court's view of the defendant he does not acknowledge.

Herbert L. A. Hart is unusual among jurisprudents in mentioning slavery as in any way special, and he does so in a way instructive by his failure to relate the law to the institution that the lawyers created. In his inaugural lecture at Oxford in 1953, where he brought Wittgenstein's analysis of the normative use of language into specific conjunction with the use of legal concepts, he observed, "The status of a slave is not (*pace* Austin) just a collective name for his special rights and duties: there is a sense in which these are the 'consequences' of his status: it is the sense in which the obligation to leave the wicket is a consequence of being 'out.' " The comparison with cricket was enlightening in showing how legal terms acquire meaning from an institutional background: in that respect, they are like the terms employed in sports, religion, etiquette, politics, and morals. In Hart's purely formal analogy, however, no difference was made between the special duty of a slave to submit to his owner's will and the special duty of a batter to leave his wicket.

Later, in *The Concept of Law* Hart looked at the subject more substantively. He quoted from *Huckleberry Finn,* where Aunt Sally asks Huck if the explosion of a steamboat has injured anyone. Huck replies, "No'm: killed a nigger." Aunt Sally observes, "Well it's lucky because sometimes people do get hurt." For Hart the passage illustrated how "in slaveowning societies the sense that the slaves are human beings, not mere objects to be used, may be lost by the dominant group." The sense "may be lost." Hart, using a passive construction, avoided assignment of responsibility to the work of legislators, judges, lawyers in suppressing the sense of human beings, and said not a word on how the legal system made a person a non-person.

In a footnote Hart enlarged on his treatment: *Huckleberry Finn* is "a profound study of the moral dilemma created by the existence of a social morality which runs counter to the sympathies of an individual and to humanitarianism." A profound study of moral dilemma! So a law-review Note might describe Swift's *Modest Proposal*. How Mark Twain would have been amused. In his novel, Jim, around whose flight the plot turns, is a fugitive slave who is a fugitive for nothing, because unknown to him, he has been emancipated by a will. In a denouement as sudden and ironic in its implications as the ending of *Tartuffe,* he is changed from an enchained felon to a free man by disclosure of the will. Could Mark Twain have satirized the magic of legal rule more sharply? Hart missed the point because he overlooked the creation of slavery by legal rules. He did not see that it makes a difference when the rules suppress persons.

Economy is the prime intellectual justification for such rule-bound absorption. Jurisprudents have thought of themselves as dealing with the elemental constituents of the system, holding the key, as Austin expressed it, to "the science of law." The reduction of law to science, however, means the treatment of law in terms of forces which are calculable like the forces dealt with in physics. Once set on this course, it is difficult to escape the model set out in classical form by Austin—law becomes a set of commands accompanied by threats by one with authority to carry out the threats.

Constraint by the threat of force is no doubt characteristic of a legal system. But two other functions, neglected by Austin, are equally characteristic: to channel and to teach. By marking out certain types of agreement as privileged—contracts in general, marriage in particular, corporations and trusts in Anglo-American law—the legal system affords ways in which human energies and material resources may be pooled and increased. In Hart's amendment of Austin, this function is performed by "power-creating rules." But his emphasis is wrong. The human beings attracted, by the legal privileges attached, to enter a contract or form a marriage are not so much given power to have legal consequences follow their agreement as they are brought to enter cooperative relationships where almost everything will depend not on power and sanction but on reciprocal trust and good will; the legal system has not provided power so much as directions for acting in harmony—a musical script, not a set of batons.

Teaching—the main activity of appellate judges; for what

else are 95 percent of their written opinions?—is even harder to accommodate within an Austinian or Hartian reduction. Teaching is, necessarily, person to person, informing and evoking. It cannot be equated with Pavlovian conditioning as an exercise in applied force. Addressing both Holmes's bad man (a real but not very typical representative of the population) and also the larger audience made up of the uncertain, the confused, the conforming, and the aspiring, the documents composed by constitution writers, legislators, and judges are educative. Their success is far more by persuasion that they are right than by coercion. To think of law as a science of power, unlocked by a key, badly obscures this function.

That the holder of the key is himself powerful is, of course, suggested by Austin's image. Hart, with apparent relish, adapts and applies this image—his own theory is declared by him to be "the key to the science of jurisprudence." With Holmes the notion that "command of ideas" is "the most far-reaching form of power" is explicit. One is reminded of the Astronomer of *Rasselas,* who, because he could predict the movements of the stars, believed that he controlled them. But our scientists of law and jurisprudence are too rule-bound even to predict with accuracy.

Fascination with rules may mean obeisance to force or the delusion of having mastered force. It may also lead to a veritably religious veneration for the rules and their imagined author. The sovereign and his command may be deified. It is hard not to think of Tillich's Ground of Being when Kelsen speaks of the *Grundnorm.* Or what shall one say of Holmes's state of mind when he exclaims that through "the remote and more general aspects of the law, you not only become a great master in your calling but connect your subject with the universe and catch an echo of the infinite, a glimpse of its unfathomable process, a hint of the universal law"? As the believer raises his eyes, the particular persons who shaped the rule, argued the rule, applied the rule, submitted to the rule, seem to have disappeared. A type of deity remains.

Contrariwise, to regard the law as a set of rules and only as a set of rules may trivialize the subject. From Hobbes to Hart, how British philosophers have liked to treat law as a game! No doubt, games afford instructive analogies for reflection on the law. No doubt, the more rule-bound a sector of law—the old-fashioned property learning on remainders and reversions, for example—the more game-like it is. Yet to regard law only as a game is to forget that in the process human opportunities and liberties and life itself may be taken.

THE INDISPENSABILITY OF IMPERSONALITY

That rules should be the ordinary stuff of legal analysis follows from their indispensability for social control and social construction. Those who rule are communicating to an indefinite number of persons in an indefinite number of situations. Those who rule cannot be present in each situation to respond to each situation afresh. They must in advance pick out grossly identifiable, repeatable elements of human conduct and set out what patterns should or should not be permitted or encouraged and what responses to different patterns would be appropriate.

As control, communication is most effective if the recipients do not look beyond the message. Traffic moves well if drivers stop when they see Red and start when they see Green. For a driver to pause, speculating about the persons who set up the lights, would only cause congestion or an accident. The system works best if the signal received is impersonal, unambiguous, complete.

The simple situation where the users moving machinery are controlled by mechanical methods is a model for the use of rules in more complex ways. At the center of the entities by which modern society acts—the business corporation, the government agency, the university—are the rules which define responsibility and allocate power. The essential character of these organizations lies in their separation of structure from person, of office from man. The perpetuity which attends them is a derivative of their lack of human personality. They cannot be identified with any single human being. Their different human components blend into a single abstraction, "the company," "the government," "the school."

Rules mark out the process by which office is achieved. Rules identify the officeholder. Rules delineate the boundaries of the office. Rules create the roles within which the officeholder acts with authority.

Everyone has encountered not only the bad side of such creations, their anonymity, but the good side, their adherence to purposes beyond the individual. If there is conflict within them, the lawyer knows that his loyalty runs not to any person but to the institution. If there is failure or corruption, the fault is to be attributed to the individual, not to the structure he is supposed to serve. That officeholders and office are distinct makes possible the resolution of conflict, survival after failure, correction after corruption. To introduce the person as an element in law of this kind seems subversive of the system.

The paradigmatic form for law, trial in court, reinforces the necessity to exalt the role of rule. In the paradigm, the judge hears conflicting parties and decides upon the evidence which they present. The evidence is related to his decision through his selection of a rule. If the judge looks at who the parties are, he is not looking at the evidence. A judge who takes into account who the parties are will favor one or the other. A biased judge is no judge at all.

If the judge looks at the rules, he is acting in accordance with the paradigm, which requires two persons to be in controversy, and a third person, who prefers neither, to decide. The judge indicates his impartiality, he proves his good faith, by looking not at the persons but at the rule. The rule is neutral, "above" the contestants and the judge.

God Himself in Deuteronomy is this kind of judge, who "regardeth not persons nor taketh rewards." He continues as this kind of judge in Christian thought. Master and slaves,

Paul reminds the Colossians, shall be judged where there is "no acceptance of persons." The divine model is offered to human beings. The judges of Israel, Moses teaches, "shall not accept persons." You are transgressors of the law, James says, "if you show respect toward persons."

The medieval moralists teach in the same vein. The sin of "respect of persons," Thomas Aquinas declares, is a sin against justice and peculiarly the sin of a judge. In the extreme case, if the judge knows from testimony not on the record that the defendant in a capital case is innocent, and the testimony on the record makes him guilty, the judge, Thomas teaches, must act within his role, suppress his personal knowledge, and pronounce the death sentence. "Put aside favor and fear, have God alone before your eyes," Innocent III tells the judges of the Church, "and walk the royal road without respect of persons." The religious tradition, Jewish and Christian, is single in its ideal of impersonal judgment.

Invoking the rule, the judge decides fairly. Justice blindfolded in the classic representation, "God alone before his eyes" in the medieval formulation, the rule impartially applied in the modern model—the paradigm of justice forbids "acceptance of persons."

The paradigm goes beyond the court to government generally. "Relieve the judges of the rigor of text law, and the whole legal system becomes uncertain," Thomas Jefferson writes at the close of the Revolution: "Chancery is a chaos, irreducible to system, insusceptible to final rules and incapable of definition and explanation. Were this true, it would be a monster whose existence would not be suffered one moment in a free country wherein every power is dangerous which is not bound up by general rules."

The place of general rules in a constitutional democracy could not be more succinctly put. Where monsters have appeared in American government, they have appeared to issue from the sleep of rule.

THE COMPLEMENTARITY OF
RULES AND PERSONS

Indispensable but insufficient to the legal process, living only in the minds of persons and applied only in the interaction of persons, rules cannot be the sole or principal object of legal study, legal history, and legal philosophy without distortion. What is distorted is the place of persons in the process. An individual, unless he or she is expressing a whim, must articulate a rule when arguing or deciding a case. But the process consists in the interplay of the persons forming the rule with the persons applying it and the persons submitting to it.

Observing that rules alone are inadequate, Roscoe Pound in 1917, in an article defiantly entitled "Juristic Science and the Law" (defiantly because he was a believer in juristic science), declared it a prime mistake to think of law "as wholly made up of rules." Above the rules were what he called "standards," such as the standard of due care, and "principles," by which rules were measured and applied. The principles were described as "the living part of the legal system" and "its most significant institution." A comparable move has been more recently made by Ronald Dworkin, Hart's successor at Oxford, amending Hart by distinguishing rules (specific directives applicable on an all or nothing basis) and principles (statements of reasons and values which are typically weighed in their application). Analogously, the brothers Kadish, philosopher Mortimer and jurisprudent Sanford, have justified discretionary departures from rules by "principles of acceptance" broader than specific, mandatory directions. In each case the expansion of rules recognizes the place of morality in the legal system: so Pound speaks of standards containing "a large moral element"; Dworkin declares his move to be a critique of positivism; the Kadishes justify departures from rules in the name of larger "ends." In no case, however, are these moves (which are so useful in the contexts in which they are made) a satisfactory substitute for the presence of persons in the system. Principles are no more "living" than rules; the personification by which they become "living" is obvious. To invoke principles instead of acknowledging that at some point persons act is to remain rule-focused.

Rules and persons may be conceived of as an antinomy— "government of law, government of men." But the principle of contradiction, that necessity of reason, makes us uncomfortable with conflicting accounts put forward as descriptions of the same process. Rules and persons may be conceived of as alternative perspectives, to be chosen depending on the view we want. This is better, but unduly encourages the attitude that the views are equally good and that either is sufficient—a slovenly and unacceptable indifferentism. The process is rightly understood only if rules and persons are seen as equally essential components, every rule depending on persons to frame, apply, and undergo it, every person using rules. Rules and persons in the analysis of law are complementary. By the same token, the paradigm of the impartial judge and the paradigm of the personally responsible judge are equally necessary.

That like cases should be treated alike, that equality of treatment excludes bribery or bias—these are axioms of justice. Yet there is no reason to suppose that justice is the only virtue required of a lawyer, legislator, or judge. If they are not to cease to be human, they must cultivate the other virtues of humanity. Justice to persons, Augustine reminds us, may be identified with love—an active service to another, who is loved.

Abandonment of the rules produces monsters; so does neglect of persons. Which monsters are the worse I will not argue. Our jurisprudence, however, has emphasized the first danger. "The intense desire," Pound observes, "to exclude the personality of the magistrate for the time being at almost any cost has left its mark on the law beyond any other factor in law making." Our history, as I shall illustrate, shows that the second danger is as great, the specific evils it has produced as enormous. Lawyers, lawmakers, judges do not act as responsible persons by mere faithful attention to rules.

In discussing Goya's masterpiece, *The Third of May, 1808,* Kenneth Clark writes that the artist

> shows one aspect of the irrational, the pre-determined brutality of men in uniform. By a stroke of genius he has contrasted the fierce, formalised repetition of the soldiers' attitudes, the steely line of their rifles, and the hard shapes of their helmets, with the crumbling irregularity of their target. As I look at the firing squad I remember that artists have been symbolising merciless conformity by this kind of inhuman repetition since the very beginning of art. One finds it in the bowmen on Egyptian reliefs, in the warriors of Asshur-nasir-pol, in the repeated shields of the giants on the Siphinian Treasury at Delphi.

Rules are formalized repetition. They enforce a conformity which may be merciless and inhuman. They embody power. ''But,'' as Clark adds, ''the victims of power are not abstract.'' Goya, as he might also have added, keeps the faces of the soldiers hidden by their shakos; it is the victims' faces which the artist has made visible.

In this book, in reaction to rule-oriented writers, I stress the place of persons with an emphasis redoubled because I seek to distinguish persons from masks. But it would be a travesty of what I believe to suppose that law could exist without rules. At the intersection of rules and persons, the process to be understood occurs. A chief difficulty to understanding, however, is the presence of masks, formed by rules and concealing the persons.

MASKS DEFINED AND DISTINGUISHED FROM ROLES

By masks in this context I mean ways of classifying individual human beings so that their humanity is hidden and disavowed. I do not mean the disguises, psychological or literary, by which one may conceal the psyche. The presentation of the self in everyday life is not in my sense a mask. Humanity is not thereby put aside. By mask I mean a legal construct suppressing the humanity of a participant in the process. Mask is the metaphor I have chosen for such constructs, because the human face is where emotion and affection are visible if not deliberately concealed.

"Property," applied to a person, is a perfect mask. No trace of human identity remains. Other legal concepts depend more obviously upon context and usage for their efficacy as masks. "Sovereign" and "court," "plaintiff" and "defendant" may, for example, function to suppress humanity. "As all who knew him are aware, the man was even greater than the judge. His passion for justice . . . appeared in his voice and words, as his love for humanity was apparent in his face," Warren Seavey writes of Cardozo—it is the unmasked face, the human voice, to which he refers.

What is the difference, then, between a mask and a role? The distinction, I believe, is both difficult and crucial. The lawmaker and the judge and the litigant are all carrying out positions assigned them by society, all are the players of roles. They have not been identified with those parts. The masked person has identified with, or been identified with, the mask.

A football team, for example, of uniformed, helmeted, numbered men is engaged in an athletic role. Their role authorizes action not normally tolerated—tackling and blocking of others, knocking them to the ground; yet obviously their role does not authorize the deliberate infliction of injuries. The equipment that accompanies a role is meant to give security and ease in its performance. It may, however, have a dehumanizing effect. So the introduction of better protection, including noseguards, has had the twin effect of making football players more aggressive, and more vulnerable to injuries where unprotected, as they are at the neck—the carapace effect, common to football players and automobile drivers. If the dehumanization were carried further and the players wore visors concealing their faces, wore jerseys which were anonymous and fungible, and took their function to be the achievement of victory although victory meant the physical destruction of their opponents, they would be masked.

The analogy suggests how a role may be turned into a mask. It suggests the importance of the carapace effect. It fails, however, to bring out sufficiently the essential contribution of roles to any community. No one can do everything and be everything. I must contribute to the community as lawyer, teacher, father, husband. In each role there is an art I must master. But as Socrates pointed out to Thrasymachus, the art is subordinated to the service of others. In his example, the role of the physician is perverted when the doctor's purpose is to make money. It may be that the role becomes a mask whenever the purpose of serving others is forgotten; the judge who has forgotten the purpose of justice is almost surely masked.

Roles are as necessary for the display of human love as clothes for the display of human beauty. The naked individual rises to the communal expectations invested in the role— black-robed on a bench, he is different from the bureaucrat behind a desk. No more than clothes does a role obscure the human visage. But as a hat can be pulled down to cover a face, so a role, misused, becomes a mask obliterating the countenance of humanity.

MASKS SUBJECTIVELY AND OBJECTIVELY CONSIDERED

Masks of the law are of two kinds—those imposed on others and those put on oneself. "Property," applied to slaves, "sovereign," applied to lawmakers, are instances of the first kind. "The court" in the mouths of judges, "the law" in the mouths of judges and law professors are instances of the second. No doubt the extent to which these terms exclude humanity is a matter of context and degree.

Applied to oneself or accepted from another for oneself, the legal mask may be internalized—it then becomes indistinguishable at a psychological level from other disguises of the self. "The law" as a personified entity may become an invisible companion like a teddy bear or a lamb who is the alter ego of a child; the child is not responsible for Lambie's actions; he may even regret them; "however," this is what Lambie had to do. Analogously, a judge may speak and even think of the law as an invisible companion telling him what he must do.

The play of children as described by Piaget affords another analogy for the lawyers' use of masks: at what he describes as "the second stage of their development," between four and seven years of age, children take the rules of their game as fixed from above. Their own cooperative action is masked as preordained necessity. Just as this stage of development continues to exist in adults who partially outgrow it, so "the law" is often viewed as preordained necessity by adult users of the law.

To analyze the masks as mere subjective phenomena, however, would be to miss their distinctive characteristic. They are not purely private projections or creations. They are socially fashioned. They are more social even than such expressions of group hostility as "wog," "gook," or "pig," which also function to deny humanity. They have been stamped with official approval by society's official representatives of reason. They are—to repeat the tautology—a portion of the law. Examining the use of masks by George Wythe and Thomas Jefferson, Oliver Wendell Holmes, Jr., and Benjamin N. Cardozo, I do not suppose that as individuals they invented the terms they used as masks. Wythe's and Jefferson's relationship with their own slaves, Holmes's experience of battle, Cardozo's experience of his father's failure may have affected their choices, but they chose from what was current in the legal universe.

Mask, *persona,* itself a term that first had meaning in drama, suggests that the true character of the masks of the law may be aesthetic. In a work of literature the word of the author is objectified. He speaks through many tongues. He "do the police in many voices." He is hidden by the form he has chosen. Is not a statute or a judicial opinion also a work of literature, the author or authors objectified in the form? At the highest level, is not legal writing great literature? "Many a common law suit," Cardozo wrote of Holmes, "can be lifted from meanness to dignity if the great judge is by to see what is within . . . the sordid controversies of the litigants are the stuff out of which great and shining truths will ultimately be shaped." Judges like Holmes and Cardozo remain hidden as they transmute the tawdry materials of life into aesthetic masterpieces. To accomplish their end, it might be supposed that they had to mask themselves as "the court."

The analogy between literature and law is, however, incomplete. Besides the aesthetic objective, there is masking of a different kind. The Stendahl behind the multiple façades of *The Charterhouse of Parma* does not deny his humanity. The masked author of a judicial opinion sometimes does. The work of literature acts only upon those who respond to it. The statute or piece of legal writing, even the judicial masterpiece, may deny the humanity of those upon whom the writing bears.

In Plato's famous presentation in *The Republic* of the case against justice, Thrasymachus maintains that law always represents "the interest of the stronger": otherwise those strong enough to make the laws would not enact them. His position has great plausibility. His objection presents in its starkest shape the claim, now most strongly advanced by Marxist analysts, that law is determined by class interest. The masks of the law, it could be argued, are invented and employed by the ruling class to cover their own aggression, to cover over the faces of those they exploit. In a Marxian account, they may be regarded as reification. More generally, in any sociological analysis, the masks may be seen as devices reflecting the structure of society and the degrees of its acknowledgment of humanity in different groups.

Socrates' reply to Thrasymachus is that the interest of the strong is not self-evident. It cannot be determined without knowing the impact of the decisions upon the decision makers. The answer has a general validity. Law is not something applied to subjects which leaves those applying it unaffected. Judge-made law, for instance, is educational—no mere umpires unaffected by the afternoon's sport, the judges are the ones most likely to be educated, and after them, the lawyers. The American legal realists emphasized the role of judges in making law. They did not sufficiently consider how making law implicated the makers. It is the law's values, perspectives, and blind spots which they shape themselves to share.

Socially employed and individually appropriated, masks are not mere instruments of power. The analogy of the visored team suggests that the masks of the law are like the accoutrements of war; and where life or liberty are taken, law seems close to war. Yet it is to suppress vital differences to treat law, even unjust law, as an act of "violence." The legal process—it is its chief justification and principal success—aims at compromise, avoidance of violence, peaceful direction of conduct. As a social reality, law is inadequately understood if it is identified with that use of force which terminates a life or makes a prisoner. Law exists in a society as a set of communications which, most of the time, are efficacious by being communicated. To treat masks as armament would be to mistake their use.

The metaphor of mask opens out to psychological or sociological investigation where the masks are analyzed as pure projections of the psyche or as pure reflections of structured power; and the metaphor invites the development of the analogies with literature, games, and war. Yet masks in the law have their own character and function which it is the work of one writing about the legal process to examine. What has been called "magic" bears closest resemblance. Soedjatmoko notes:

Observing that words sometimes make human beings behave in accordance with the sense they convey, many people believe words to possess an inherent power which may affect situations and dead objects as well, and priests to possess the gift of handling such powerful words. We call the practice of speaking powerful words "magic" if the speaker himself believes that his words bring about the desired effect. The ancient Javanese did believe in verbal magic, as is evident from stories which we find in their literature. Considering, then, that some Javanese texts are unintelligible unless we suppose the author to have practiced magic, and that many other texts are easier to understand and fit better into a framework of facts if interpreted on the basis of that supposition, we shall have to reckon with the possibility that in Java "poetical style" and magical function were concomitant.

These observations are made of folkways on an Indonesian island. I find it difficult to distinguish the use of masks by our lawyers and judges, whose utterances show their own belief, as long as they act as lawyers or judges creating masks, in the power of their words.

Neither individual projections nor objective artifacts, neither social roles nor literary disguises, the masks of the law are magical ways by which persons are removed from the legal process. By rational criticism, by historical reconstruction, the persons may be restored.

THE REMOVABILITY OF MASKS

The users of any system—scientific, theological, legal—encounter points where their premises and their practices are inconsistent. These gaps in the system must be bridged or the system changed. To bridge the gaps, those who accept the system employ fictions. As Lon Fuller has demonstrated, fictions find as "pervasive" an application in jurisprudence as in physics: fictions are a necessity of law.

Masks are a variety of fiction. At the points of a legal system where it is too much to recognize that a human being exists, a mask is employed. The intolerable strain is relieved. It may be supposed that as fictions in general are a necessity, so the subspecies of fiction, masks, are inevitable.

The conclusion does not follow. Useful or at least harmless pretenses can be distinguished from masks—all the more necessary to make the distinction because the legal universe contains so much make-believe untested by reference to reality. In the making of masks lawyers have let their fiction-making capacity run amok. As the stories which follow suggest, masks are monsters as dangerous as those issuing from the sleep of rational rule. Masks are a type of "human self-alienation." Masks conceal persons.

To remove the masks is to distinguish between them and the persons. By the latter, I mean particular flesh and blood and consciousness. I take as a starting point that we are such beings, that we encounter such beings, and that encountering them we recognize those who are in shape and structure, in origin and destiny, like ourselves. I assume that we have the experience of responding to persons.

> Among the Bali, an individual is initially named by a unique nonsense syllable. Within the family, and in situations involving actions having effects on the family, he is called by the number designating his sibling ranking. His duties, his privileges, the principles which guide his choices, are determined by his place in a sibling-order. When he assumes offices and duties, his titles *are* his names and in that context, he *is* the bearer of that office, the actor of that role. The policies and to some extent even the memories that determine his choices as a bearer of office are entirely distinct from those that guide him as a member of his family. If he keeps the roles distinct, they need not come into conflict; but of course if he tries to conjoin them, "his" various role-policies can come into opposition.

So the anthropologist Clifford Geertz—he is quoted by Amelie Oksenberg Rortz, exploring the meaning of "person."

The problem suggested is not only to be found among the Bali but among our own lawyers and judges. Are they identical with their function, the memories which guide them those of their office? More generally, are persons merely a collection of roles—husband, father, lawyer, etc.? I take persons to be ontological realities, perceptible through the roles, distinguishable from both roles and masks. Recognition of persons involves a conceptual scheme, but it is a conceptual scheme which is the condition of discourse. To say with Hans Kelsen, "The concept of physical (natural) person means nothing but the personification of a complex of legal norms," is to put the matter backward, an inversion leading to an imaginary universe corresponding to nothing in existence. If a lawyer could not distinguish between real persons and fictional persons such as corporations or trees, he would not be capable of communication.

"Persona" once meant the disguise adopted by the actor. It came to mean an intelligent, self-subsisting being, "the most perfect" in the universe. In the history of the Latin term is packed the latent relation of mask and person. In the evolution of "persona" is the development I see taking place in the law, masks concealing persons and being replaced by them, the acceptance of masks being the greater sin. God, it is now seen, is not a respecter of masks.

The history of this process seems calculated to cause vicarious anger or vicarious guilt. But can any good come of it? The melancholy record of fratricidal inhumanity is the nightmare from which Stephen Dedalus shouted he was trying to awake. If Wythe and Jefferson, Holmes and Cardozo—the best lawyers of their age, our best—put on masks, who could have done differently? These are the phenomena whose terror Mircea Eliade evokes, explaining the need of redemption from time. "History!" writes Bokonon. "Read it and weep!"

Non-persons exist in contemporary American law. What need, then, of history to re-create the problem? Can the problems even be perceived in history unless one has already perceived the present posing of the issues? Is not the turning to history a withdrawal from curable ills to a past which is beyond change? The answer to each of these questions must consist in the enormous advantage that distance from an evil yields: the incentive to disguise, rationalize, or accommodate weakens or disappears. Looking intently at the past can improve our present vision.

If despair or terror or escape are not ultimate human responses, history of this kind can serve a heuristic function. It invites us not to contemplation but to inquiry—inquiry into institutions now structured by law and served by lawyers as slavery once was. It directs us to consider the part of the active participants in these structures—the lawyers first, then the judges, lawmakers, and administrators. It leads us from inquiry to recognition of the persons who speak to us through rules and of the persons to whom the rules are spoken.

2

Virginian Liberators

GEORGE WYTHE, Chancellor of the Commonwealth of Virginia, was a lawyer, a signer of the Declaration of Independence, Speaker of the Revolutionary Assembly, and a teacher of law. In 1760 Wythe took Thomas Jefferson—seventeen, just half his age—as his pupil and introduced him to the universe he was to inhabit as a lawyer and legislator in Virginia. Successively, Wythe was his instructor in legal theory, his initiator into legal practice, his sponsor in lawmaking and, in Jefferson's own description, his "faithful and beloved Mentor in youth" and his "most affectionate friend throughout life."

When Jefferson became Governor of the new Commonwealth in 1779, he abolished a Chair of Divinity in the old royal college of William and Mary and put in its place a Chair of Law and Police, on which he seated Wythe, who became in fact what he was in Jefferson's mind, the first professor of law in the United States.

Only a generation before, William Blackstone at Oxford had become the first Professor of the Laws of England. Though Wythe never wrote an American equivalent of Blackstone's *Commentaries,* Jefferson's admiration for the Professor of Law and Police at William and Mary was undiminished: "I know of no place in the world," Jefferson, sonless, wrote in 1785, "where I would so soon place a son."

George Wythe reciprocated this affection and trust and in turn expressed his feelings by a symbolic act. "I give my books and small philosophical apparatus," he wrote in the first codicil of his last will, "to Thomas Jefferson, president of the United States of America: a legacie considered abstractlie not deserving a place in his musaeum but estimated by my good will to him, the most valuable to him of any thing which i have power to bestow."

By the same will, Wythe, sonless, created a trust (a cestui que trust as Law French pointedly expresses it) for a beneficiary who was half black, half white. Michael Brown by name, he had been Wythe's slave; emancipated, he now lived in Wythe's house. Wythe named Jefferson as trustee, making him fiduciary for Brown, who had once been "personalty" in Virginia.

The larger legacy to Jefferson, the greater demand upon his loyalty, was the intellectual bequest. Jefferson not only cherished Wythe's image as the embodiment of justice but he described him in his lifetime as "one of the most virtuous of characters." After Wythe's murder, he declared that "a more disinterested person never lived." His virtue had been "the purest kind, his integrity inflexible, and his justice exact." John Randolph said that Wythe's "judgements were all as between A and B, for he knew nobody, but went into Court as Astrea was supposed to come down from Heaven, exempt from all human bias." In Jefferson's lapidary summation, Wythe was "the honor of his own and the model of future times."

Wythe drafted the oath to be taken by every chancellor of Virginia, himself the first. The chancellor swore to "do equal right to all manner of people, great and small, high and low, rich and poor, according to equity and good conscience, and

the laws and usages of Virginia, without respect of persons."
The old royal judges' oath for the General Court in Chancery
had been almost the same, concluding, however, with the
words "without favor, affection, or partiality," which Wythe
replaced with "without respect of persons." His change invoked Jewish and Christian tradition and the ideal of the
mighty and impartial God of Deuteronomy.

For the seal of the Chancellor, Benjamin West proposed
that Wythe use the story of Sisamnes, a Persian judge who,
according to Herodotus, had taken bribes. The king had discovered his fault, had had him slain, his skin flayed, the skin
made into strips, and the seat of justice covered with the
pieces. In his stead, his son was appointed and reminded by
the king never to forget in what way his chair was cushioned.
Wythe accepted the seal.

His own impartiality was put to the test after the Revolution in the great case of *Page* v. *Pendleton*. Page, the debtor
of the estate of John Robinson, an Englishman, attempted to
discharge his debt by paying paper money of Virginia worth
one thousandth of the same sum in specie, and a statute of
revolutionary Virginia declared such paper to be good in paying creditors who were English nationals. Chancellor Wythe
held the statute invalid, overridden by the peace treaty between Great Britain and the United States. But even if the
treaty did not exist, he said, to enforce the statute would be
to break his oath to do equal right to all manner of people.
English citizens were as much people as Virginians. Payment
of just debts was an obligation of natural law; to destroy this
natural duty was beyond "legislative omnipotence." He
turned to the classic words of protest against unjust, man-
made law: "As Antigone says to Creon," he wrote, "the
laws of nature are 'unwritten law divine.' " Then, thinking of
the Chancellor's seal, he added that a judge who upheld such
a statute out of patriotism "deserves perhaps the punishments
of Sisamnes."

Edmund Pendleton, who benefited by his ruling as the executor whose fees depended on the size of the estate, had been his rival at the bar and, after the Revolution, when both had become judges, his antagonist on the bench. As First Judge of the Court of Appeals, Pendleton oversaw Wythe's Chancery and reversed over half of his decisions. Overruling is painful for any judge, and overruling one out of every two times intolerable—to no judge more than Wythe, whose learned lucubrations seemed to issue almost physically from his great domed head. He attributed these overrulings to the malice of an enemy.

Like so many country boys, Pendleton had found the practice of law to be a path to wealth for a youth of industry, agility of mind, and ability to articulate ideas vigorously. He had risen in the world with the help of a great patron, John Robinson, whose estate he now administered and whose embezzlements as Treasurer of the Colony he had ignored. For Pendleton, law was a process whose end was profit.

Wythe saw the law as a temple in which he functioned as a priest. Votary and scholar, he worshipped alone. Pendleton was a profaner. They loathed each other. When the opportunity came to Wythe in *Page* v. *Pendleton* to injure Pendleton, he did not abandon his ideal of knowing no one from the bench. He turned the blind eyes of the just judge to the enemy enriched by his decree.

It is natural to see this selfless man as pure lawyer, the first and most influential of American law professors. In addition to Jefferson, his pupils included James Monroe, John Marshall, Henry Clay, all the bright young men of the most politically powerful state in the union—a teacher who reached, to speak in the fashion of the bar, the apogee of his profession when he became a judge. Thomas Jefferson is just the opposite. Who thinks of him as a lawyer? He seems too manifold in his interests, too vital in his passions to be so circumscribed. But he did inhabit Wythe's legal universe. For both of them it was the world they needed if they were to act with equity and good conscience, without respect of persons, while making the slave law of Virginia.

THE UNEQUIVOCAL EMANCIPATORS

Virtue as an Amazon, in her hand a spear, at her feet a foe, beneath the scene the legend *Sic semper tyrannis*—this was the seal of the Commonwealth of Virginia, approved by George Wythe. Like the seal of the Chancery, the image is dramatic and uncomfortable. It makes clear, it seems, a passion against tyrants as strong as the Chancellor's hatred of corrupt judges. Yet it is not clear that George Wythe recognized the owners of slaves as among those always to be overthrown by Virtue.

It has been said he was "a warm opponent of Negro slavery." "With other eminent Virginians of the period, he was opposed to slavery and by his will emancipated his servants." "Among the eminent Virginians of the time, only George Wythe seemed to take the position that Negroes held the full attributes of humanity, and therefore possessed rights which were anterior to any claims that white men might have . . ." These three quotations are from works published in 1907, 1943, and 1964 by twentieth-century historians increasingly more positive and specific about Wythe's devotion to the liberty of blacks. But is there any evidence from his own day? He left no express statement of his views. The only slaves he did liberate—and not by will—were Michael Brown and two others of his immediate household. Still, Thomas Jefferson wrote the English emancipationist Richard Price in 1785 assuring him that Wythe's sentiments on the subject of slavery were "unequivocal." What were those sentiments, and how did they relate to Jefferson's own?

In Maryland, Jefferson told Price, slaveowners lacked "the courage to divest their families of a property which however keeps their conscience unquiet." In Virginia, justice was "in conflict with avarice and oppression." In that conflict, "the sacred side" was daily gaining recruits, who had "sucked in the principles of liberty as it were with their mother's milk." Young men of this sort were under Wythe's instruction at William and Mary, and Wythe, "one of the most virtuous of characters'' was unequivocal. What Jefferson means seems clear, yet the denial of equivocation itself represses a doubt. Neither he nor Wythe had, at that time, divested their family of any slaves.

Jefferson had made his own views clear enough in *Notes on the State of Virginia,* a work nearing completion when he answered Price. The first Emancipation Proclamation on the American continent, issued November 7, 1775, by Lord Dunmore, the royal governor of Virginia, freed the rebels' slaves (as Lincoln did, not quite a century later) without compensation: a war measure in each case. Jefferson did not commemorate Dunmore's historic act. He did observe that slavery transformed slaves into enemies and destroyed their love of country: ''For if a slave can have a country in this world, it must be any other in preference to that in which he is born to live and labour for another.'' To the objection of national security, he added that of religion or ideology: ''And can the liberties of a nation be thought secure when we have removed their only firm basis, a conviction in the minds of the people that these liberties are of the gift of God? That they are not to be violated but with his wrath?'' These objections of a national character were preceded by one both social and personal, cast in terms of Jefferson's most prized value, education: ''The whole commerce between master and slave is a perpetual exercise of the most boisterous passions, the most unremitting despotism on the one part, and degrading submissions on the other. Our children see this, and learn to imitate it, for man is an imitative animal. This quality is the germ of all education in him . . . The man must be a prodigy who can retain his manners and morals undepraved by such circumstances.'' Written with sexual undercurrents and the tone of self-examination, this passage was followed by this declaration: ''And with what execration should the statesman be loaded who, permitting one half the citizens thus to trample on the rights of the other, transforms those into despots and these into enemies, destroys the morals of the one part, and the amor patriae of the other.''

Who was the statesman to be loaded with execration? Who had permitted one half the citizens to be despots? The passage seems intended as a criticism of those who had formed an institution which Jefferson had found impregnable. To *Notes on the State of Virginia* Jefferson appended a draft constitution for Virginia, declaring "all persons," born after December 31, 1800, to be "free." But how had he and Wythe acted when, as lawyers, they made the law before the Revolution? What had they done when, as legislators, they wrote the law after the Revolution? These unequivocal emancipators became statesmen making slaves. Their transformation was effected by accepting the law's power, fictions, and masks.

THE LEGAL STRUCTURE OF
PRE-REVOLUTIONARY SLAVERY

On the eve of the Revolution, slavery in Virginia did not exist as a relationship of brute power. A social institution, it was given its shape by a hundred assumptions and omissions, intentions and neglects, customs and conventions. Law formed a part of these multiple pressures and, although far from the whole institution, was essential to it. The statutes on the control of slaves provided not a set of detailed instructions which the slaves meticulously obeyed but a message primarily directed at the white community. The statutes defining the legal status of slaves determined the dispositions to be made at a slave's birth and at a master's death. Slavery was not a transient condition: the law gave it immortality. Control statutes and status statutes together were indispensable to the creation and maintenance of the institution.

The statutes on control were designed on the model of a criminal code regulating public behavior. No slave was to leave his or her owner's plantation without a pass. No slave was to carry a club, staff, or other weapon. No slave was to own a horse, hog, or cow. No slave was to run away and lie out, hiding and lurking in swamps, woods, or other obscure places. No slave was to resist his or her owner administering correction. No slave was to lift his or her hand in opposition to a Christian, provided the Christian was not a Negro, mulatto, or Indian. No slave was to attempt to rape (the possibility of successful rape was not contemplated) a white woman. No slave was to prepare or administer medicine. No slave was to meet with four or more other slaves. No slave was to attend a religious service except with his or her "white family." The statutes were accompanied by provisions specifying punishments for their violation, ranging from whipping to castration to death. Gender was consistently specified—never perhaps, prior to the movement for women's liberation in the 1960's, was a legislative body as attentive to both sexes as the Virginia House of Burgesses in its regulation of slaves. If ever law had the nature ascribed to it by John Austin—a general command issued by one with power to inflict an evil on the subject who disobeyed—these decrees met the definition.

The statutes, the legislature prescribed, were to be read aloud at the door of each parish church twice a year, on the first sermon Sundays in March and September, so that the slaves could make no pretense of ignorance if they disobeyed. In form, the control measures consisted in command and threatened sanction, communicated to those subject to the command. Enforcement of the statutes, in fact, was haphazard and sporadic, and to view them in an Austinian way as the effective regulators of slaves' behavior is to overlook their more important function. True, even the most brutal of the laws was occasionally carried out by officials of the colony. The law against the practice of medicine had been enacted with the purpose of preventing the poisoning of masters by slaves; in 1761 it was applied to Cupid, a male slave, who had given medicine to Frank, a female slave. Edmund Pendleton and his co-justices in Caroline County, finding that Cupid's act fell within the literal prohibition of the statute, decreed that he should be hanged—a prime case of a clear rule being applied mechanically because no lawyer intervened in the process. But the House of Burgesses itself recognized the play of personal discretion in the application of the code. Statutes vital to security, notably the regulations on the meetings of slaves, carried particular penalties for law officers who failed to enforce them and for owners who tolerated their violation—a tacit admission that law enforcement had to be selective.

Other statutes openly took account of discretion in the process. A master might appear, if he chose, in defense of a slave charged with a capital offense "to make what just defense he can for such slave, so that such defense do only relate to matters of fact and not to any formality in the indictment or other proceedings of the court." There was to be no lawyers' trifling with procedural regularity—to that extent rule was to hold sway—still, it was in the owner's discretion whether his slave should stand friendless at the bar or be shielded by the owner's person. Castration as a penalty for habitual hiding out was, for another example, optional at the owner's request. Discretionary provisions of this kind pointed to an audience for the statutes different from the slaves they purported to address.

The control statutes were to be inscribed in the registry book of each parish—it was not for the benefit of the unlettered blacks that this formal dissemination was required. The reading at the church doors was to be in English—no thought was taken for those recently imported Africans whose knowledge of English would be rudimentary. Statutory phraseology was often intricate—no care was given to the slaves' unfamiliarity with legal terminology. The gestures of communication, tied to the actual Sunday worship of the Church of England, had a strong flavor of ritual. The ritual was designed less to impress the slaves than to reassure the owners.

The pedagogy of the statutes pointed to the slaves as creatures who must be coerced, upon whom it was right to exercise force. The statutes measured the amount of violence that masters might employ. The owner's boisterous passions were to be modeled to the community's norm. Violence on the slaves was authorized and rationalized by being put in the form of a rule. Punishments were set as though each penalty had been measured to the act prohibited. The model of this approach was an act of 1723 whose ostensible purpose was to put slave witnesses "under greater obligation to tell the truth." If their testimony was shown to be false, not by "due proof," but merely by "pregnant circumstances," then

> every such offender shall, without further trial, be ordered by said court to have one ear nailed to the pillory, and there to stand for the space of one hour, and then the said ear to be cut off; and thereafter, the other ear nailed in like manner, and cut off, at the expiration of one other hour; and moreover to order every such offender thirty-nine lashes, well laid on, on his or her bare back, at the common whipping-post.

Sadistic in its precision of detail, this statute appeared to focus on the witnesses. It was to be read to them before they gave testimony, in the only case in which they could give testimony—the trial of another black. The spirit of the law was captured in the summary accompanying the printed text of the statute: "Evidence, Punishment for." Knife, pillory, and lash were combined to force truth from an enemy class. The stronger message of the statute was to the judge. Directed to read it to black witnesses, the judge was reminded of their unreliability, their subjection, their amenability to physical threats. Compelled to bring these brutal threats into the actual conduct of his court, he was instructed in the act of administering justice.

The communication made by the statute to the judge in the paradigm case of a trial was the communication transmitted by other control laws to sheriffs, deputy sheriffs, constables, prosecutors, county courts, and owners. More powerful in intensity than the standards mumblingly communicated to the slaves was the clear word brought to the masters: the community is with you in your exercise of domination.

"Without force, the alienability of the title to the human capital of blacks would have been worthless," write Fogel and Engerman, stressing in their fundamental reevaluation of Southern slavery that the plantation system required a judicious blending of economic incentive with coercion. But what made it possible for slavery to continue for more than a generation? Without acceptance of the rule that the slaves could be transferred by their owners and by the testaments of their owners, neither force nor economic incentive could have maintained the system. To regulate birth and overcome death, and incidentally to determine the transmission and distribution of slaves, a special world had to be created in which rules had a force, a magic, of their own. This second function of the law of slavery depended on a mass of concepts, decisions, and statutes, whose exact application to human beings required the industry and imagination of lawyers.

"Slaves," said the index to the first laws of Virginia, "See Negroes." From the beginning of the colony, "slave" and "Negro" were terms of art indicating a special legal status. The content of these terms was largely given by the popular understanding of what a slave or Negro was. From the beginning, Africans were distinguished from Europeans by complexion, physiognomy, customs, language, and treatment. Lawyers did not single-handedly determine their definition. Yet when it came to the key questions posed by death and birth, answers could not be given by popular perception. What happened to an African when the one for whom he worked died? What happened to a child born of an African? Answers to these questions issued from the use of concepts and rules which, even before they were written up as a code, had the character of law. Africans in Virginia, having arrived by means of purchase, were viewed as *property*.

"For the better settling and preservation of estates within this dominion"—so their desire for immortality was confessed—the Burgesses in 1705 decreed that plantation slaves "shall be held, taken,and adjudged to be real estate (and not chattels)." The object of the statute was to secure the perpetuity of ownership in plantations, insuring that slaves would descend with the land they worked. Designation of plantation

slaves as real estate dramatized the triumph of landed propri-
etorship over death. The dead owner's slave was not cast into
a state of nature. The slave was to pass "to the heirs and
widows of persons departing this life, according to the manner and custom of land of inheritance held in fee simple."
Slaves in the possession of merchants and factors were ex-
empted from the operation of the statute and were to be held
"as personal estate in the same condition as they should have
been, if this act had never been made." Whether real estate
or personal estate, slaves were property, subject to all the
rules by which the rights of the dead were imparted to their
spouses or to their descendants.

The other puzzling and necessary feature of slavery as an
enduring institution, the inheritance of slave status by children, was also accounted for by the concept of property.
Originally, so the jurists defending slavery supposed, persons
became slaves by being captured in war. Their captors could
kill them. Enslavement was a substitute for death. The captor
who had the power to kill had the lesser power to enslave.
This sort of argument, familiar to lawyers as *a fortiori* reasoning, looked at comparative quantums of power. It did not
look at the human persons affected. Like Oliver Wendell
Holmes, Jr., in a later age, those devising it treated the measurement of power as decisive. They thought that the captor
acquired a just title when he spared the captive to be a slave,
and those who bought from the captor got good title from
him. Even on its own terms, the argument failed to justify the
enslavement of infants who had not been captured in battle
and who had never been subject to death at the option of a
captor. The concept of property, applied to the child, elimi-
nated that logical difficulty. The slave's child was the product
of property already owned and belonged to the owner of the
mother, just as the offspring of a mare belonged to the owner
of the mare.

Before birth, the unborn child was identified with the
mother's body. This identification, so it was argued in a
Virginia will case of 1736, avoided a "very inconvenient"

result. If the unborn child could have been devised apart from the mother, the "owner of the mother, we may suppose, would not be very careful either of the mother in her pregnancy, or the child after it was born, and some time it must remain with its mother: this might occasion the loss of many an infant, which is certainly a most humane consideration."

Overcoming the death of the master, determining the status of the offspring, the legislators and courts of Virginia presented a doctrine on the morality of slavery. They taught that it was good. In the pedagogy of the law, slaves were identified with the soil—the literal foundation of prosperity in the colony—or, generically, with property. As long as the teaching of the lawgivers was accepted, slavery could not be criticized without aspersion on the goodness of wealth itself.

The burden of moral instruction was not carried solely by the single statute of 1705 defining plantation slaves as real estate and merchants' slaves as personalty. The care and consideration lavished by the lawmakers on all forms of property proclaimed to the dullest intellect that ownership was desirable. Locke's notion that a purpose of government was to protect property could justify all measures taken to secure the stability of the slaveholder's domain. The masters' ties of commerce, marriage, and kindred, so often intertwined with the masters' property arrangements, and dependent upon them, confirmed the position of the slaves. Property was the most comprehensive and most necessary of social categories. Catalogued within it, slaves fell within a classification which announced that it was right and good to maintain their enslavement.

The concept of property performed a further function. It put the slaves at a distance from the world of men and women. "Slave" and "Negro" functioned in the same way, but neither term by itself carried a primary meaning suggesting the non-human. "Property" obliterated every anthropoid feature of the slave. Consistently inculcating this description, the statutes assured the owning class that they did not need to attend to the person of the slave in any conveyance, lease, mortgage, or devise they cared to make of their human possessions.

Addressees of the property statutes were only in an incidental way the slaves themselves. In theory, as real estate or personal estate, they could not be addressed at all. Definition as property determined their physical location, their employment, their sexual opportunities, and their familial relationships whenever they were made the object of sale, lease, mortgage, foreclosure, gift, bequest, intestacy, or entailment. They could not, however, apply this law to themselves. If they grasped the general idea that they and their children were always at the direction of another, they had deciphered the message of the law for themselves.

The law treating slaves as property conflicted with the control statutes which treated the slaves as responsible, triable, teachable human beings. Like any other legislative body, the House of Burgesses was not only changeable, partisan, or absentminded on occasion; it was attempting to give legal form to a variety of values. Unless one value was made absolute, each value was crossed by a competing value. The result in the shape of legislation bespoke different underlying assumptions, preferences, and purposes. Only a bookish historian, or an orator making a point in debate, can suppose that legislation must be a work of logical symmetry in which disharmonious statutes never jostle one another.

Inconsistency was not fatal to the dominant message communicated to the trustees and executors, lawyers and judges, auctioneers and sheriffs who had to manage the transfer of particular persons when ownership in them passed, and to the testators and heirs, donors and donees, buyers and sellers, mortgagors and creditors, who wanted to know the terms upon which ownership in particular persons could be conveyed. To all those interested in the disposition and distribution of slaves, the message communicated was single: individuals do not have to be looked at when a conveyance is made. Whoever they were, those conveyed would be distributed in accordance with the general property rules appropriate to the sale or lease or gift or mortgage or pledge or devise made.

The law was a double code: a rule of conduct for those transferring the ownership of slaves; a set of instructions whose detailed message was unintelligible to those whose lives depended upon it.

THE LEGAL STRUCTURE AND REALITY

Sexually, slaves did not differ from other animals who were classified as property. Legally, no special provision was made for them as sexual animals, with the exception of the law against the attempted rape of a white woman. Nothing in the control statutes or in the property concept recognized that they had the human capability of marrying. The Virginia anti-miscegenation statute applied only to the marriage of an Englishman or woman with a free or indentured Negro. No provision was necessary for marriage with slaves—how could property marry? The incest statute of the colony made no attempt to regulate slaves' matings—how could property violate the law of Leviticus? The statute on rape was silent where female slaves were concerned—how could property have rights against its owner?

The sexual nature of slaves caused one difficulty when they were classed as real estate. A slave, as Jefferson observed, "must lock up the faculties of his nature, contribute as far as depends on his individual endeavors to the envanishment of the human race, or entail his own miserable condition on the endless generations proceeding from him." When Jefferson spoke of a slave "entailing his condition," he used a figure of speech. Entailment was the act of an owner assuring by a legal document that his property would descend only to the heirs of his body and not be alienated by his descendants. A slave could only assure that the issue of his or her body descend as property to some owner by begetting a child. Jefferson indulged in a lawyer's irony when he termed this perpetuation of enslavement entailment. By the law of property, however, an owner might entail his slaves to pass to his blood heir with his plantation. Properly entailed slaves descended like other realty. As a consequence of their sexual nature and as a consequence of the law, if entailed slaves did not lock up their faculties, an heir might find himself possessed of more slaves than he could use upon his land; their entailment would prevent their being sold or pledged. In the technical language of the legislature, appropriate for animal breeding, the land would be "overstocked."

Between 1705, when the definition of plantation slaves as real estate was enacted, and the Revolution, legislators and lawyers argued how far the metaphor of real estate should be pressed. Lenders wanting the largest tangible assets of the plantations as collateral wished that the slaves be as freely transmissible as other forms of personal property. Owners seeking credit had a corresponding need for slaves to be readily disposable. Against these interests ran the dynastic desire of the planters to have the slaves descend with the land to their families in perpetuity.

In 1727 the conflict led to the legislature creating a new hybrid. Slaves, even on the plantations, were to be personal property, except where plantation slaves were inherited as intestate property without a will or where by a deed or a will the slaves were specifically annexed to the land. In the next generation this compromise proved unsatisfactory. The Burgesses of 1748 declared the acts of 1705 and 1727 void as if they "had never been made." Slaves were to be realty no longer. Conscious of their power to alter or maintain metaphor, the Burgesses also declared that no one who had acquired a right to a slave as real estate was to forfeit his acquisition. The English Crown negatived the 1748 changes, and in 1752 the Burgesses petitioned the king to let them reintroduce the law. Their argument had the air of eighteenth-century reason. "Slaves," the Virginians argued, "are in their nature personal estate, and not real."

Before the statute of 1727 there had been no express provisions on the entailment of slaves, so their entailment appeared to depend on the common law of England and the judges' interpretation of the thirteenth-century entailment statute, *De donis*. In 1768 John Randolph, Attorney General of the Colony, argued in *Blackwell* v. *Wilkinson* that the statute of 1705 made slaves real estate, so that they could be entailed exactly like other realty. Edmund Pendleton and George Wythe (for once acting together) appeared for the defendant, who had disregarded a series of entailments made before the statute of 1727, and maintained that only slaves specifically annexed to land could have ever been entailed. A slave apart from land did not fall within *De donis'* classification of entailable objects, "for 1st. He is not a manor. 2nd. He is not lands. 3rd. He is not a tenement." Like the Burgesses in their petition, Pendleton and Wythe contrasted the real nature of the slave with the definition of 1705 of the slave as real estate. The real nature of the slave, they successfully argued, was that he was *personalty*.

Under these decisions and earlier Virginia precedents, Jefferson noted, "our property has ever since been transmitted." He made the reporting of these matters "arising under our peculiar laws" part of his professional work before the Revolution. Still a junior at the bar, he was counsel in a case in 1770 which tested how far the legislature might go in determining reality. He acted for one Howell, whose great-grandparents had been a black man and a white woman. As punishment for their fault, their daughter, Howell's grandmother, was bound by Virginia legislation to servitude until she was thirty-one. While so bound, she gave birth to a daughter, Howell's mother, also bound by law to servitude until she was thirty-one. While in this state, she gave birth to Howell, who was sold by her master to one Netherland, who proposed to keep Howell in servitude until he, too, was thirty-one. He was so kept until he was twenty-eight. Three years away from freedom, Howell sought to be free at once.

Under the law of nature, Jefferson argued, "we are all born free." If it were natural to inherit a parent's status, then the child of a father who was a slave would be a slave, but that was not the law of Virginia. The legislature had merely added that for two generations the descendants of a black father and a white mother should be slaves until they were thirty-one. A legislature, "wicked enough," Jefferson agreed, could extend the penalty to the third generation; the Burgesses, he argued, had not done so.

George Wythe appeared for Netherland. Presumably he was going to argue that the status of Howell was determined by the status of his mother. Before Wythe could begin—so Jefferson reported his own abrupt defeat—the court interrupted him and gave judgment for Netherland.

In *Blackwell* v. *Wilkinson,* Edmund Pendleton and George Wythe argued that the real nature of slaves at law was personalty. In *Howell* v. *Netherland,* Thomas Jefferson and George Wythe assumed that the legislative determination of whether one was free or not was final. When Jefferson, Pendleton, and Wythe were a committee to remake the law of Virginia, how would they legislate the nature of slaves?

On October 12, 1776, Jefferson presented and moved a bill for the revision of the laws of the Commonwealth of Virginia. It was his persuasion, as he put it in retrospect, "that our whole code must be reviewed, adapted to our republican form of government, and, now that we had no negatives of Councils, Governors & Kings to restrain us from doing right, that it should be corrected in all its parts, with a single eye to reason, and the good of those for whose government it was framed." In the summer he had written that it was self-evident that "all men" were "created equal" and "endowed by the Creator" with the "inherent and inalienable" right to liberty. In the fall the Assembly adopted his motion, and the committee was appointed to carry it out.

Virginian lawyers of the eighteenth century, even when they were revolutionaries, it might be supposed, were so imprisoned by traditional legal assumptions about slavery that they had no choice but to ratify the legal institution. However universalist their proclamations of liberty, they lacked, it might be imagined, a concept which would correspond in law to what they announced as ideology. Suppositions of this sort would be mistaken. Only a dozen years old, new but already popular and prestigious, the *Commentaries on the Laws of England,* by the Professor of the Laws of England at Oxford, provided both a legal critique of slavery and a concept on which to base a law of universal liberty.

English law, Blackstone taught, consisted in the rights of persons and the rights of things. He began with the rights of persons. Who were they? "Natural persons," he answered, "are such as the God of nature formed us." The possibility of expanding the category by creating artificial persons or corporations was acknowledged. No suggestion was made that the category could be artificially contracted. From the time God formed the human being in the womb, Blackstone declared, a person existed. Man-made law was directed to persons. Its purpose was to protect them "in the enjoyment of those absolute rights, which were vested in them by the immutable laws of nature."

Purpose of this kind was contradictory to the institution of slavery. When Blackstone came to "Masters and Slaves" in his treatment of "Persons," he wrote: "War itself is justifiable only on principles of self-preservation; and therefore it gives no right over prisoners, but merely to disable them from doing harm to us by confining their person; much less can it give a right to kill, torture, abuse, plunder, or even to enslave, an enemy, when the war is over." He rejected the classical basis for title to a slave. "Much less," he added, was the justification for enslaving a captive's offspring valid; no legal basis existed for the perpetuation of enslavement into succeeding generations.

Disposing of the arguments made by Roman jurists and their Western European successors, such as Grotius and Pufendorf, Blackstone merely adapted the reasoning of Montesquieu in *L'esprit des lois.* It may even seem that he did less than Montesquieu, for Montesquieu's matchless irony in the argument he makes in favor of "the right to make the

Negroes slaves'' put the attack on slavery in its most fundamental form, an evocation of shared personhood:

> Il est impossible que nous supposions que ces gens-là soient des hommes, parceque, si nous les supposions des hommes, on commencerait à croire que nous ne sommes pas nous-mêmes chrétiens.

> [It is impossible that we should suppose those people to be men, because if we should suppose them to be men, we would begin to believe that we ourselves are not Christians.]

This is *ad hominem* in the highest sense—it is addressed to every human being and then especially to those human beings who as Christians have been told to love others as themselves. If the force of the argument is accepted, slavery is not only unjust, it is uncharitable, it is against a multitude of virtues, it is against man's dignity. Appealing to the intuition of personhood, Montesquieu avoided the measurement of quantums of deprivation in the way of the Roman lawyers; he also forestalled the quibbling of social-contract theorists such as Locke, who could treat slaves as outside the basic contract of society. It is not without significance that in our own day John Rawls, basing justice on a social compact, can envision slavery and serfdom as ''tolerable only when they relieve even worse injustice'' and can then instance the substitution of slavery for death in war as a ''transition case'' in which ''enslavement is better than current practice.'' The Roman jurists and the European slave traders would have asked little more. This kind of rationalization is excluded by Montesquieu.

Yet Montesquieu, succumbing to the determinism which was half his strength, ended by accepting slavery in lands where despotism reigns and in countries where it is too hot to work by choice. The sugar planters of Haiti did not need more rationalization than he afforded. Blackstone contained as strong a philosophical argument against slavery as Montesquieu—all of us whom God has formed in the womb are persons—and he tied this argument in an unqualified way to his account of the purpose of law. His conclusion was peremptory and absolute: English law "abhors and will not endure the existence of slavery within this nation." Making law inconsistent with slavery, he put an ax to the roots, for—in the absence of a legal system—slavery was impossible.

No less than Montesquieu, Blackstone limited his conclusion. He spoke of an "English master" (in the 1770 and subsequent editions an "American master") who brought his slave to England. Until foot was set on the soil of the British Isles, Blackstone did not challenge that one was master, the other slave. He announced the universality of freedom where fourteen thousand or so slaves existed and by implication denied it in the colonies, where half a million or so were at work. He turned from the large and awful reality which he felt powerless to correct to the small and local situation which English judges might alleviate. His limitation was inconsistent, his displacement of focus incoherent. Yet displacement of this kind is not uncommon among academic theorists—it is the badge not of hypocrisy but of impotence.

The general thrust of Blackstone is clear: the purpose of law itself is liberty for every person formed by God. When in 1772 Lord Mansfield granted habeas corpus to Somerset, a Virginia slave being held on a ship by his master as cargo consigned to Jamaica, his decision was rightly interpreted by popular sentiment as judicial corroboration of Blackstone and an almost fatal blow to enforcing slavery by law in England. Hedge as Blackstone himself did when consulted by Somerset's counsel, qualify as Mansfield did by subsequent dicta, Blackstone's reasoning was incompatible with slavery as an institution. The modern reputation of Blackstone as the bulwark of nineteenth-century property owners obscures the revolutionary opening his book offered the Virginia lawmakers.

Thomas Jefferson has reported how Blackstone was presented to them: Edmund Pendleton, the most conservative committeeman, proposed "to abolish wholly the existing system of laws, and prepare a new and complete Institute." The committee, he said, should "take Blackstone for that text, only purging him of what was inapplicable or unsuitable to us.'' The *Commentaries* would serve as their ''model.'' The opening Blackstone offered was tendered formally to Jefferson and Wythe.

THE CONTROL STRUCTURE
OF THE REVOLUTIONARIES

Pendleton was supported in the committee by Thomas Ludwell Lee. He was voted down by Wythe, Jefferson, and George Mason, the author of the Virginia Declaration of Rights. In retrospect, Jefferson recalled two reasons for refusing to make the laws afresh with Blackstone as basis. First, new laws would have to be ''systematical.'' To be systematical they would have to be ''the work of one hand.'' No committee member had time to do the whole job. Second, every word of a new set of statutes ''would become a subject of question and chicanery until settled by repeated adjudication.'' Quibbling lawyers ''would involve us for years in litigation.'' The result would be to ''render property uncertain.''

The first reason could not have been controlling. The old law was not systematized. Why should the new have been? The second supposed a strong distrust by lawyers of other lawyers and the courts. Jefferson may have felt this way, but did Wythe? The key difficulty is focused on in Jefferson's ''render property uncertain.'' The property which would have been made most fundamentally uncertain was property in slaves. John Quincy Adams accurately described the committee's dilemma: If they had started afresh, ''they must have restored slavery after having abolished it; they must have assumed to themselves all the odium of establishing it as a positive institution, directly in face of all the principles they had proclaimed.''

Slavery, nonetheless, had to be dealt with. In understandable disgust with the ways of men in committee, Mason resigned. Lee was assigned the topic and died. Wythe, Jefferson, and Pendleton remained. Jefferson did the text on the control laws. The bill was reported to the legislature in 1779. Managed by James Madison, it was adopted without substantial alteration in 1785.

As, in a deist's view of the universe, God rules on grand and simple lines, so Jefferson discarded the detail which had made the old control laws exact and hideous and substituted a simple scheme of elegant generality. Instead of specifically proscribing meetings of groups of slaves, the practice of medicine by slaves, hiding out by runaway slaves, and the lifting of a slave's hand in opposition to a white Christian, he prohibited "riots, routs, and unlawful assemblies, and seditious speeches." Instead of specifically designating thirty-nine lashes, castration, or death as sanction, he made each crime punishable by whipping at the discretion of a justice of the peace. The statute on false testimony of slaves disappeared. The new provision on seditious speeches was a far broader control of the use of language. Milder but more comprehensive, functionally the new statute did not differ from the colonial grotesquerie it replaced. Its message to the white community—the message of the legislature, the message drafted by Jefferson and approved by Jefferson, Pendleton, and Wythe—was: We are with you in the use of measured force.

The opening clause of the new legislation parodied the revolutionaries' statement on the inalienable liberty of human beings. "Be it enacted by the General Assembly," the committee bill said, "that no persons shall henceforth be slaves within this commonwealth, except such as were so on the first day of this present session of the Assembly, and the descendants of the females of them." This was not unlike saying, "Be it enacted that no persons shall henceforth be convicts within this commonwealth except such as are already convicted and those subsequently found guilty by process of law." No one was born a hereditary slave in Virginia unless he was the descendant of a female slave. Still, the provision was not wholly innocuous or tautological: it banned the importation of slaves. But the ban on imports, increasing the value of slaves already within the commonwealth and to be born within it, did not touch the institution. The new statute proclaimed the lawfulness of slavery in Virginia, provided for its perpetuation, and left the slaves the option of "locking up their faculties" or providing the slaves of the next generation.

Jefferson's first draft of the law on slaves, done in June 1776, was not remarkably different. In a bill for "new-modelling the form of Government and for establishing the Fundamental principles thereof in future," Jefferson wrote: "No person hereafter coming into this country shall be held within the same in slavery under any pretext whatever." Unless "coming into this country" meant "being born," what Jefferson proposed in 1776 was what he obtained in 1785.

The extent to which Wythe and Jefferson despaired may be measured not only against the principles of Blackstone but against the work of Edmund Burke, who in 1780 drafted and in 1792 proposed a code for the amelioration of the conditions of slavery in the British colonies. Burke proposed an officer to act as a species of ombudsman for the slaves and a plan by which the government would purchase the freedom and provide for the education of able slaves; with special attention to "the government of a family" as "a principal means of forming men to a fitness for freedom," he provided for the marriage of slaves and a way in which a father had the right to redeem himself, his wife, and his children from slavery. The difference between Burke's draft and the Virginians' statutes is this: accepting the slaves as human beings, Burke worked toward their enjoyment of human liberties; Jefferson and Wythe treated the slaves as human beings for the purposes of the control laws; they proposed no law by which their enjoyment of human liberties was recognized.

Six years after the committee reported its bill, one year after it had passed, Jefferson in his *Notes on the State of Virginia* wrote that the committee had approved a bill to emancipate all slaves born after the passage of the act, to educate them at public expense, and to transport them, at eighteen in the case of girls and at twenty-one in the case of boys, to a new land where they would constitute a free and independent people. In his *Autobiography*, written in 1820, Jefferson reported more laconically that the committee agreed on the principles of a bill, which Jefferson, omitting education, now reduced to "freedom" and "deportation."

No text of an emancipation bill survives. Unequivocal advocates of emancipation, why did Wythe and Jefferson fail to bring the bill in? "It was thought better," Jefferson wrote in 1820, "that this should be kept back, and attempted only by way of amendment . . . It was found that the public mind would not yet bear the proposition, nor will it even at this day." The passive voice and the impersonal "it" concealed responsibility for judgments which could have been made only by Jefferson and Wythe themselves.

To have emancipated the children of over two hundred thousand slaves in Virginia would have been enormously expensive. To have transported them elsewhere would have been herculean. To have replaced their labor would have been nearly impossible. The public mind would not bear it. Even Burke in England had waited twelve years. Yet in 1803, the next generation, St. George Tucker, the incumbent of Wythe's old chair at William and Mary and Pendleton's successor on the Court of Appeals, did not find emancipation unthinkable when he published a commentary on Blackstone acknowledging the justice of his views on slavery and the extraordinary irony of revolutionaries "imposing upon our fellow men, who differ in complexion from us, a slavery, ten thousand times more cruel than the utmost extremity of those grievances and oppressions of which we complained." Tucker indeed had published a plan for gradual emancipation in 1796 without prejudicing his later appointments to the university and the bench. Was the situation so much more rigid in 1777? Estimates of possibility often depend as much on the will as on the judgment. Let, however, Jefferson and

Wythe's estimate of possibility in 1777 be accepted. Can they be blamed for not attempting the impossible? Obviously not. But not attempting the impossible, they reinstituted slavery by law. For that decision they were responsible—that is, it must be recognized that they as human beings performed the acts by which slavery was continued as a legal institution. They chose to participate in the system. With their own hands they put on the masks of the law and imposed them on others.

THE VIRGINIA PARADOX

Subtly but perceptibly, a difference exists between being property and being a person in whom property exists. The committee's first draft of topics to be covered spoke of "Property in Slaves." The committee did not pursue the distinction. The committee became altogether silent on the nature of slaves in the new commonwealth. No need existed to deal with the problem Wythe and Pendleton had wrestled with in 1772, the nature of entailed slaves—other legislation had abolished all entailments. To define the nature of slaves now was to enter on the most treacherous ideological ground, to distinguish between human natures. Saying nothing, the committee intended, so Jefferson reported, "to make slaves distributable among the next of kin, as other moveables." Jefferson put this proposal as among "the most remarkable alterations" made by the revolutionaries. The committee, in fact, kept the law established by the General Court in 1772 on the basis of Wythe and Pendleton's argument.

In 1791, now Chancellor, George Wythe sat on the case of *Turpin* v. *Turpin*. Peterfield Turpin in February 1789 had written a will giving his brother Horatio ten named Negro slaves. At the time he wrote the will, the slaves belonged to his father. A month later, his father actually transferred them to him. On Peterfield's death, Horatio claimed the bequest. Philip, another brother, contended that Peterfield could not have willed what he did not own when he wrote his will; the slaves should be divided between the brothers as intestate property. Wythe found the teaching of his sources divided. In *Bockenham's Will,* Holt had found "absurd and repugnant" the fiction that a testator made his will over again at the moment he acquired new property: a will spoke as of the time it was written. On the contrary, Justinian's *Digest,* "ordinarily thought a reasonable rule of decision," upheld bequests of property acquired after the will was made. With no authority to guide him in choosing between a Roman Emperor dead twelve centuries and an English Chief Justice a century in his grave, Wythe invoked "the principles of law and reason" and held for Horatio.

His opinion was the model of a learned judge's. Ranging back to the Roman rules collected in Byzantium, he used history as it usually has been used by lawyers, to state an ancient formula abstracted from context. Analyzing opposing authorities and dismissing those he disagreed with as contrary to the principles of law and reason, he used reason—as it often has been used by judges—to mean congruence with other assumptions of the legal system. Personifying the dead Peterfield as though he and not the Chancellor spoke in deciding where the property was intended to go, he used personification as it is commonly used in the interpretation of wills, to announce a policy approved by the court.

To decide the case Wythe did not need to ask anything about the slaves. He did not bother to record their names. They moved as personalty. "As the law is now," he wrote, "and always has been, a bequest of slaves transfers the property of them in the same manner as if they were chattels."

"As if they were chattels"—Wythe acknowledged the fiction, as he acknowledged the fiction that permitted the dead Peterfield to speak from the time he had acquired the slaves, although he had actually spoken before he had them. "As the law is now and always has been"—he admitted that the revolutionaries had left the nature of slaves unchanged.

In 1798 William and Susanna Fowler sued to recover from Lucy Saunders a number of slaves she had inherited from her father, who in turn had received them from his father-in-law at the time of his marriage. The Fowlers claimed that Lucy's father had had only a life estate, and that an outright gift by his father-in-law would have been in fraud of a statute of 1758 regulating gifts of slaves. Wythe held that the statute did not apply to transfers made in consideration of marriage; Lucy's father had validly acquired the slaves in consideration of marrying Lucy's mother. "The property of slaves, whatever be their number" he wrote, "may be transferred with as little judicial ceremony as a single quadruped or article of house or kitchen furniture." So these things were moved from Saunders's father-in-law to Saunders to his daughter without Wythe having to know their names or consider their identity.

In 1805, the last year of his life, the Chancellor heard the case of the child, grandchild, and great-grandchild of an Indian woman, Butterfield Nan. She was free and her descendants sought to establish their own freedom through descent from her, so that one Hudgins, who claimed to own them, would not sell them out of the Commonwealth. Freedom, Wythe said, was "the birthright of every human being"— such was the teaching of "our political catechism," the Virginia Bill of Rights. He did not conclude slavery could not exist. He did conclude that whenever "one person claims to hold another in slavery," the burden of proof falls on the owner. Here, he could see with his own eyes that the grandchild of Butterfield Nan was "perfectly white." He declared her descendants free.

In 1768, in *Blackwell* v. *Wilkinson,* Wythe had argued that the real nature of a slave was "personalty." In 1770 he had won *Howell* v. *Netherland* by standing on the power of the legislature to cancel freedom. In 1792, in *Turpin* v. *Turpin,* he had ruled that slaves passed by will "as if they were chattels." In 1798, in *Fowler* v. *Saunders,* he had declared that a transfer of slaves was like a transfer of a quadruped or kitchen utensil. As a lawyer and as a judge, he had not challenged the power of legislatures and judges to suppress a birthright. When, in the last case of his life involving slavery, he gave the descendants of Butterfield Nan the benefit of a procedural rule, he did not change his view that the law determined who was property.

"As Antigone says to Creon, the laws of nature are 'unwritten laws divine.' " What other American judge would have identified with Antigone? But if a legislator was guilty of breaking unwritten divine laws in diluting a debt, how could a legislator approve a statute perpetuating slavery? How could a lawyer look on persons as kitchen utensils? How could a judge decree the transfer of a person as a quadruped? "With what execration should a statesman be loaded . . . ?"

The split between the ideals of the American Revolution and the maintenance of slavery was evident to contemporaries like Tucker; it has now been comprehensively explored by David Brion Davis, who has probed with particular sensitivity Jefferson's "uncertain commitment" to universal liberty. The liberators were divided, knew they were divided, and were able to function because they entered a universe with distinctive rules.

Jefferson did not apply his reproach to Wythe. Wythe did not apply it to himself. No Creon because he maintained the law of slavery in Virginia, he took the legal universe to be self-contained. When he entered that special world, he accepted the masks of the law—they were the law's creations, not his. He did not see it as his fault that these fictions effected the distribution of slaves and the perpetuation of slavery. "Compassion," he wrote, commenting on his imposition of liability on an innocent surety, "ought not to influence a judge, in whom, acting officially, apathy is less a vice than sympathy." Acting officially to distribute slaves, Wythe was no longer the unequivocal advocate of emancipation.

The Virginia paradox was this: Wythe believed that human beings are by nature free. He believed that the legislature is not omnipotent over nature. He believed that the legislature can enslave human beings. Rule-centered, he perceived with sharpness the injustice of an unjust rule; he did not perceive the injustice of removing human beings from consideration as persons. The Virginia paradox is the legal paradox, generally.

At least half of the property cases before the Chancellor involved the disposition of slaves. He could not have compassion for each of them as a person and still be a judge. His role in a slave system necessitated the use of masks. If he acted at all in his judicial office, those he disposed of had to fall within an appropriate subdivision of property. He needed to suppress humanity in the objects he transferred. He had to impress upon them the mask of property. The operation was not wholly external. If he were on the seat of Sisamnes, that chair of agony, he could not pay attention to his torment. He had to act with apathy. He had to suppress humanity in himself. He had to put on himself the mask of the court.

When one reads of the earnest efforts of young eighteenth-century lawyers to master Roman law, one could weep at their futility—what possible relevance had the learning of fifth-century Byzantium to the affairs of America? Tears would be misplaced. Learning the Roman law was far from ineffective indoctrination in the fiction-making power of a legal system. Citation of Roman law, as Wythe cited it in *Turpin* v. *Turpin,* was not mere harmless display of erudition; it was active evocation of the magic of the law. Roman law could make a horse a consul and did make a horse a priest; it could and did extinguish a person's past; and if it did these ''impossible'' things, it could and did unmake persons. Legal education has often been education in the making and unmaking of persons. Wythe was a superb teacher.

The essential was that no exceptions be permitted to break the spell. The control statutes, modeled on criminal law, had judges' options, sheriffs' options, prosecutors' options, owners' options. No one had options under the property concept, save the owner who had the option, following a prescribed ritual, to end the spell altogether and make his slave free. If emancipation was not granted, the property concept was absolute and all-enveloping for purposes of distribution and perpetuation.

"Relieve the judges from the rigor of text law," wrote Thomas Jefferson, interrupting a calm exposition of the common law to Philip Mazzei in 1785, "and permit them, with praetorian discretion, to wander into equity & the whole legal system becomes uncertain." Discretionary innovation, he went on to say, was the cardinal sin of Lord Mansfield, "admirably seconded by the celebrated Dr. Blackstone, a judge in the same department, who has endeavored seriously to prove that the jurisdiction of the Chancery is a chaos, irreducible to system, insusceptible to final rules, & incapable of definition and explanation. Were this true, it would be a monster whose existence would not be suffered one moment in a free country wherein every power is dangerous which is not bound up by general rules."

Blackstone was the prime authority that slavery was illegal; Mansfield had indicated that slavery was not sure of enforcement in England. Jefferson, however, did not point to Blackstone and Mansfield as the authors of a monster on this account; Jefferson's own attack on slavery in *Notes on the State of Virginia* echoed the argument in Somerset's case which Mansfield had found cogent. His opposition to equitable innovation was put in fundamentally jurisprudential terms. His words can be read as a plea for the necessity of rule in a constitutional democracy. (I have done so in Chapter I.) In the context of his thought, however, they are linked to his refusal to make a basic revision of the law of Virginia, lest he make the law uncertain. Uncertainty broke the spell. The passion of his attack came from a devotion, Wythe-like, to the fragile world of masks; for the use of masks made bearable the institution of slavery. The monster who would have made the law uncertain would also have destroyed the masks which made the institution possible.

George Wythe is the first of all the lawyers of the United States who from 1775 to 1865, North and South, kept slavery in existence. He is first not in that he caused the others to follow him, but in that, as professor of law, as legislator, as Chancellor of the Commonwealth of Virginia, he taught the others. His pupils followed in his path. Jefferson wanted to end the evil of slavery. So did Henry Clay, James Monroe, and John Marshall. Deploring the evil, they overcame their objections to it as Speaker, President, and Chief Justice, respectively, and sustained the system, accepting the power of the law to convert persons into personalty. They could believe in the natural law of freedom, and champion emancipation, and enforce slavery, so long as the legal universe was a special world with its own rules.

Like Wythe himself, they personally owned slaves. Their acceptance of the masks of the law did not blind them to the personalities of those they knew domestically. Sally Hemings, for example, his wife's half-sister and his slave, was a person Thomas Jefferson responded to when on an April day in Paris he spent two hundred francs on "clothes for Sally." Yet when he died her ownership moved under the property clauses of his will and her eventual fate had to depend on the claims of Jefferson's creditors not consuming the estate. The masks he had accepted, constructed, sustained, permitted him to distribute Sally Hemings in a fashion that would have been impossible if in the act of transmission he had to confront another living person. At the critical moments the masks of the law covered the faces of the slaves. Only an act of violence could shatter the concealing forms.

Slavery survived in Virginia after the Revolution not as an act of brute power and not as a discredited social habit, a colonial vestige repudiated by an enlightened ideology. It survived as a full-blown social institution with the control mechanisms and metaphors for transfer and distribution of the colonial regime intact. As an institution its survival was assured by the cataloguing power, the rule-making capacity, the indifference to persons of—the law? That is to depersonalize those responsible; better say—the lawyers. Without their professional craftsmanship, without their management of metaphor, without their loyalty to the system, the enslavement by words more comprehensive than any shackles could not have been forged.

WYTHE'S MURDER

No one has written on Wythe without commenting on the manner of his death in 1806 and its sequel. Wythe had emancipated his mulatto slave, Michael Brown, and his housekeeper, Lydia Brodnax. He left his houses and land in Richmond and his stock in trust to support them. By his first codicil, Wythe divided the stock between Brown and George Wythe Swinney, the heir of all his other lands and slaves, his namesake and his favorite grandnephew. Jefferson, as I have noted, was to be the trustee of the portion meant for Brown.

Nemo est haeres viventis—"No one is the heir of a living man." That old Latin tag used to be repeated over and over again by Barton Leach, teaching Property I at Harvard Law School. Who is the heir of Mr. Smith? *Nemo, nemo, nemo*—the whole of estate law depends on determining the heir only at the testator's death. The legal usage wars with the social reality. In households bound by the ordinary ties of blood and affection, the heir knows who he is.

Insolvent, in the need of the inheritance, and resentful of Brown, George Wythe Swinney saw that to bring into play the rules of property he would have to put aside respect for persons in the most fundamental sense. By a single act, he shattered the fragile legal rule protecting life: he sprinkled arsenic in their coffee, poisoning both Brown and Wythe. Jefferson's mentor and Jefferson's *cestui que trust* perished by his act.

Wythe lived long enough to disinherit Swinney, but his murderer was untouched by the criminal law. The effective barrier to prosecution came from the law permitting the testimony of blacks only against blacks. The statute controlled the form of justice in the judicial system in which Wythe had sworn to do equal right to all manner of people. It was invoked by Swinney's counsel, William Wirt (Wythe's former colleague as co-chancellor, Monroe's later Attorney General), to prevent the chief witness, Lydia Brodnax, from testifying. Charged with his testator's murder, Swinney was acquitted. His indictment for the murder of Brown was not processed.

Justice murdered; a muzzled black woman standing by; a white man in judicial robes and a black man dying; above them, gloating, a youth of fair appearance. Another seal for the courts of Virginia. Yet Wythe himself, although all his life a teacher, unlike Socrates by his death taught nothing.

IMPERSONATIONS DISTINGUISHED

The last case in *Wythe's Reports,* taken out of order and set by Wythe himself as a climax, is *Hinde* v. *Pendleton,* decided by the Chancellor in 1799. Among the property of the Robinson Estate, of which Pendleton was the active executor, was a woman who was in the possession of Mrs. Thomas Hinde as a gift from her father. Four children were born to the slave, and then it was discovered that, before the gift to Mrs. Hinde over thirty years earlier, title to her had been conveyed to Robinson, and the Robinson Estate was the true owner of the woman and the produce of her body. Pendleton ordered the auction of the mother and her children. Fearing that the neighbors would not bid against the Hindes, he told the agent not to let them be sold under a reasonable price. The agent took the instruction as authority to employ a by-bidder, a person who, as one of the auction crowd, would bid up the price while secretly acting for the seller. The Hindes were compelled to bid 52,000 pounds, "confessed to be enormous" (an athletic male slave sold for 13,000 pounds), to win the woman and her children. When they discovered the trick, the Hindes sued in equity to reduce their obligation to the fair market price.

Pendleton defended the employment of a by-bidder as "not

unlawful or exceptionable in general.'' Alternatively, he maintained, if the sale were tainted, it should be rescinded altogether, and he as executor should get back mother and children to dispose of as he chose. Wythe, whose judgments, in John Randolph's words, were "all as between *A* and *B,* who knew nobody,'' had before him his worst enemy in the posture of authorizing and extenuating a commercial deception and offering an alternative of great meanness. He described Pendleton in the opinion not by name but as "the active defendant'' and the by-bidder's "prompter.''

The by-bidder, Wythe went on, "instead of being who would be a buyer, as he pretendeth to be, is in truth the seller disguised, lending his own person to the seller, his office is dramatic no less than the office of an actor in theatrical exhibitions, they both represent others; and the object of both is to deceive. In this latter character however they differ thus: they use their art to persuade, one that he is, the other that he is not, whom he personateth.'' The practice did "not consist with the praecepts in any system of ethics hitherto approved.''

The practice was peculiarly exceptionable here. In an ordinary case, a man bidding against a secret by-bidder would be constrained by the true value of what he bid for. Here Mrs. Hinde "manifested a tender affection for the slaves, and such anxiety to retain them, which was increased by a reciprocal abhorrence in them from a separation, that she seemed resolved to buy them at any price.'' Her husband was at Pendleton's mercy: "to gratify a wife, for a family of servants, endeared to her probably by an intercourse of obsequious attention and faithful ministration on one side, in return for benign treatment and provided care on the other, he bid the pretium affectionis, which is unlimited, and which therefore was What The By-bidder And His Prompter Pleased.'' The last seven words were capitalized by the Chancellor. He did not set the sale aside as Pendleton asked in the alternative. He restrained the defendants from collecting more than the fair market price.

The case occurred only because a woman and her children

could legally be auctioned like quadrupeds or kitchen utensils. The heart of Wythe's opinion was that human emotions had been exploited. If the Hindes were willing to pay the price of affection, it was because the family on the block had shown "reciprocal abhorrence" at separation and had won love by their attention and ministration. The sting of the opinion, striking the by-bidder and his prompter Pendleton, was directed at this sordid manipulation of the relations between persons.

In this climactic opinion of his career, the Chancellor observed the conventions. He was the court pronouncing the law governing the acts of litigants. Yet no one reading what he wrote could doubt that George Wythe was aware that it was Edmund Pendleton who had prompted this despicable conduct and defended it. In this splendid climax, where the content of the legal rule depended explicitly on ethics, where distinction was drawn between theatrical and deceitful personification, where every word said of the by-bidder's dramatic office might have been said of his own as a judge disposing of persons, the mask of the slaves was half lifted, and the mask of the court was half removed.

3

The Overlord of American Law and the Sovereign of Costa Rica

THE DECISION which made the United Fruit Company free to become both the sponsor of Chiquita Banana and *el Pulpo,* the octopus of Latin American revolutionary literature and politics, was given in 1909 at the apex of the American legal system by Oliver Wendell Holmes, Jr. If the company had been asked to defend its role without regard to the law, it might have answered, in the words of Charles Gould in *Nostromo,* "Only let the material interests once get a firm footing, and they are bound to impose the conditions on which alone they can continue to exist . . . A better justice will follow." Justice by corruption was a North American plan for Central America in 1904, when the United Fruit Company struggled with the American Banana Company and Joseph Conrad wrote *Nostromo.* It was a plan still operating in 1974 when the most recent owners of the company paid over one million dollars to persuade a Central American President to relax an impost on bananas.

Conrad's subtle and comprehensive insights might have enabled him to invent the participants in the actual battle in Costa Rica: Minor Cooper Keith and his assignor, Don José Astua; Herbert L. McConnell and his advocate, Don Ricardo Jiménez; and the Boston lawyer, Bradley Webster Palmer,

who was at the center of the network of legal relations constituting the largest Yankee enterprise in Central America. The
author of *Nostromo* could also have explored with sensitivity
the fissured soul of Palmer's partner, Moorfield Storey, critic
of American imperialism and spokesman for the enterprise;
and he might have described as an elemental force the New
York lawyer Elihu Root, who incarnated American regard for
legality and money. But Oliver Wendell Holmes, Jr., the person on whose adoption of a comprehensive mask the outcome
of the struggle in Costa Rica finally turned, has a complexity
and a dimension larger, I believe, than that of any character
in *Nostromo*.

HOLMES'S PLACE IN LEGAL HISTORY

Holmes, like Blackstone and Wythe, had the great advantage of being a law professor who became a judge, so that his
teaching could take the form of opinions in particular cases,
and he could shape action by theory. That law is a type of
teaching, suasive far more than coercive, is never better demonstrated than when a professor is on the bench. Towering as
a teacher above his contemporaries, Holmes was, in
Cardozo's words, "the great overlord of the law and its
philosophy."

He was the founder of "non-Euclidean legal thinking,"
the first person "completely to undermine the conception that
law resembles pure geometry." A Vesalius teaching that
anatomy should be studied by dissection; a Machiavelli
showing how politics could be studied as objectively as any
other natural phenomenon; a Galileo replacing speculation
about the stars with inspection of the skies through a telescope—such was the estimation of Holmes, and the analogies
with other scientific revolutionaries drawn by Jerome Frank,
writing in the 1930's as Holmes passed his ninetieth year.
According to Frank, Holmes had effected his fundamental

revolution in perspective in 1897, in "The Path of the Law," a dedicatory address at Boston University Law School, when he told the students of law: "The object of your study, then, is prediction, the prediction of the incidence of public force through the instrumentality of the courts." He then gave his celebrated definition: "The prophecies of what the courts will do in fact, and nothing more pretentious are what I mean by law."

From Holmes "we all derive," wrote Karl Llewellyn, speaking for that small band of scholars of the late twenties and early thirties loosely classified as the American legal realists. Under his banner, Llewellyn, Frank, and the others proceeded to urge the study of what courts did in fact. To understand the behavior of judges, they contended, was to examine the stimuli to which the judges were exposed and the judges' reaction to the stimuli. Precedents were among the phenomena to be inspected—the realists were not so naïve as to imagine that rules had no part in a legal decision; as Frank pointed out, rules could even be "controlling." They noted, however, that rules did not confine the most creative judges at their most creative moments; rules did not bind the corrupt or the prejudiced; rules operated with the greatest impact on honest judges of middling intelligence. They insisted that rules should not be the sole object of legal study and legal research. The stimuli to be examined were far more numerous and included bribes, political allegiances, and the personal experience of the judges. Comprehensive understanding of all the factors affecting a decision would alone yield an intelligent account of what courts did in fact, and would alone make possible intelligent prediction of their future doings.

How imperceptible were the efforts of the realists, how wide the gap between what they urged and what their colleagues and students in the law schools did! A principal reason for their failure was this: Vesalius had dissected corpses; Machiavelli had analyzed the politics of the Italian peninsula;

Galileo had used a telescope; the father of their revolution had spoken the words they repeated—his practice showed his meaning to be other than what they imagined.

Wound at Ball's Bluff

At Ball's Bluff, Tremlett's boy George told me, I was hit at 4 $^1/_2$ p.m., *the heavy firing having begun about an hour before, by the watch*—I felt as if a horse had kicked me and went over—1st Sergt. Smith grabbed me and lugged me to the rear a little way & opened my shirt and ecce! the two holes in my breasts & the bullet, which he gave me. George says he squeezed it from the right opening. Well—I remember the sickening feeling of water in my face—I was quite faint—and seeing poor Sergt. Merchant lying near—shot through the head and covered with blood—and then the thinking begun.

. . . I was taken into the large building which served as a general hospital; and I remember the coup d'oeuil on which I closed my eyes with the same sickening which I had felt on seeing poor Merchant. Men lying round on the floor—the spectacle wasn't familiar then—a red blanket with an arm lying on it in a pool of blood—it seems as if instinct told me it was John Putnam's (then Capt. Comdg Co H)—and near the entrance a surgeon calmly grasping a man's finger and cutting it off . . .

Much more vivid is my memory of my thoughts and state of mind for though I may have been light-headed my reason was working . . .

Perhaps the first impulse was tremulous—but then I said—by Jove, I die like a soldier anyhow—I was shot in the breast doing my duty up to the hub—afraid? No, I am proud—then I thought I couldn't be guilty of a deathbed recantation—father and I had talked of that and were agreed that it generally meant nothing but a cowardly giving way to fear. Besides, thought I, can I recant if I want to, has the approach of death changed my beliefs much? & to this I answered—No. Then came in my Philosophy—I am to take a leap in the dark—but now as ever I believe that whatever shall happen is best—for it is in accordance with a general law—and *good & universal* (or *general law*) are synonymous terms in the universe.

> I remember Hayward's saying "It is a beautiful face," or something of the sort & looking up & seeing Willy Putnam, calm & lovely, and being told or knowing he was dead. I was soon moved to a Wall Tent with John Putnam where all was quiet . . . and things went smoothly barring my impatience . . .

So Holmes described his first experience of mortal jeopardy.

"Wounded in breast at Ball's Bluff, October 21, 1861, in neck at Antietam, September 17, 1862, in foot at Marge's Hill, Fredericksburg, May 3, 1863"—so ran Holmes's autobiography in *Who's Who in America.* The experience of fighting, of trying to kill, of being nearly killed, of upholding the Union by force, affected his vision of the law.

He was familiar, he wrote in 1880, with "objections to treating a man like a thing, and the like." He was familiar with them, he said, and continued: "If a man lives in society he is liable to find himself so treated." Conscription was the great example. If the state had power to send you to your death, what could the state not do? Characteristically, Holmes blurred the difference between the state exposing you to risk and the state deliberately killing you. Quantitatively measured, the actions were not distinct. In 1927, sixty-six years after his experience in the Civil War, conscription was still the great example: "We have seen more than once that the public welfare may call upon the best citizens for their lives." Surely then the state had power to sterilize the feeble-minded lest we be "swamped with incompetence." Characteristically, he argued that the greater power, quantitatively determined, embraced the less.

His vision of the universe put personal relations on the same level. "It seems clear to me," he declared in *The Common Law,* "that the *ultimata ratio* not only *regum,* but of private persons is force, and that at the bottom of all private relations, however tempered by sympathy and all the social feelings, is a justifiable self-preference." For a married man of forty, that is a strong statement; it is scarcely an unconsidered one.

The principles whose evolution he described in *The Common Law* appear at points to be identified with forces or with force. The conclusion, as well as the form, of his account of the law of negligence is Darwinian: "The general principle of our law is that loss from accident must lie where it falls." In the contest for survival, the strongest force prevails, and it is not a judge's business to be tenderhearted to the vanquished or the maimed.

In later essays, Holmes was sometimes a meliorist and a reformer, and advocated an approach to law closer to engineering than biology. The law was to be improved, and improved by measurement. Quantitative judgments should replace haphazard guessing. What was to be measured? "The relative worth of our different social ends." How was such worth to be measured? By determining the intensity of our social desires. Who would determine them?—opinion polls and survey research were not yet in vogue. The measurement of intensity would have to be done by "the great judge," who accurately appraised the requirements of the community. That social ends terminate in individual persons, that social desires exist in individual persons, was not observed. Ends or desires were taken globally as forces capable of calculation by the judicial expert.

Nevertheless, law for Holmes was not raw power but force somehow subordinated to rule. He did not advise law schools to study the place of bribery, nepotism, favoritism, and party pressures in the American judicial process. "If you want to know the law and nothing else, you must look at it as a bad man, who cares only for the material consequences which such knowledge enables him to predict," Holmes wrote in "The Path of the Law." But a bad man would have wanted to know what judges were venal, and a more sophisticated bad man would have wanted to know what his lawyer's nexus to the judge was. Holmes, holding himself aloof from this impure world, studiously ignored the effect of such calculation. He did not call for "Corruption I" to stand in the law-school curriculum next to "Corporations I." He did not propose that "Political Influence" be a topic following "Procedure." He did not ask that "Lawyers as Lobbyists" be studied along with "Constitutional Law." His famous definition of the law as prophecies of what the courts will do in fact was, abstractly taken, capable of the exegesis the American legal realists later gave it. In context, the definition was immediately qualified by the declaration that the means of predicting the incidence of public force was "a body of reports, of treatises, of statutes . . . These are what properly have been called the oracles of the law." Not the study of force, but the study of documents was what Holmes advocated. If he had been asked to explain why, he would have said that in these pages one could find force directed by rule.

"Good and universal (or *general law*) are synonymous terms in the universe" (his italics), Holmes thought near death at the battle of Ball's Bluff. The same faith formed the climax of "The Path of the Law." Through "the remoter and more general aspects of the law," Holmes affirmed, "you not only become a great master in your calling but connect your subject with the universe and catch an echo of the infinite, a glimpse of its unfathomable process, a hint of the universal law."

Cynics may see in the climax of "The Path of the Law" the rhetoric appropriate to a speech of dedication. Doing so, they disregard Holmes's intuition, the mystical vision which sustained him as a judge as much as when he was a soldier wounded in the breast. Others, only slightly less cynical, may see in this conclusion a strain of theology inappropriate for a lawyer. That there "is scarcely a dialectic problem which is discussed in the modern law school, of which one does not find at least a hint in the argumentative technique of the theology of the last century" was for a realist like Thurman Arnold the crowning absurdity of legal education. Holmes himself, with a comparable scorn, called Christopher Columbus Langdell "perhaps the greatest living legal theologian," and did not intend the description as a compliment. But some vision of the construction of the universe will be found to underlie anyone's account of law. Skeptical as he was about attempts to explain the cosmos, Holmes's theology was close to being identical with his vision of law. Skeptical and impious as he could be about any particular piece of legislation—the Sherman Anti-trust Act, for example, was "humbug"—he venerated the law, and its source for him was sacred.

To rise above force, to distinguish lawless might from legal right, to convert power into principle, an authority had to be supposed which issued the rules recognized as law. That authority Holmes personified—it was his second great personification (the law itself the first)—in the sovereign. The attributes of this being he took from his nineteenth-century predecessor, John Austin. The sovereign was a deist's god, the necessary supplier of motion in a system whose components were force and rule. If not expressly said to be omnipotent and omniscient and benevolent, he was supposed to possess the knowledge and the power of the system, and his commands were not open to challenge by those within it. Like his deistic prototype, he could not be coerced. Like his prototype, he could not be affected by the orders which he issued for his subjects. Like his prototype, he was personified as male. Under this loose and comprehensive mask, individual judges, politicians, officeholders, legislators were coalesced into a single solemn source of law.

Once, as a young man, Holmes had criticized Austin's conception: "It is admitted by everyone that who is the sovereign is a question of fact equivalent to the question who has the sum of the political powers of a state in his hands." These powers were not necessarily unitary, but might be held by "organizations of persons not sharing in the sovereign power, and by unorganized public opinion." Those organizations and that opinion could make law, too. For lawyers, law was not what the sovereign commanded but what was "enforced by the procedure of the courts"; to say that the rules emanated from the sovereign's will was "a mere fiction."

This critique, appearing in the *American Law Review* in

1872 and reflecting Holmes's first teaching of jurisprudence at Harvard, appears as an anticipation of his famous 1897 definition of the law as prophecy. It points to a realism like Jerome Frank's, to an analysis of who participates in the procedure, to a focus on how political power is divided. But if law is a calculus by lawyers of forces, how shall a judge phrase his doing of the sums? In the act of deciding, he is not predicting a future combination of forces, he is declaring what is now the rule; if he is not speaking for himself, who is he speaking for but the sovereign? When Holmes had been a judge for almost thirty years, when law had become his theology, the sovereign seemed to him one and irreducible. When a case came before him in which he had to choose between the realist critique of his youth and his settled judicial doctrine, he chose orthodoxy. The distance between orthodoxy and reality was to be measured when the struggle in Costa Rica was terminated by his opinion.

The threads of the case are intricate—perhaps only one man, Bradley W. Palmer, ever held them all in his hand. Yet what Holmes decided can scarcely be appreciated without gathering the threads, not as Bradley W. Palmer would have arranged them, but in a pattern disclosing the interplay of litigants and lawyers and the officials of three governments.

FORMATION OF THE ANTAGONISTS

In 1899 Minor Cooper Keith, an Englishman, builder of Limón, Costa Rica's sole Atlantic port, developer of that country's banana industry, concessionaire of the national railway, and son-in-law of José María Castro, the Costa Rican Republic's President (1846–8, 1866), and Andrew W. Preston of Brookline, Massachusetts, the principal importer of bananas to the northeastern United States, pooled their interests in a single entity, the United Fruit Company. Boston-based, but drawing capital from New York and a scattering of stockholders in all parts of the United States, the company acquired ten of its competitors at once and bought control in four others. Buying high when it had to discourage competition in Central America, selling low when it had to discourage competition at home, United Fruit came to control all of the bananas exported from Costa Rica and (with its associated companies) to control eight tenths of the bananas imported into any part of the United States. In its first year of operation it made a profit of $1.8 million on a capital of $16 million; by 1902 its earnings were over $2 million. In 1906, the year when litigation with American Banana became serious, they reached $3.7 million. At the height of the legal controversy, the company must have seemed to be the source of only golden eggs: in the year ending September 30, 1907, earnings, on invested capital of $18.5 million, reached $6.2 million.

At the center of this New England enterprise was Bradley W. Palmer, lawyer. He was not a great adventurer in Latin American politics like Minor Cooper Keith, "the uncrowned king of Central America." He was not the leader of a large industrial enterprise like Andrew W. Preston. He was not the supplier of capital, or an operating officer like the other two members of the executive committee. But with Keith, Preston, and the two others, he was the executive committee, and as the others changed, Keith, Preston, and he remained. He was, beyond doubt, indispensable. Who else but a lawyer who knew the company's interests intimately could have structured the mergers, carried out the acquisitions, and drafted the contracts which gave United Fruit its preeminent position?

Bradley Webster Palmer was not himself a Bostonian. Coming from Wilkes Barre, Pennsylvania, he would have appeared to his New England colleagues as a Westerner. His parents had been prosperous enough for him to attend Exeter, Harvard College, and Harvard Law School, so that his purely academic qualifications would have been acceptable in Boston, and when he was in fact accepted into the partnership of Moorfield Storey and J. L. Thorndike, his career at the Boston bar was assured. Aged thirty-three in 1899, when he put

United Fruit together after being Preston's counsel in the predecessor importing company, he had the energy and determination of the lawyer who has made his way in the metropolis by painstaking devotion to legal details and his client's business.

Besides being a director and a member of the executive committee, Palmer was the record keeper of the company— the Secretary, writer and guardian of those minutes which constituted the company's paper life. Normally a lawyer not on the company payroll—outside counsel—is not listed as an officer. In United Fruit's annual reports, the firm of Storey, Thorndike, and Palmer was described as General Counsel under the heading "Executive Officers."

Herbert L. McConnell of Mobile, Alabama, was an importer of bananas from Bocas del Toro, Colombia, an island off the Colombian coast in the Department of Panama, with $20,000 invested in his enterprise. Faced with the competition of United Fruit, he sold out to the trust at the end of 1899. In a contract negotiated by Bradley W. Palmer, McConnell was conceded a minority share in his old enterprise and the right to stay on as its manager as long as Andrew Preston thought him fit; he agreed to keep imports from Bocas del Toro to two steamerloads a year, and he agreed not to compete in any way with United Fruit.

In four years, McConnell received $12,450 in salary and $77,666 in dividends from the trust. He acquired a new sense of how profitable the banana business could be. In the words of Bradley W. Palmer, "This sudden accession of wealth by one who had theretofore been in very moderate circumstances, and engaged in small affairs, turned his head." A bachelor, he was willing to gamble. In 1903 he claimed in his own name uncultivated lands suitable for bananas along both sides of the Sixaola River.

McConnell's new property lay at the northeastern top of the Isthmus of Panama, in territory once claimed by Costa Rica but awarded by arbitration in 1900 to Colombia. McConnell began to clear the land, plant crops, and open railroad transportation to Gadokan, the nearest harbor. In

1904 he transferred his personal investment to a new corporation, the American Banana Company, whose prospectus estimated that its annual profits would be $414,000 on an invested capital of $750,000. The company's subscribers were all citizens of Mobile or Birmingham, Alabama.

Counsel for this enterprise were Gregory L. Smith and Harry T. Smith of Mobile, lawyers prominent enough locally to have the First National Bank of Mobile and the regional office of the Louisville and Nashville Railroad as their clients—their access to capital and to the principal means of moving bananas north from Mobile must have appealed to McConnell. They reciprocated by investing in his venture, Gregory Smith subscribing to $5,000 worth of the stock, Harry Smith to $2,000, each prudently paying in only $1,000 on their subscriptions.

The method of operation of the banana men may be inferred from these reports to McConnell from R. K. Warren, his manager at Bocas del Toro. June 10, 1903: "Parades, who is still *alcalde,* is in with the U.F. Co. gang, and they have made application for *our land.* We will circumvent them with 'Grease.' " June 19, 1903: "I have just spoken with the *alcalde* (Parades), and he said he wanted to see me at my room. I told him I was ready at any time. If *greasing* to the extent of four or five hundred silver is wanted, I will yield. If it is for a greater sum, I will submit it to you before agreeing." October 13, 1903: "The United Fruit Co. owns this *Alcalde.*" These communications fell into United Fruit's hands and were circulated by it to reflect upon McConnell. It would require an act of faith in the rectitude of Boston businessmen to suppose that the characterization of United Fruit's ownership of an official was merely rhetoric.

BATTLE IN SAN JOSÉ AND WASHINGTON

United Fruit did not at first react ferociously. A proposition McConnell himself described as "most reasonable" was tendered him, but his plans were too large for him to make an accommodation. Calmly but pointedly, Minor Cooper Keith wrote McConnell on June 23, 1903: "Both Mr. Kyes and Mr. Leet are naturally doing all they can to block your operations in the Sixaola River, and as a business man you can clearly understand that we cannot discontinue such obstruction on our part until we have some definite assurance from you that you intend to respect the contract made with our company and work in unison and harmony with us." In September 1903, as his plantation neared full bearing, soldiers of Costa Rica occupied it.

He appealed to the State Department. His land was in Colombia, how could Costa Rica be permitted to invade it? Secretary of State John Hay cabled the American Minister to Costa Rica, William Lawrence Merry: IF FACTS ARE AS REPRESENTED, USE GOOD OFFICES WITH COSTA RICA TO PERMIT THE CONTINUANCE OF WORK. Merry contacted the Acting Minister of Foreign Relations, Don José Astua Aguilar, who informed him that Costa Rica claimed no jurisdiction over the territory and that Costa Rica did not demand that McConnell's work stop. Don José gave no hint that he himself was the owner under Costa Rican law of McConnell's property.

By 1904, however, Don José appeared in his proprietary role. He was the owner, so the papers presented to a Costa Rican court showed, under what became known as the Astua Denouncements—land claims filed in March 1900 in the name of Don José Astua Aguilar, his wife Carolina, and his children José Antonio, Graciela, Cora, Mercedes, and Margarita, and in the name of Don Rodolfo Rojas and his four daughters, each person asserting title to one thousand hectares, or a total acreage twice the area owned by United Fruit for banana production in Costa Rica. The claims covered the very ground on the Sixaola occupied by McConnell's plantation. The Astua Denouncements treated the land as Costa Rican, not Colombian.

Don José and Don Rodolfo and their families, it further appeared, had assigned their claims in various shares to Minor Cooper Keith and his brother Johnny (said by Minister Merry to represent "the political interests" of United Fruit in Costa

Rica), and Johnny's four children, and to Mariano Guardia, a bookkeeper for United Fruit, and to Edgar J. Hitchcock, an employee of the Northern Railway, the Keith concession which had become a wholly owned subsidiary of United Fruit. Another assignee of the Astua Denouncements was Don Luis Anderson, who later succeeded Don José as Foreign Minister of Costa Rica. These assignments were transitory—the intermediate assignees conveyed their land to the Northern Railway itself. No doubt the documents constituting the Astua Denouncements had, from the beginning, this objective—to put title to the banana lands into the control of United Fruit; it may be equally inferred that Don José, Don Luis, and the others who cooperated in the claim and the assignments, and who were not otherwise on the company's payroll, did not go uncompensated for their assistance.

Acting through Don Ricardo Pacheco, a former Foreign Minister, United Fruit began the process of confirming its subsidiary's title in a Costa Rican court. The judge ruled that McConnell had no standing to intervene in the process. In anticipation of the outcome, in the fall of 1904, soldiers of Costa Rica again occupied the McConnell plantation. Minor Cooper Keith's later testimony was that he could not "remember" whether he had suggested this course of action to any official of the republic of Costa Rica or not.

While this struggle in Costa Rica was in progress, the territory on the Sixaola was affected by a change in the status of Panama—a change due largely to the enterprise of a New York lawyer, William Nelson Cromwell; but that is another story. On November 2, 1903, the Congress of Colombia adjourned without ratifying the treaty which gave the United States the right of way on the isthmus. On November 3, a revolt against Colombian rule broke out in Colón. An American cruiser arrived with instructions to prevent the landing of any government troops. On November 6 the United States recognized the revolutionaries as the "Republic of Panama," and on November 18 the new nation executed the treaty which gave the United States the Canal Zone.

Panama now stood in place of Colombia as the country in which McConnell believed his land lay and on whose protection he depended. The Panamanian constitution, promulgated early in 1904, recognized that if the United States of America guaranteed the independence and territorial integrity of Panama, the United States had the right to "intervene in any part of the Republic of Panama to re-establish public peace and constitutional order in the event of their being disturbed." On February 14, 1904, the United States guaranteed the Panamanian Republic's independence and territorial integrity. By the end of the year the Panamanian Army had ceased to exist, and the United States of America possessed the only military force on the Isthmus of Panama.

Article 4 of the constitution of Panama declared that Panamanian territory comprised the area awarded Colombia in its 1900 arbitration with Costa Rica. That area apparently included the disputed banana plantation on the Sixaola. The United States now had the right under the Panamanian constitution to reestablish order in Panama, it had the obligation by treaty to guard Panama's integrity, and it had the force on hand to do so.

Observing this North American presence on the Isthmus, McConnell addressed a formal memorial to the State Department on December 21, 1904. He pointed out that a United States War Department map of Panama showed his land to be part of Panama, not to mention that the constitution of Panama formally treated the area as Panamanian. He asked damages of Costa Rica for $200,000 actually lost and for the capital value of his enterprise, estimated by him to be $2 million (his $400,000 of estimated profits capitalized at 20 percent). A Democratic Congressman from Alabama, George W. Taylor, added his voice to the protest. In response to these pressures, Secretary of State Hay on February 8, 1905, instructed Minister Merry to arrange "some satisfactory *modus vivendi*" between McConnell and Costa Rica. Hay disregarded a communication received from the United Fruit Company that it was the true owner of McConnell's land.

Upon this intervention, Astua assured McConnell on April 12, 1905, "of the benevolent attitude of the President"—an assurance which, in the circumstances, would have been read as the politest of political threats. Accompanying these words was an offer to McConnell on the part of the Costa Rican government of a twenty-five-year lease of the lands he claimed to own, "respecting, however, the rights of third parties"—in short, respecting the Astua Denouncements. McConnell rejected this derisory concession. Negotiations continued. On May 10, 1905, Johnny Keith informed the Costa Rican Minister of Public Works that McConnell's contract not to compete prevented him from entering into "the business of the cultivation and sale of tropical fruits." He, Keith, had information from New York as to what the State Department would do. It was "probable" that the Department "will not insist on the carrying out of its instructions to support or assist the project of Mr. McConnell."

Still the issue was not resolved in Washington. In October 1905 McConnell filed a new protest with the State Department, now pointing out that Don José, "with whom all our negotiations took place," was the head of the family whose claim was at the foundation of United Fruit's Costa Rican title. He appealed to the State Department to protect the rights of American citizens in Panama, adding that the United States had a special duty to the Republic, "the youngest and weakest in the family of nations."

In January 1906 the new Secretary of State, Elihu Root, cabled Minister Merry that the United States did not "cede" the right of the courts of Costa Rica "to prejudice the ultimate rights of American citizens" until it was decided who was the final sovereign of the land. This terse declaration, communicated to Foreign Minister Astua, caused him to object that Costa Rican courts must have authority to decide title to land over which it exercised *de facto* sovereignty—otherwise, "the axiom that the courts are the law brought into effect and life would be rendered futile." Perhaps Don José, too, was a legal realist.

In Costa Rica, as later in the United States, McConnell seemed destined to have counsel not quite as politically powerful as those opposing him. In the negotiations with Astua, McConnell was represented by Don Ricardo Jiménez, in Minister Merry's opinion "one of the best lawyers in the country." Don Ricardo had been Minister of Foreign Relations. In 1910, he was to become President. In 1905 and 1906 he was out of office.

"It seems," Don Ricardo wrote the trial judge on April 26, 1906, "that it is the duty of the President, of his Ministers, of the State Attorney, and of the Justices, to hasten to satisfy the slightest desires of Mr. Keith." A stronger or more candid comment on the relation of the United Fruit Company to the government of Costa Rica could not have been made. "Nevertheless," he continued, "so great is my belief in the force of reason that I refuse to accept this theory, and insist on petitioning again and again that Mr. McConnell be done justice." These courageous words had no effect upon the court confirming Northern Railway's title: McConnell was still not permitted to be heard. But in May 1906 a panel of the Supreme Court of Justice decreed that McConnell had at least a right to intervene in the contest. By this time, however, McConnell had determined that his hope lay not in the justice of Costa Rica but in the justice of the United States.

THE CHOICE OF COUNSEL

Bradley W. Palmer was not only General Counsel of United Fruit, he was a partner in "the new sort of firm, generally and clearly recognized as a distinctive entity," in which partners shared fees as well as space and, working within the organization of a single entity, developed their own specialties. Founded in 1887 by Moorfield Storey and John L. Thorndike to do the legal business of the Union Pacific Railroad, the partnership had gone from railroad mortgages to municipal bonds, and when it lost the Union Pacific after New York management ousted Charles Francis Adams, its growth was not ended. In the five years in which United Fruit had been its client, the firm had almost doubled its membership, and Palmer had drawn from Warren and Brandeis his old classmate and Brandeis's most gifted partner, Harvard Law School's future dean Ezra Ripley Thayer. As Storey, Thorndike, Palmer and Thayer, the partnership stood in the top rank of Boston legal enterprises. When its great client was threatened, Palmer turned to the firm's chief litigator and public figure, its founder, Moorfield Storey.

Four years Holmes's junior, Storey had missed the War but had shared the same environment of Boston and Harvard. "When beginners at the law," Storey reminded Holmes, "we had ample time for excellent fooling in the Law Library and ampler digestion even for banquets at Point Shirley." A member of the small dining club whose members had included Holmes, Henry Adams, and the two Jameses, he had succeeded Holmes in the intellectual labor (remunerated by $300) of co-editor of that forerunner of student law publications the *American Law Review,* and in that capacity had published some Holmes articles, including his critique of Langdell. He then entered practice with Brooks and Ball, "primarily business lawyers," with which Dickensian firm, his biographer records, he "acquired early a familiarity with business methods and points of view, besides a keen sense of the place and value of money in American civilization." If one bears in mind that his biographer was Mark Howe, Marquand's model for his biographer Horatio Willing in *The Late George Apley,* the force of this understatement may be appreciated. Service with the District Attorney's office, according to the same authority, cultivated his "prosecuting state of mind" and "capacity for sharp distinctions between right and wrong." His friendship with Charles Francis Adams, the Union Pacific's president, led to his handling the railroad's legal business and the founding of his own firm.

Storey organized the Massachusetts Reform Club to combat the lax moral standards of the Grant Administration, and the political corruption facilitated by lawyers was the target of his prosecuting state of mind when he became a leader and then president of the American Bar Association. From civic corruption, he extended his verbal attacks to immorality in international affairs. His speeches on the American taking of an Asian country read today as a remarkable anticipation of the criticisms to be made of the American involvement in Vietnam. Of the responsibility for army atrocities in the pacification of the Philippines, he wrote that the then Secretary of War, Elihu Root, "was silent in the face of certain knowledge, and by his silence he made himself responsible for all that was done with his acquiescence. The responsibility for what has disgraced the American name lies at his door." With equal vigor he attacked Root's successor, William Howard Taft. When Roosevelt took Panama, Storey told the Massachusetts Reform Club, "It is not safe to let a strong man decide what is just to the weak. Such a doctrine means anarchy. Justice is the same for individuals and nations."

With this frankness and censoriousness and an intolerance of imperfections such that he was in his lifetime called "the last of the Puritans" ("last" was premature; Santayana was to use Storey's nephew, W. Cameron Forbes, as his "last Puritan"), he had a keen consciousness of hypocrisy as a vice in others. A favorite verse for quotation was James Russell Lowell's Yankee gibe at England as John Bull:

> Ole Uncle S. sez he, "I guess
> John preaches wal," sez he;
> "But, sermon thru, an'come to *du*
> Why, there's the old J.B.
> A-crowdin' you and me!"

Theodore Roosevelt and Elihu Root, he suggested on various occasions, were this kind of sanctimonious sermonizer. Root had asserted the United States' respect for the independence of Central American countries, for whom the United States would be a trustee. "We may feel," said Storey, "that the

United States will follow too closely the rules laid down by a distinguished trustee in Boston who said that there were three things a trustee should never lose sight of—first, the safety of the trustee; second, the convenience of the trustee; and third, the compensation of the trustee.'' Storey offered this local analogy in the Godkin lectures of 1920 at Harvard. The critique of American foreign policy as greedy imperialism had been his theme since 1898.

When James Bradley Thayer published a complacent article, ''Our New Possessions,'' on the law to be used in the areas conquered from Spain, Storey wrote him: ''I confess, however, that you are one of the last men living from whom I expected the suggestion that we should not apply the New Testament, the Declaration of Independence, and perhaps, you would add the Ten Commandments to 'concrete problems,' but use them to keep our 'inner states wholesome and sweet,' while we apply 'horse sense' to practical matters. I believe the exact contrary, and I care little for principles or religion which are left for private use and not applied in dealings with others.'' His formula of confession, ''I confess that you . . .'' suggested the extent to which he suppressed his own conflicts and projected them onto others.

When, in the 1911 Storrs lectures at Yale Law School, he addressed the complaint of Roosevelt that ''many of the most influential members of the bar . . . make it their special task to work out bold and ingenious schemes by which their very wealthy clients, individual or corporate, can evade the laws which are made to regulate in the interest of the public the use of great wealth,'' Storey had a clear answer. The lawyers the President criticized were ''really telling their clients what the law permits and how to make their practice comply with its requirements. This is not evading, but obeying the law.'' Reverence for the law, he said, invoking Lincoln, must become ''the political religion of the nation.''

Storey called his Storrs lectures ''The Reform of Legal Procedure,'' an emphasis on law as process anticipating Cardozo. But he treated law as a set of commands on paper, not as a process in which he was a communicant. No piece of paper can resist manipulation. In this understanding of law, Moorfield Storey was very like Holmes's bad man—it was after thirty years of interacting with the Boston bar that Holmes had fashioned this image. Like Holmes's creation, Storey as a lawyer was sanction-oriented, unmindful of the educative and channeling functions of the law. Although the antitrust laws had been on the books for about twenty years, Storey saw no incompatibility between principle and practice when his partner formed New England's largest trust. His firm, he observed in his autobiography, "did not undertake to advise on questions of business, but only of law."

When Bradley W. Palmer let Storey know that United Fruit needed a champion in a suit charging it with violation of federal law, Storey was willing to act. Palmer—in Storey's autobiography, written after forty years of association with him, "B. W. Palmer," "Mr. Palmer," "my partner Palmer"—was no boon companion. He was, in Storey's phrase (faintly patronizing, even ambivalent), "a very busy business lawyer." He acted not to oblige Palmer, not merely to make money for the firm. He was carrying out his own view of what fidelity to a client required and what the commands on paper permitted. When the exigencies of litigation led to his co-champion being found in the New York law firm of Strong and Cadwalader in the person of Henry W. Taft, brother of Root's successor as Secretary of War and a conduit to the Roosevelt Administration, he did not look at the persons for whom he acted or those by whom he succeeded.

By its own calculation of continuity, Strong and Cadwalader was eighty-five years old in 1905 and among the very oldest of law firms in New York City. Longevity of this kind was remarkable in what had changed in those years from a provincial seaport to an international center of capital. More remarkable still was the adaptation and expansion of the firm from the trial work done by George Washington Strong to the counseling of savings banks and testators done by George Templeton Strong to the underwriting business attracted by John Lambert Cadwalader. In 1899 the firm added to its regular clients James Speyer and Company, bankers and underwriters of Latin American republics. In the same year, his fortieth, Henry W. Taft joined the firm as the fifth of its five partners.

From Cincinnati, this younger brother of William Howard Taft had risen without great difficulty in a practice which valued the industry of a young man of proper Protestant antecedents who had been a member of Skull and Bones at Yale. As a partner of Strong and Cadwalader, Taft was as sensitive as Storey to the decline he noticed in the esteem in which lawyers were held. The very term "corporation lawyer" had become one of opprobrium. The fault, he told the students of Harvard Law School, was that of "a relatively small portion of the entire membership of the bar" who had involved themselves to unprecedented degree in business (if he had cared to use the example, Bradley W. Palmer would have been an instance). It was unjust to go from their conduct to blanket condemnation of the bar. Corporation counsel were rightly condemned only when they identified themselves with their clients and when they aided these clients to evade the law. Lawyers at their noblest—he did not exclude himself from this role—were "constructive statesmen." That role, he assured the students, was not inconsistent with earning a living.

"The crowning service of the American lawyer," was, in his opinion, "to teach respect for the law because it is the law"—the sentiment was one with Storey's on "the political religion of the nation." He had himself in 1906 assumed the onerous public duty of Special Assistant to the Attorney General to bring against the American Tobacco Company the first criminal prosecution under the Sherman Antitrust Act. When Bradley Palmer wanted New York counsel to defend United Fruit on charges of violating the Sherman Antitrust Act, Henry W. Taft was a not inapposite choice.

Besides expertise and his familial tie to the Administration, Taft had the friendship of the incumbent Secretary of State,

Elihu Root, whom Theodore Roosevelt (then his grateful beneficiary) described as "a great corporation lawyer," and of whom either Thomas Fortune Ryan or William C. Whitney—his relations to each of these plunderers of the street railway system of New York were such as to make the story plausible of either—was supposed to have said, "I have had many lawyers who have told me what I cannot do; Mr. Root is the only lawyer who tells me how to do what I want to do."

So acute was his analysis of legal ambiguities, so balanced his presentation of alternatives, so farsighted his solutions, and so clear his discrimination between the criminal and the permissible that no client Root counseled ever went to jail. No fellow professional of his day could have seen him as one of the minority who had brought discredit on the bar. Henry Taft did not. They had met in 1899, and their relations, both personal and professional, had become "more and more friendly." Root brought to his opinions, at the time he gave them, the indispensable conviction that what the law permitted was right, or as Taft put it, he "raised the tone of any discussion and expelled any idea of sordidness or appeal to unworthy motives." He brought to his work a faith he publicly professed in "the principles underlying our institutions," a faith "that those principles are founded in eternal justice." Yet he possessed the ability, almost equally indispensable for a good lawyer, of looking at his own work self-critically. "We conduct and try our cases too much," he wrote privately, "as if we were playing a game, in which the Judge was umpire to award a prize to the most skillful player." The most skillful player could make the observation. As Edmund Pendleton was the epitome of a successful lawyer in colonial Virginia, so Elihu Root was the personification of corporate law in New York City.

The legal system of the United States, Henry Taft declared, rose far above the defective systems observable in Latin America. It was indeed the best the world had ever known. In this system, he observed, Root was "the leader of the bar.'' He was so deservedly, for ''he had excelled not alone in the practice of his profession in a local atmosphere, but he had added thought upon the relations of this country to foreign countries . . .''

Taft and Root had one client in common whose interests in foreign countries depended on the aid of the United States. In February 1904, Root, then Roosevelt's Secretary of War, had returned to what he called ''the best field for activity in the world,'' the practice of law in New York. He remained in practice until July 1905, when he became Roosevelt's Secretary of State. In this period he represented James Speyer and Company, the regular client of Henry Taft, in arranging a bond issue for the Republic of Costa Rica. When Root returned to office, Taft resumed his regular work, in September 1906 writing President Roosevelt directly to complain when the Republic of San Domingo, then under the special protection of the United States, had cut Speyer and Company out of participation in an issue of Dominican bonds. When Bradley Palmer needed New York counsel in 1906, he could not employ Elihu Root, who had become the Secretary of State. He did not employ Speyer's other counsel, Guthrie and Cravath, famous though they were for trial work. Not only because he had prosecuted the tobacco trust, not only because Speyer would have recommended him, not only because his brother was in the Cabinet, not only because he could write directly to the President on behalf of a client, was Henry Taft the lawyer Palmer chose: he was the best substitute for Elihu Root.

Opposing counsel was not less respectable but was less well connected than Taft, and slightly less prominent than Storey—Everett Pepperell Wheeler, sixty-five years old, the senior partner of Wheeler, Cortis, and Haight. A graduate of Harvard Law School, he had been chairman of the New York Civil Service Commission in the days of reform, 1883 to 1889, and again from 1895 to 1897, being president of the Reform Club in the city in 1889 and 1890, when Storey was a reformer in Massachusetts. He was also the incumbent chairman of the international law section of the American Bar Association, and a widower who had recently married the daughter of President Gilman of Johns Hopkins University. If expertise in the rights of nations was as important in the case as it appeared, Wheeler seemed as good an expert as a client could obtain. If wisdom and vitality were needed to manage the case, Wheeler was a rejuvenated man of experience. If the ability to fight hard against great forces was a sine qua non, Wheeler had fought corruption in the most corrupt of urban centers.

THE DIRECTIVE OF ELIHU ROOT

In a formulation famous as the Roosevelt Corollary to the Monroe Doctrine, Theodore Roosevelt had stated the general position of the United States vis-à-vis Latin America. Elihu Root, out of the Cabinet but chief draftsman of the formula, was authorized by the President to disclose the President's letter of May 20, 1904, setting out the Corollary. The President declared:

> If a nation shows that it knows how to act with decency in industrial and political matters, if it keeps order and pays its obligations, then it need fear no interference from the United States. Brutal wrongdoing, or an impotence which results in a general loosening of the ties of civilized society, may finally require intervention by some civilized society, and in the Western Hemisphere the United States cannot ignore this duty . . .

In January 1905, when Root, still out of the Cabinet, had represented Taft's client James Speyer and Company, he had written Secretary of State John Hay in regard to the interests of Speyer in Costa Rica. It was important, he wrote, for bondholders that their debtor be tranquil and stable. It was important for American bondholders that the United States have a right to intervene if their debtor defaulted. It was, Root wrote Hay, important to have "the next door neighbor of Panama under the financial control of Americans, with a power of ultimate control by the United States.'' It is unlikely that the importance of American control of Costa Rica seemed less to him when he became Secretary of State himself. He could not have been unaware that the financial stability of Costa Rica depended on its exports, that its two exports were coffee and bananas, and that the United Fruit Company controlled its exports of bananas.

In March 1906, two months after he had cabled Minister Merry that Costa Rican courts should not ''prejudice the ultimate rights of American citizens,'' Elihu Root addressed the situation caused by McConnell's claim against United Fruit. His audience was the American Ministers to Panama and Costa Rica. He employed terms which raised the tone of the discussion, seemed to expel any idea of sordidness, and were to be decisive in the subsequent lawsuit between the American Banana Company and United Fruit.

Seven years before he wrote this letter, Root's protégé Roosevelt was the logical choice to be the Republican candidate for governor of New York. But Roosevelt, seeking to avoid a New York City tax, had said under oath seven months before, ''I have been and am now a resident of Washington.'' The constitution of the state required that the governor be a resident of New York for five years preceding the election. Root consulted his senior at the New York bar, Joseph Choate, who told him, ''I don't see anything for it, Root, but for you to go up to the Convention and jump it on them.'' Root addressed the convention on the question at length, explaining that ''under well-settled and familiar law . . . there are two kinds of residence.'' Roosevelt had meant to affirm temporary residence in Washington, not deny permanent residence in New York State. As Root recalled almost forty years later, ''I mixed my argument with a lot of ballyhoo and it went over with a bang.'' The convention chose Roosevelt as its candidate; he went on to become governor and President. Jumping it on them—the straightforward assertion of the conclusion one wanted, suitably ornamented by legal language—had been essential to Roosevelt's career; its usefulness was not confined to a political convention. So here Root jumped it on them.

Root wrote:

> In the Department's conception of this matter Costa Rica exercises at present a temporary de facto sovereignty over the territory included in the McConnell concession, subject of right to be divested at any time at the will of Panama, but actually continuing until such time as the pending boundary treaty is ratified. She exercises the powers of government that are necessary for the orderly administration of the district, but should not use the sovereignty in such a way as to impair the rights of the jure sovereignty of the territory. Her functions of government are limited by her tenure, which is of a temporary and precarious character. Her duty is to preserve the property, not to destroy it, and to hand it over to her successor without the commission of any acts tending to impair the ultimate rights of the de jure owner . . .
>
> In a word, Costa Rica stands in a postion of an usufructuary entitled to the fruits and profits of the territory during the period of tenure, and it cannot be admitted that Costa Rica can in any way destroy or impair the substance of the usufruct . . . It follows that Costa Rica can rightfully exercise no jurisdiction within the territory which Panama could not exercise; and as Panama cannot rightfully deprive possessors of title to property acquired under Colombian laws, which remained in force after the secession of Panama, without due process of law, it would be equally unjust for Costa Rica to attempt to do the same thing.

The Secretary of State had now set out the respective rights of the two republics with the exactness, complexity, and terminology of a conveyance of real estate, a nice mixture of legalism and nonsense. What did he want done?

> . . . the ultimate attributes of sovereignty belong to the ultimate owner, and for this reason it is proper that Panama should see to it that rights and titles which have accrued concerning lands within this area should not be prejudiced by the

State having accidental and temporary jurisdiction. It is suggested that this result may be reached by discreet representations by Panama to Costa Rica, perhaps by remonstrance or
otherwise, rather than by a physical attempt to assert such jurisdiction.

Panama, then, was not to fight but to protest. Still, American property in Panamanian territory "was to be protected
and preserved" by Costa Rica. After seven tight paragraphs
of legal analysis and terse verbiage, was this Root's conclusion, a victory for McConnell? He concluded:

In this connection, however, it is proper to state that the
Department disclaims any intention to interfere in this case to
the prejudice of the United Fruit Company or any other American interest already acquired in the territory immediately in
question.

The Secretary disclaimed intent to injure the acquired
rights of United Fruit. But the heart of the question of boundaries was whether United Fruit would have to surrender the
Astua award. United Fruit had a judgment from the judicial
system of Costa Rica confirming its title. If United Fruit was
not to be prejudiced, the Secretary had decided in favor of
United Fruit. Elihu Root made plain that United Fruit was not
to be prejudiced.

THE INITIATIVE OF COUNSEL IN ALABAMA

United Fruit struck the first blow in the American courts.
Almost from the company's inception, Palmer had worked
with a New Orleans lawyer, Walker B. Spencer, a Tulane
graduate his own age; and Spencer's firm, Howe, Fenner,
Spencer, and Cocke, was given the title of Associate General
Counsel (thirty years later United Fruit was still listed as the
Spencer firm's principal client). In November 1904 Spencer
and his partner Cocke appeared before the federal judge in
Mobile. In the name of McConnell's old company, Camors-

McConnell, now under United Fruit's control, they asked that McConnell be enjoined from breaking his contract not to compete with United Fruit. United's president, Andrew Preston, also sued in his own name, but on second thought withdrew as an individual plaintiff. McConnell was represented by the Smiths, the Mobile lawyers who had invested $1,000 apiece in American Banana. They defended on the ground that the contract McConnell had signed was part of United Fruit's illegal effort to restrain trade in bananas.

The federal district judge for Southern Alabama, Harry T. Toulmin, held any restraint of trade was "collateral" to McConnell's promise not to compete; whether United Fruit had broken the law or not, McConnell was bound to carry out his contract. The judge issued a temporary injunction forbidding McConnell to carry on his business. The Fifth Circuit Court of Appeals in New Orleans affirmed the temporary injunction and on rehearing reaffirmed it. With its second decision on February 6, 1906, United Fruit seemed assured by the courts of the effective end of McConnell's competition. To make doubly sure, a small stockholder in Mobile brought a suit charging fraud in American Banana's prospectus.

In the midst of these contests, near the crest of United Fruit's success, a remarkable history was issued over the signature of "B. W. Palmer" and published privately in Boston under the title *The American Banana Company* and the subtitle "An account of the operations of Herbert L. McConnell in planting banana lands on the Sixaola river, and of his acts in Costa Rica and Colombia (later Panama) relating thereto, with an explanation and copies of documents and correspondence." The book could only have been compiled by the author treating as his own the letters between McConnell and Warren and only by the State Department making available its correspondence of the past four years.

The American Banana Company was not a popular history; it consisted mostly of decrees and documents. The book was not a brief; it had no legal theses to sustain. The firm name was not used, and Palmer did not identify himself as counsel for one of the book's protagonists. An unusual piece of propaganda, then, the book's intended audience must have been executives of United Fruit, to reassure them, and potential investors in American Banana, to demonstrate that American Banana's position was hopeless. Combining an air of objectivity with a ruthlessness of editorial aim, the work was a remarkable exhibition of Bradley Palmer's tenacity and thoroughness.

VICTORY IN NEW YORK

In September 1906 American Banana sued United Fruit in the federal court in New York. Setting out the formation of United Fruit, its monopolistic acquisition of competitors, its selective underselling of bananas and selective overbidding for bananas, its regulation of the price of bananas through its subsidiary the Fruit Dispatch Company, Everett Wheeler charged that the taking of the Sixaola plantation was yet another step in the creation of a monopoly in the commerce of bananas to the United States. He asked two million dollars in damages. Under the Sherman Act his client would be allowed these, plus court costs and "a reasonable attorney's fee," all tripled, if it should prevail.

Strong and Cadwalader by Henry Taft, with Moorfield Storey and Walker Spencer of counsel, answered for United Fruit. They denied that United Fruit had bought out competitors for the purpose of controlling the trade in bananas. They declared that they did not have knowledge sufficient to form a belief as to whether the Fruit Dispatch Company regulated the price in bananas. They denied that United Fruit had instigated the seizure of McConnell's plantation. Swearing to the truth of these professions of ignorance or outright denials, the lawyers vouched for the innocence of their client. "The lawyer who stands in a community for incorruptible honesty," Storey told his Yale audience, "acquires an influence which is invaluable. When it is known that his presence in

Court means that he thinks his client is right, that mere presence has great weight with jury or with Court. The services of such a man are sought by all, and the client is fortunate who secures them.'' Storey and Taft were willing that United Fruit be so fortunate.

Before trial Everett Wheeler took the depositions of seventy-five persons, including Ascensión Esquivel, the President of Costa Rica. He then asked United Fruit to produce copies of the letters or cables it had sent to its agents or to members of the Costa Rican government at critical points in 1904 and 1905, and to disclose the sums of money it had sent to its agents in Costa Rica in 1904 and 1905. When United Fruit declined to do so, Wheeler went before E. Henry Lacombe, a product of the New York Corporation Counsel's office and a federal judge since 1887, well known to Wheeler, and sought an order. He obtained a decree that United Fruit meet his demands at the trial and not excuse itself by claiming that the documents were outside of the jurisdiction in Costa Rica, but Lacombe refused Wheeler the right of inspecting them before trial, and Wheeler could not get Francis Cabot Lowell, the federal judge in Boston, to amend Lacombe's order. If, in the impeachment proceedings against President Nixon, inspection of the recordings he had made had been postponed until his trial before the Senate, and that body, instead of hearing the facts, had considered first the issue, raised from time to time by his statements, that ''the Presidency,'' not Richard M. Nixon, had performed the various acts of which he stood accused, we would have a contemporary analogue to what now occurred in the case of American Banana.

Trial, according to Storey, ''is an ordeal which a man dislikes to face, and experience does not make it more attractive. The young lawyer rushes into court, confident in the justice of his cause. His older brother is dragged in, knowing how uncertain the result of a trial always must be, never so much alarmed as when his case seems absolutely sure and he can see no ground on which his opponent can win. He realizes with Mr. Justice Curtis, that 'Every new witness is a new peril,' and he knows all the chances of battle.'' At this stage of the American Banana litigation, the reasons for avoiding trial became very strong. If trial were reached, the operations of United Fruit in Costa Rica would have to be set out before the world. Settlement must have seemed preferable. But as an alternative to settlement or trial, there remained demurrer—admit all the facts alleged in the complaint and argue that even if admitted they did not create liability for United; concede the facts and win on the law. Storey and Taft elected this alternative.

Before Charles Hough, a veteran district judge who had presided over Taft's prosecution of the tobacco trust, Taft moved that the complaint be dismissed for failure to state a cause of action. Hough granted the motion on March 9, 1908. The perils of trial, the risk of disclosing vital records, were removed for United Fruit.

Hough treated the matter more as an action for tort at common law than as a case charging violation of the antitrust statutes of the United States with impact on imports to the United States. Wheeler had alleged that the sending of Costa Rican soldiers in 1903 had been "at the inducement" of United Fruit, and that the occupation of the plantation in 1904 had been "at the instigation" and "at the inducement" of United Fruit. Supposing for the sake of argument that United Fruit had committed a tort, Hough wrote: "There was but one tort and if one offender can be sued, it is of the essence of the doctrine that the other must be equally suable. But neither Costa Rico nor its officers could be brought into our courts . . ." Although Hough consistently misspelled the name of the country, he felt that Costa Rica was a sovereign and so immune from suit.

A JUDGE FROM BEYOND THE BRAZOS

The case in Alabama had meanwhile taken an unexpected turn. The judges of the Fifth Circuit—A. P. McCormick of

Dallas, Texas; Don A. Pardee of Atlanta, Georgia; David D. Shelby of Huntsville, Alabama—ruled on March 5, 1907, after a full hearing, that Judge Toulmin had erred in finding McConnell's defense of antitrust violations irrelevant. McCormick had not been a member of the panel which in 1905 and 1906 had affirmed Toulmin's injunction. He now gave the opinion of the court. The claim of someone who had made a promise that the promise was illegal was "a very dishonest one," he wrote, but the contention must be considered.

McCormick had been born in Brazoria County, Texas, when Texas was part of Mexico. He had graduated from Centre College, Kentucky, in 1854 and had then practiced law in Brazoria, becoming successively probate judge, state district judge, member of the legislature, and for the past twenty-four years federal judge. Seventy-three years of age and the father of ten living children, he possessed the independence of temper that sometimes accompanies long judicial tenure. His perspective was that of Western America. If Pascal had made his famous epigram on the geographical limits of justice with reference to the United States, he could have replaced "across the Pyrenees" with "across the Brazos."

Corporations, "these unnatural persons as they may be called"—so McCormick modestly began—had "devoured individual natural persons having capacity and inclinations for trade." He went on to analyze them less as imaginary persons than as actual monsters: Having devoured natural persons, they were, he wrote, "wonderfully strong. Age does not impair their strength. They perenially recruit it from the highest ranks of the legal profession, with veteran experts in strategy, both grand and elementary." He did not mention Henry Taft or Moorfield Storey or Walker Spencer by name—he may not have known of the former two, but the latter would have been in his line of vision. In any case his view of the role of corporation lawyers in the process of preventing enforcement of the antitrust laws was clear: "There are necessary delays in litigation, inherent weaknesses in its best machinery . . . and all these elements are capitalized to the last extent by these highly organized unnatural persons . . ." The state was "overtaxed" in its efforts to restrain them.

McCormick's conclusion was a remarkable rejection of the rule that a judge should be blind—or, rather, I should say, invoking a tradition of equity jurisprudence with which so much that I have written here has affinity, he set aside a mask and transcended the rule that a judge should not look at persons. "The courts, especially the courts of equity," McCormick concluded, "should not pose always as the fabled goddess, but keep an eye single to these exigent conditions and aid the state, as they rightfully may, by withholding help or grace from graceless and hurtful acts." No grace for the graceless—a fit formula for refusing the aid of a judge to perfect a wrong.

With this admonition in his ears, Judge Toulmin, on July 15, 1908, held that the contract which McConnell had signed was illegal and unenforceable in a court of justice. McConnell was now free to go on the offensive.

THE CONGRESSIONAL ARENA

While appeal from Judge Hough was pending in New York, Wheeler opened a flanking attack in Congress. He gave an Alabama Senator, Joseph Johnston, a copy of the complaint against United Fruit, which Johnston used as the basis to propose a resolution in the Senate directing the Department of Commerce and Labor to investigate United Fruit as a monopoly. Buttressing the complaint was a report obtained by Wheeler, already in the files of the Department of Commerce and Labor—an account dated March 6, 1906, from the German consul in San José to his government, in which the consul matter-of-factly laid out the dominance of United Fruit in Costa Rica. Its income was five times that of the national government's. The only port of entry on the

Atlantic Coast was in the company's hands. Besides controlling the entire export of bananas, it controlled the principal railroad and the nation's communication system. United Fruit, the consul concluded, had "a mighty, unassailable position as the uncontested lord of the land."

Andrew Preston was provoked by Johnston's move to tell the *Boston Herald* that United Fruit welcomed, indeed "courted," an investigation. In Washington the company moved to block it and succeeded. Nothing happened, except a two-hour hearing on Johnston's proposal before a subcommittee chaired by Senator John Kean, Republican of New Jersey, president of the National State Bank of Elizabeth, the Elizabethtown Gas Company, and the Elizabethtown Water Supply Company, and no special champion of the antitrust laws.

"I say," Wheeler told the committee, "they came over there without warrant of law and drove us off the plantation . . ." In over forty years of fighting civic corruption in New York, he had not known a more flagrant wrong. United Fruit had engaged in conduct "little short of treason"—levying war in Central America on fellow citizens of the United States. The company, he told the Senators, was a citizen swollen to such greatness as to be "absolutely regardless of law."

He described United Fruit overbidding for bananas in Central America and selling them cheap wherever local competition existed in the United States. Storey replied, "[T]hese are things which the Sherman Act is intended to promote." Such practices, he said, constituted competition, "the fiercest competition—there is no law against it." McConnell was the worst sort of American businessman, a bad loser in an economic contest, a contract breaker who did not know enough to stay with a benevolent employer. "We do not," said Storey, "owe this man one cent, and we do not feel like being blackmailed into paying it."

The sharpest exchange between the two lawyers recalled the confidence of Don Ricardo Jiménez that there was a truth, a reason which would ultimately prevail. "What do you expect to get out of it?" asked Storey, referring to the proposed investigation. "We expect," Wheeler replied, "to get justice."

The Senate did not act, the Department of Commerce and Labor did not investigate, the Department of Justice did not prosecute, the Administration in which Root was Secretary of State and William Howard Taft Secretary of War did not touch the Banana Trust. Wheeler continued his quest in the courts of the United States, in October 1908 asking the Second Circuit Court of Appeals to reverse Judge Hough.

APPEAL

Walter C. Noyes of New London, Connecticut, a graduate of Cornell Law School, judge of the Court of Common Pleas of New London for twelve years, had within the year been appointed to the Second Circuit by President Roosevelt. Joined by Judge Lacombe and Alfred C. Coxe of Utica, New York, on December 15, 1908, he upheld Hough's dismissal of the complaint for failure to state a cause of action. From the mass of balanced phrases in Root's letter of April 16, 1906, Noyes selected Root's recognition of Costa Rica's "temporary de facto sovereignty." He wrote: "The acts complained of were adopted by the government of a sovereign state in its political capacity and in the exercise of its de facto sovereignty. The question of their legality or illegality cannot be determined by the courts of another country."

Wheeler took the case to the Supreme Court of the United States in January 1909 and argued it orally against Storey and Taft less than three months later, on April 12 and 13. In his written brief he attacked the heart of the two decisions against him in the lower courts. United Fruit's case rested on this proposition: "I was shrewd enough to use as my tool in breaking the law of the United States certain persons wearing the livery of a foreign government and by clever representations I induced that government to assume responsibility, and therefore I am immune.'' Such play-acting, he urged, should not shield American lawbreakers.

Wheeler's chief precedent, a decision by Blackstone, came from the eighteenth century: A man troublesome to the East India Company was arrested by the ruler of the land, an Indian Nabob, and imprisoned. On his eventual release, he returned to England and sued the company for causing the arrest. Whatever the form of government, Blackstone had written in his famous book, ''there is and must be in all of them a supreme, irresistible, absolute, uncontrolled authority, in which the *iura summi imperii,* or the rights of sovereignty, reside.'' As judge in this case, he ruled that the Nabob was such an authority, exercising ''an absolute despotism'' and ''accountable to no human power.'' An English jury, nonetheless, found that the Nabob had acted ''contrary to his own inclination, through fear of offending the defendant, and under his awe and influence.'' He had been the company's cat's-paw. As a judge, Blackstone held the company liable: it was not protected by the Nabob's possession of sovereign authority.

Wheeler quoted Blackstone's words: The Nabob was ''a mere machine,'' ''an instrument and engine of the defendant.'' The officials of Costa Rica were, analogously, ''the tools'' of United Fruit. Their act of despoiling McConnell and transferring his land to the company was an act for which the company was liable.

In reply, Taft and Storey kept the focus on the sovereignty of Costa Rica. The Nabob had been in fear of the East India Company and had acted against his own inclination. Here at issue were the deliberate decisions of the Government of Costa Rica, enforcing the law of the land. What wrong was alleged when the plaintiff charged United Fruit with urging that government to carry out its own statutes? The plaintiff could not look at the motives of United Fruit when the act which was the gravamen of injury was that of the sovereign.

They used hornbook law, *Webb's Pollock on Torts,* to show conclusively that the sovereign was immune from suit.

JUDGMENT BY HOLMES, J.

Decision was handed down two weeks after argument, April 26, 1909. By a vote of 9–0, United Fruit was victorious. Dismissal of the action was affirmed. Holmes gave the opinion of the court, in which all joined, save Harlan, who accepted the outcome but not the reasons. What was instructive in the decision was not the doctrine, which had already been invoked by the district and circuit courts, but the use of the doctrine by "the great overlord of the law and its philosophy."

Holmes himself described the case to Lewis Einstein, shortly after he had decided it, as one "about the U.S. Fruit Company," but nothing in his opinion focused on the company. The previous fall he had told the same friend, "If I had to bet, I should bet that monopolies on the whole, i.e. the trusts and the like, were very much for the public interest; and I feel sure that the popular prejudice stands on no reasoned grounds." He stood ready, he wrote Sir Frederick Pollock privately, to enforce the Sherman Act, but he thought it "a humbug based on economic ignorance and incompetence." With this view of the law involved, he made the opinion an exposition of two interrelated grounds central to his own jurisdiction, on either or both of which he justified dismissal.

First, the statutes of the United States did not reach the acts of United Fruit. "Law," wrote Holmes, paraphrasing "The Path of the Law," that small summa of his judicial philosophy, "is a statement of the circumstances in which public force will be brought to bear upon men through the courts. But the word commonly is confined to such prophecies or threats when addressed to persons living within the power of the courts. A threat that depends upon the choice of the party affected to bring himself within that power hardly could be called law in the ordinary sense.'' By ''the ordinary sense,'' Holmes meant the sense he had given law in ''The Path of the Law.'' He did not explain why it lay within the choice of United Fruit, a corporation incorporated in the United States with its affairs directed from Boston, to bring itself within the power of the United States. In this portion of the opinion he appeared to regard United Fruit as an entity operating in Costa Rica which could choose or not to be subject to the jurisdiction of a federal statute.

Second, ''The fundamental reason why persuading a sovereign power to do this or that cannot be a tort is not that the sovereign cannot be joined as defendant or because it must be assumed to be acting lawfully . . . The fundamental reason is that it is a contradiction in terms to say that within its jurisdiction it is unlawful to persuade a sovereign power to bring about a result that it declares by its conduct to be desirable and proper. It does not, and foreign courts cannot, admit that the influences were improper or the results bad. It makes the persuasion lawful by its own act. The very meaning of sovereignty is that the decree of the sovereign makes law.''

With great economy of intellectual effort, always a consideration with him, Holmes disposed of a case whose messy facts would have been difficult to substantiate at a trial and which would have put a $15 million international business to the trouble of disclosing its methods of business at the suit of an unsuccessful troublemaker. At the same time, Holmes exempted the foreign actions of American monopolies from ''the humbug'' of the Sherman Act. To have achieved these results and to have put as the court's his own theory of law were notable accomplishments.

When his opinion was drafted and circulated to the Justices, Chief Justice Melville W. Fuller returned it with a note:

> Yes, but very hard extension of the rules. Panama is no more an independent state than Nabob—
> But this is a fine opinion and worthy of the writer, which is saying a good deal.

With the pithiness of a man from Maine, the Chief Justice made three capital points and one unconsciously revealing error: (1) an opinion worthy of Holmes, for it was a splendid essay in his jurisprudence; (2) a very hard extension of the rules, for the rules were what Holmes dealt with and the rules were stretched to enclose the messy facts; (3) the government whose sovereignty was the crux of Holmes's decision was no more independent than the Nabob—Holmes's central fact was wrong. That the Chief Justice described the country as Panama and not Costa Rica showed as pointedly as possible how these dependencies of American empire were fungible from the perspective of Washington.

Melville Fuller, seventy-eight, was a great friend of Holmes, and he did not fight. Holmes did not alter his opinion an iota.

SOVEREIGNTY AS A MASK

That Holmes was a rich man (possessed, by inheritance, marriage, and investment, of assets worth $406,038 in 1909) would not have consciously been permitted to affect his decision. In his own investments he had scrupulously taken pains "to avoid the great enterprises such as interstate RR on account of possible cases before me." United Fruit was a great enterprise he had avoided, and he would have loathed the suggestion that any general preference for the rich played a part in the process of his thought. With similar scrupulousness he abhorred friendship as a basis for decision. Storey might believe that "his presence in Court means that he thinks his client right" and that his mere presence had "great weight" with the court. But it is doubtful that Holmes focused in such a way upon the advocates before him. Whatever recollections Storey's presence stirred (they had seen almost nothing of each other for decades), of "excellent fooling in the Law Library and banquets at Point Shirley," Holmes was not to be won by a familiar voice. "The Puritan still lives in New England, thank God!'' Holmes had said in a famous Memorial Day address. But that the voice was Bostonian, and Moorfield Storey ''the last of the Puritans,'' were not controlling. Neither the character of counsel nor the inescapable fact that United Fruit was a ''New England enterprise'' (perhaps the most successful New England enterprise of the turn of the century) was a factor Holmes entered in his equations. New England might be—he had said it in the same Memorial Day address—''mother of a race of conquerors,'' and their conquest might now extend to a Latin empire. American Banana might be a small Southern venture troubling this empire like a mosquito, and he might be an old Civil War hero. No doubt a judge from Brazoria would have taken a different view of the case. No doubt a judge sensitive to the impact of American power on the people of another nation would have spoken more circumspectly. Still, Holmes's focus was not on his class, his friends, his ancestral stock, or his region. Wythe-like, he knew neither A nor B. He acted now on an abstract plane, where no entry was allowed except to general concepts.

''In an hour,'' Holmes wrote as the United Fruit case awaited decision, ''I go to our weekly conference and shall find out whether this week's effort satisfies my brethren. I have put my heart into it, and some of them have been flattering but I have not heard from all. It is part of the slightly exasperating discipline, that somebody is likely to light on a characteristic phrase or a generalization that expresses in a sentence the result of years of reflection and want it struck out, and doubts and doubts and doesn't know.''

Holmes was ''the overlord of the law and its philosophy.'' But, as Cardozo acutely observed, he was ''sceptic even of himself''—it was half his charm as friend and correspondent. Yosal Rogat, in a brilliant comparison of Holmes to Henry Adams and Henry James, has pointed to the analogous sense of alienation in each of them from American politics and the rough-and-tumble post–Civil War world. The detachment bred of this alienation was entirely consistent with intense commitment to the inner universe Holmes had constructed: indeed it was its precondition. Doubt he might, yet he had intellectual passions. Here, as he confessed, his heart was in the opinion. Its central formulations were generalizations expressing in a sentence the result of years of reflection. The colleagues who doubted and doubted and didn't know were objective embodiments of doubts that troubled Holmes, doubts which he must yet deny.

In *American Banana,* on the motion to dismiss, where the plaintiff's allegations had to be accepted as true, Holmes had before him the story of domination of a small country's government by a predatory American business which had brutally suppressed a challenge to its monopoly. Holmes's emotion was not directed to these facts but to the effort of Everett Wheeler to make United Fruit accountable. The case of the chairman of the international law section of the American Bar Association depended, Holmes said, on "several rather startling propositions." It was "surprising," he added, "now to hear it argued that the acts complained of fell within the jurisdiction of Congress." "Startling" and "surprising" were terms of caustic criticism. When he came to the case of the Nabob, "the mere tool" of the defendant company, Holmes observed, "That could hardly be listened to concerning a really independent state." He continued, "But of course it is not alleged that Costa Rica stands in that relation to the United Fruit Company." It had not been alleged in so many words in the complaint. It had been so argued by Wheeler and so noted by the Chief Justice, and Holmes had hardly listened.

It is more than accidental that in the letter describing the case as one "about the U.S. Fruit Company," Holmes had written just before that sentence these characteristic words: "But then personality is an illusion only to be accepted on weekdays for working purposes. We are cosmic ganglia; so I believe as much as I believe anything. And personality is merely the gaslight at the crossroads with an accidentally larger or smaller radius of illumination." Holmes turned from the ganglia to his inner universe, the result of years of reflection. What excited him was that "the very meaning of sovereignty" was at stake.

"The common law," Holmes wrote in a famous dissent, "is not a brooding omnipresence in the sky but the articulate voice of some sovereign or quasi-sovereign." In the first half of this sentence the common law is caricatured as a Calvinist deity reigning on high. In the second half of this sentence, a sovereign with an articulate voice is posited as pronouncing the common law. The caricature is heightened by the marvelously self-contradictory phrase "omnipresence in the sky." Rejecting this deity both in his traditional form—it was Holmes's father who had declared that Calvinism, "the wonderful one-horse shay," had fallen apart—and in its caricatured form as the source of law, Holmes replaced him with his own deity—the sovereign with the articulate voice of the courts. The law announced by a judge was not a lawyer's prophecy. A judge could not say he was announcing his own will as the law. A judge must then be the articulate voice of a sovereign. But who was this being distinct from the judge speaking? The personification of the sovereign, impalpable, hypothetical, mysterious as the rejected brooding omnipresence, became inescapable and disturbing.

Sovereignty, Holmes wrote in *American Banana Company* v. *United Fruit Company,* "is pure fact." It was what he had said in 1871, lecturing at Harvard College. The strenuousness of the assertion now suggested what its author was suppressing, skeptical when criticizing Austin, but now accepting Austin.

In what sense did Holmes treat the determination of sovereignty as "pure fact" in the case before him? It was a fact that soldiers of Costa Rica had taken physical possession of McConnell's plantation. It was taken as true for purposes of deciding the case that United Fruit had instigated and induced this occupation. It was a fact that Elihu Root recognized that Costa Rica had temporary de facto sovereignty in the area. It was also a fact that Elihu Root recognized that Panama had de jure sovereignty with the right to determine title to land in the territory. It was a fact that the United States had the only military force in Panama. It was a fact that the President of the United States had publicly asserted that the United States would suppress brutal wrongdoing in Central America. It was fact that the United States had the right to intervene any- where in Panama to suppress disorder and the United States had a treaty obligation to defend the territorial integrity of Panama. In which fact did the "pure fact" of sovereignty consist?

If brute power was decisive, why was not United Fruit's control over the Costa Rican officials more decisive than the soldiers' control of the plantation? Alternatively, why was not the American military hegemony on the Isthmus of Pan- ama the most decisive fact of all? If it were not brute power but a different kind of "fact," a combination of power and legal description of the power, why were certain words of Secretary Root decisive and not others? Root had recognized the most limited, divisible authority in Costa Rica. Why was not his legal description of Panama's power to determine title decisive?

If Holmes had cared to range further outside the record before the Court and examine material in the hands of the United States Government and printed in the *Congressional Record,* was not the trade report of the German consul in Costa Rica as instructive as Secretary Root's letter to the American Minister in Panama? Did not that report assert as a matter of well-known fact that in Costa Rica "the uncon- tested lord of the land" was United Fruit?

Sovereignty for Holmes was not a notion capable of this kind of investigation. As in any science, "pure fact" took its contours from a conceptual scheme. In this case, the roots of the scheme were theological, disclosed by Holmes's refusal to inquire into the divisible nature of sovereignty on the banks of the Sixaola. Holmes came from a tradition of mo- notheists. He would not entertain polytheism when he framed his concept of the sovereign as god. In any place where there was law, there must be but one sovereign. Holmes took a portion of Elihu Root's words as decisive because the single sovereign was a necessary hypothesis of his legal universe. That the sovereign should be subject was "a contradiction in terms." It was no accident that Holmes expressed the essence of his position as a necessity of logic. God would not be God if he were not omnipotent, according to orthodox theology. The sovereign would not be the sovereign if he did not create the law. The "very meaning of sovereignty" was at stake.

When he spoke of law as prophecy based on treatises, statutes, and the reports of cases, he did not acknowledge that all these collections of rules depended on a process in which persons such as Bradley Palmer, Moorfield Storey, Everett Wheeler, Henry Taft, and Elihu Root must play a part. His concept of law as force controlled by rules could not accommodate these actors. For Holmes's account of law to be true, knowledge of the rules must lead to prediction of the incidence of public force. If they did not, prediction turned not upon the statutes and the case reports and the treatises over which Holmes pored, but on the adventitious and the ugly and the personal—on whether a judge had practiced in New London, Connecticut, or Brazoria County, Texas; on whether a business concern had paid off the appropriate public officials of a foreign dependency of the United States; on whether one litigant had counsel with connections in the Department of State and a brother at the head of the War Department responsible for the military forces on the isthmus. Facts of this character, so important to the accurate estimate of what force could be applied on behalf of the American Banana Company, fell beneath the height at which Holmes directed his eyes.

Sticking to a "pure fact" which did not correspond to the power structure of Costa Rica or to the power structure of Panama, or to the American government's view of its power and responsibilities in Central America, Holmes had a concept separated from the real world, imaginary, a creation of the legal universe. Concealed under the mask of the sovereign were Don José Astua and President Esquivel and the United Fruit Company and Andrew W. Preston and Minor Cooper Keith. The human beings who had acted in Boston and in San José, in New York and Washington disappeared from sight.

4

The Passengers of *Palsgraf*

THE MOST FAMOUS tort case of modern times—"the most discussed and debated," as Dean Prosser put it—is *Palsgraf* v. *Long Island Railroad Company,* decided in 1928 by the most excellent state court in the United States with an opinion by the most justly celebrated of American common-law judges, Benjamin N. Cardozo. The facts of the case as stated by Cardozo were these:

Plaintiff was standing on a platform of defendant's railroad after buying a ticket to go to Rockaway Beach. A train stopped at the station bound for another place. Two men ran forward to catch it. One of the men reached the platform of the car without mishap, though the train was already moving. The other man, carrying a package, jumped aboard the car, but seemed unsteady as if about to fall. A guard on the car, who had held the door open, reached forward to help him in, and another guard on the platform pushed from behind. In this act, the package was dislodged, and fell upon the rails. It was a package of small size, about fifteen inches long, and was covered by a newspaper. In fact it contained fireworks, but there was nothing in its appearance to give notice of its contents. The fireworks when they fell exploded. The shock of the explosion threw down some scales at the other end of the platform many feet away. The scales struck the plaintiff, causing injuries for which she sues.

Cardozo held that the plaintiff could not recover. No negligence to her by the railroad had been shown. ''The risk reasonably to be perceived,'' Cardozo wrote, ''defines the risk to be avoided, and risk imports relation; it is risk to another or others within the range of apprehension.'' When the guard pushed the passenger with a package, he could not have apprehended that the plaintiff was endangered by his action. In his action he did not relate to her. As to her he could not have been negligent.

William S. Andrews, who wrote an opinion in the case no less eloquent than Cardozo's, saw negligence as a breach of duty of a man to observe care toward ''his fellows,'' not toward specific persons he should have seen as endangered by what he did. If he breached the general duty, every consequence which followed had been caused by his negligence—''we cannot trace the effect of an act to the end, if end there is.'' Still, ''practical politics'' refused to hold the negligent person liable for every consequence, and so courts drew an ''uncertain and wavering line,'' cutting off liability at a certain degree of distance in time and space—a degree of distance which could not be set with greater specificity. Here the injury to the plaintiff was close in time and space to the original act of negligence. The defendant (the railroad) was liable, and the plaintiff could recover compensation.

Disagreement between the judges did not depend on a different reading of the facts. As Andrews put it in dissent:

> Assisting a passenger to board a train, the defendant's servant negligently knocked a package from his arms. It fell between the platform and the cars. Of its contents the servant knew and could know nothing. A violent explosion followed. The concussion broke some scales standing a considerable distance away. In falling, they injured the plaintiff, an intending passenger.

Both summaries of fact were wonderfully laconic. Andrews's was the superior in impersonality, eliminating even the sex of "plaintiff." Compelled by grammatical necessity to use a personal pronoun, Cardozo did disclose that the plaintiff was female. Otherwise, neither judge said anything about her age, marital status, maternal responsibilities, employment, or income. What injuries she had suffered, whether she had been almost decapitated or whether she had been mildly bruised, could not be learned from either opinion. What compensation she had sought or what compensation she had been awarded—a jury had decided in her favor—was unmentioned.

No greater information was given about the defendant, except that it was a railroad or, as Cardozo chose to express it in his summary, possessed a railroad. The income and expenses, assets and liabilities, owners and directors of the defendant were unstated. Its officers and its guards or "servants" were anonymous. Defendant was as impersonally designated as plaintiff. *P* and *D* or *A* and *B* could as well have been written for their names.

The accident described by the judges had a timeless quality. It would have to have happened after 1830, since a railroad was involved. Otherwise it could have happened any time and, save for the mention of Rockaway Beach and the name of the railroad line, anywhere. Nothing was said of the hour, the day of the week, the month, the year. No notice was taken of when the plaintiff had begun her case, and of how many months or years it had taken her to reach the highest court of New York.

Cardozo and Andrews made no reference of any kind to the lawyers who had conducted the litigation. The editor of the printed report supplies their names—William McNamara and Joseph F. Keany for the defendant, Matthew W. Wood for the plaintiff. The judges made no comment upon their training, their competence, their presentation of the evidence, their relationship to their clients. No connection was suggested between them and the facts at the court's disposal. Nothing was said as to negotiations they might have conducted with each other. Their remuneration and the bearing of the decision upon it were not touched upon.

A fortiori, the judges said nothing of themselves—their own income and investments, their marital and parental status, their professional experience, their personal experience of New York commuter trains, their own study or debate over the case. The authors of the opinion and the dissent were, if possible, less visible than the plaintiff, the defendant, and the three lawyers. Who they were was not a fact of the case. Ignoring the lawyers and themselves, stripping the litigants to their status of plaintiff and defendant, Cardozo and Andrews had performed the standard operations of opinion writers announcing the rules of law which governed their conclusions.

THE COMMENTATORS' HISTORY

The first writers about *Palsgraf* v. *Long Island Railroad* were students doing case notes in law reviews, the year following the decision. These authors did not go beyond the facts disclosed by Cardozo and Andrews. The *Michigan Law Review* followed Andrews in stating the case without revealing the plaintiff's sex, while the *Cornell Law Quarterly* observed that Palsgraf was a woman. The *Columbia Law Review* noted that often defendants in suits for negligence were large corporations, but it said nothing in particular about the Long Island Railroad. Most law reviews noted that Cardozo had written the majority opinion. Occasionally the names of the dissenters in the Court of Appeal were listed. The lower-court judges and jurymen were not spoken of. No law student saw any point in mentioning the lawyers.

Their elders, the professional legal scholars, did not differ materially from them when they began their analysis of the case. Like the students, their interest was in the rule. The facts came, ready-made, from the opinion. Arthur L. Goodhart (a nephew of Irving Lehman, one of Cardozo's majority) first pointed to the importance of *Palsgraf* in 1930 in the *Yale Law Journal* under the title ''The Unforeseeable Conse-

quences of a Negligent Act." Goodhart, the American editor
of the leading English legal journal, the *Law Quarterly Review,* identified Palsgraf merely as "the plaintiff." Leon
Green replied to Goodhart's analysis in the *Columbia Law
Review* with an article called simply "The Palsgraf Case."
Green, the new dean of Northwestern University Law School
and a leading authority on torts, added one new fact to the
discussion—Mrs. Palsgraf had won $6,000 in the trial court.
He made nothing of his discovery.

In the next decade the case was the subject of comment,
criticism, and speculation by professors of law, none of
whom chose to tell more of the case's history. W. W. Buckland, an authority on Roman as well as English law, discussed the decision in the *Law Quarterly Review* without so
much as mentioning the plaintiff's last name. William Prosser, who was becoming known for his work on torts at Minnesota University, exhibited the same austerity in referring to
"the plaintiff." Writing ten years after the decision,
Thomas A. Cowan, then an associate professor at Louisiana
State University, declared that *Palsgraf* was now "a legal institution." Provocatively entitled "The Riddle of the Palsgraf
Case," his article solved the riddle by saying that the famous
rule did not go beyond the case's peculiar facts; but with everything made to depend on "the facts," Cowan did not
amplify those selected by the court. In 1939 the *Columbia
Law Review,* the *Harvard Law Review,* and the *Yale Law
Journal* commemorated the death of Cardozo by an extraordinary joint issue dedicated to his work. Warren A. Seavey,
Professor of Law at Harvard, analyzed Cardozo's contribution to the law of torts, of which *Palsgraf* was a capital example. Summarizing Cardozo's summary of the facts, he referred to "the plaintiff, a woman." Who the defendant was
he saw no point in including in his précis, and he saw no
need to mention the plaintiff's lost $6,000 verdict or anything
else not stated by the court.

In 1941 Albert A. Ehrenzweig, who was to make persuasive a new approach to negligence in America, made his

debut as author in an American law review with "Loss Shifting and Quasi-Negligence: A New Interpretation of the *Palsgraf* Case." A young judge in Austria, Ehrenzweig had left after the Nazi annexation, and when he wrote on *Palsgraf* was completing his third year as an American law student at the University of Chicago. He argued vigorously that liability in the case of accident to a customer should not be decided on the basis of perceived risk but should be allocated to the enterprise which generated the risk of accident: accidents caused by a business should be treated as a cost of the enterprise. His proposition was, however, general. He added no information on the Long Island Railroad, railroads in America, or Mrs. Palsgraf.

Palsgraf, meanwhile, had entered the casebooks to instruct students in the law of torts. The most conventional, that of Francis Bohlen, reporter of the *Restatement of Torts,* catalogued Cardozo's opinion under the heading "Acts Involving an Undue Probability of Material Harm to the Legally Protected Interests of Others," where the accident served as an example of an act found not to involve undue probability of harm. He filed Andrews's dissent separately under the title "Causal Connection between Misconduct and Injury Necessary to Maintenance of Action." Two essays in doctrine, Cardozo's and Andrews's expositions each served a doctrinal function in the casebook of orthodoxy. At Yale Law School, where if anywhere legal realists existed in 1931, Walter H. Hamilton and Harry Shulman presented the Cardozo and Andrews opinions without captions and with a note referring to the articles of Goodhart and Green: not a word of factual data was added. Leon Green, who held the view—atypical among teachers of torts—that torts should be analyzed not in legal categories so much as in terms of the activities where the torts had occurred, entered *Palsgraf* in his casebook under "Interests of Personality and Property," in a chapter called "Traffic and Transportation," in a subsection called "Passenger Traffic." Nothing, however, was added by Green on the number of passengers the Long Island Railroad carried, the number of accidents it annually had, or the nature of the railroad business. From the juxtaposition of the case and headings the student was expected to intuit connections which might exist between the rule and the activity of railroading. "Interests of Personality and Property," in the legal terminology adopted by Green, did not indicate any focus on the particular personality of Mrs. Palsgraf. "Personality" was employed as a synonym for "the body," and Green's general heading meant that injuries to the body would here be considered. Reproducing the text of Cardozo's opinion, Green, however, said nothing about the injuries of the plaintiff.

Ten years after the decision, the standard casebook treatment was in the orthodox vein of Bohlen. In a new edition of a Harvard Law School casebook which, in its original form, went back to James Barr Ames in 1874, Warren A. Seavey and Edward S. Thurston introduced *Palsgraf* with these captions: "Unintended Interference with the Person or Tangible Things" (the general heading), "Extent of Liability" (the chapter heading). "Person" in Seavey and Thurston, like "personality" in Green, was a synonym for "body." As in Green, injuries to the body were treated along with injuries to things without significant differentiation between them. In the classic Seavey-Thurston framework, *Palsgraf* was simply a leading case on risk.

Post–World War II law students were given a new source of facts from an unexpected quarter. Austin Wakeman Scott, Professor of Law at Harvard, and Sidney Post Simpson, Professor of Law at New York University, published the trial record of *Palsgraf* in a casebook on civil procedure. They did so not as historians but as professors of Procedure, illustrating the use of rules by setting out a case every first-year law student would know from torts. From 1950 on, there existed in this accessible form, obtainable without any special research, a multitude of particular facts unmentioned by Cardozo and Andrews. Would any law professor make use of them?

In 1953, William L. Prosser, then dean of Boalt Hall at the University of California, Berkeley, and by now the nation's leading authority on the law of torts, delivered "Palsgraf Revisited" as one of the Cooley lectures at the University of Michigan. For footnotes to the published lecture, Prosser took from Scott and Simpson these facts: "The plaintiff was a Brooklyn janitress and housewife, 43 years of age. She was accompanied by her two daughters, aged 15 and 12." The men running for the train with the package were "Italians." The scale which struck Mrs. Palsgraf was "an ordinary penny scale of the railroad platform type." It was either knocked over by the explosion, as Cardozo thought, or knocked over in the rush to escape by the crowd on the platform. The only fact from the record Prosser thought important enough to bring into the main body of his lecture was that the date was not the Fourth of July, when bundles with fireworks might have been anticipated, but August 24, 1924.

Prosser concluded a critical examination of the rule in *Palsgraf:* "It has been, I think, always the formula, the generalization which has been at fault, in a field where it seems impossible to generalize at all. 'The mule don't kick according to no rule' . . . There is no substitute for dealing with the particular facts, and considering all the factors that bear on them, interlocked as they must be."

Prosser did not say how what he had added bore on "the facts" set out by the court or "interlocked" with them. Like Cowan insisting that the riddle was solved by the facts, he said nothing on "all the factors." Presentation of the case in the casebooks and treatises on torts was unaffected by his article and unaffected by the availability of the record. None of the material he had added was picked up in the second edition in 1956 of *The Law of Torts* by Fleming James, Jr., and Fowler Vincent Harper, Professors of Law at Yale. When in 1968 a new edition of Leon Green's casebook appeared, jointly edited by Green and five other law professors, the authors stated, "The literature dealing with the *Palsgraf* case is now enormous.'' None of it apparently had added to the facts used by Cardozo.

A single addition did appear in Seavey and Thurston, now Seavey, Page Keeton, and Robert Keeton, on *Torts*—a cartoon of a railroad station platform with scales falling on a woman embracing a small girl. The cartoon, placed opposite the *Palsgraf* opinion, bore this caption: ''And Lilian began to cry I want my mama! my mama!'' The juxtaposition was mysterious, unless one had read the record of the trial and discovered that Mrs. Palsgraf had testified: ''Well, all I can remember is, I had my mind on my daughter, and I could hear her holler, 'I want my mama!'—the little one.'' Her lawyer asked, ''That was Lilian?'' and she answered, ''Lilian, yes.'' The cartoon was done by Leonard Bregman, a member of the class of 1954 at Harvard Law School. Its execution showed that students were relating the record set out in Scott and Simpson for the study of procedure to the famous opinion. Lightheartedly done, the cartoon testified to an unsuppressed interest in dimensions of the case unrecorded by Cardozo and the authorities on negligence.

Prosser's casebook had been edited jointly by himself and Young B. Smith, dean of Columbia Law School. In 1962, Smith was dead and Prosser spoke for himself with the boldness of a man who has long considered the matter: ''The Record in this case is set out in Scott and Simpson, *Cases on Civil Procedure* (1950), pp. 891–940. A study of it indicates that as described in the opinion the event could not possibly have happened.'' What he had put as an alternative in his 1953 lectures was now a certainty: the scales must have been toppled *not by the explosion* of the fireworks but by the crowd running in panic on the platform. He asked if the change in facts ''made any difference in the decision.'' The question had a certain pathos. Did it make any difference to the commentators and law teachers that the action perceived by the court ''could not possibly have happened''?

In his hornbook on torts, the bible of students, Prosser permitted his sense of the unreality of the event to show through. He explained why the case had been of such perennial interest. "What the Palsgraf case actually did," he wrote, "was to submit to the nation's most excellent state court a law professor's dream of an examination question."

Among all the persons who had shaped the rule and were ignored by the analysts, there was one exception. From the beginning *Palsgraf* was linked with Cardozo. In 1928 he had sat on the Court of Appeals for fourteen years, for four years he had been Chief Judge. He had delivered in 1921 the remarkable Storrs lectures at Yale which became *The Nature of the Judicial Process*. He had made other decisions commemorated as turning points. Law students knew his name better than they knew the name of any other judge of a state court. The student notes in the law reviews pointed out that *Palsgraf* was a Cardozo opinion. The professorial commentators referred constantly to Cardozo as its author. The excitement of *Palsgraf* was not merely that it was a brilliant examination question; it was an examination question answered by Cardozo.

The analysts did not, in the main, explore the relation of Cardozo the man to the rule he had framed. Warren Seavey, however, in his 1939 memorial essay "Mr. Justice Cardozo and the Law of Torts," made some general observations on his character which had a particular bearing on *Palsgraf*. Like most appellate judges, Seavey observed, Cardozo had "the unwelcome task" of taking away compensation awarded by a lower court. "In fact, in a majority of the tort cases in which he rendered opinions," the court denied the plaintiff recovery. The "entire record," Seavey wrote, showed that Cardozo reached these results, not "from some internal and inexplicable sense of justice" and not from "private opinions of policy," but from the consideration of "principles deduced from the cases" and the weighing of "competing interests." Cardozo "did his full part in causing the court to be a court of justice, but it was not by destroying it as a court of law. Personally solicitous for the poor and the maimed, and in criminal cases eager to find the scintilla of doubt which would keep from punishment one accused of crime, he did not become the protector of the injured merely because the defendant had ample funds to meet a judgment or had an ability to spread the loss. His scales were those of legal justice, not sentimental justice.''

In the same memorial issue of the law reviews, Judge Learned Hand paid tribute to Cardozo's wisdom, a wisdom which depended on more than detachment from self-advancement. ''I am thinking,'' wrote Hand, ''of something far more subtly interfused. Our convictions, our outlook, the whole make-up of our thinking, which we cannot help bringing to the decision of every question, is the creature of our past; and into our past have been woven all sorts of frustrated ambitions with their envies, and of hopes of preferment with their corruptions, which, long since forgotten, still determine our conclusions. A wise man is one exempt from such a handicap . . . Cardozo was such a man . . . I believe it was this purity that chiefly made him the judge we so much revere.'' The tributes to Cardozo by Hand, one of his greatest judicial contemporaries, and by Seavey, one of the greatest of law teachers, recall the tributes to Wythe, a judge who knew neither *A* nor *B,* and the biblical paradigm of the just judge who does not accept persons. The portrait of Cardozo traced by Hand and Seavey left little place for distinguishing between the rule and the man. The person of Cardozo was recognized only to identify the man so firmly with the mask that the judge appeared merely to announce the truth.

No law review, commentator, or casebook mentioned the lawyers. Their names appearing in the printed opinion were excised when the opinion was reproduced in casebooks. The jury and the lower-court judges, even the composition of the divided sides in the Court of Appeal, received little more attention. Green's casebook in 1931 was called *The Judicial Process in Tort Cases,* a title invoking Cardozo's Storrs lectures, *The Nature of the Judicial Process*. Green made no reference to the trial, the trial judge and jury, or the steps involved in the appeal—in short no reference at all to the actual process. Prosser, in "Palsgraf Revisited," gave what he called "the alignment" of judges for and against the plaintiff, a bare listing of last names. Charles O. Gregory and Harry Kalven, in a 1959 casebook, printed portions of the Appellate Division's opinions, and acknowledged their authors; beyond their names, nothing was mentioned.

The omissions of the casebooks and the commentaries are, of course, no criticism of writers for not doing what they did not conceive to be their function. They were concerned with doctrinal exposition, not with history. They were interested in a rule which could be described in terms of *P* and *D,* an examination question. But what of the legal historians? If they ventured into the modern period at all, they wrote about larger matters like decisions on constitutional law by the Supreme Court. Fifty years after the accident had occurred, forty-six years after the famous opinions, no history of the case had been written.

THE PARTICIPANTS

Counsel. If we go no further than the record of the trial and material existing in print, the lawyers become visible. The railroad was represented by Joseph F. Keany and William McNamara, who gave their addresses as "Pennsylvania Station." Keany, the senior man, had the title of General Solicitor of the Long Island Railroad and was listed as an officer of the company, subordinate to C. B. Heiserman, the General Counsel. Heiserman was also the General Counsel of the Long Island's parent, the Pennsylvania Railroad, and had his offices in Philadelphia. It may be inferred that Keany had a fairly free hand in dealing with local tort litigation.

The actual trial was conducted by Keany's junior, McNamara. He was a recent graduate of New York Law School, a proprietary institution not to be confused with New York University Law School. McNamara introduced no witnesses, cross-examined the plaintiff and her witnesses with moderate spirit but not exhaustively, and sought to bring out that a lot of people on the platform were carrying bundles. His summation to the jury, unreported, could not have taken more than fifteen minutes. He asked the judge to charge the jury that no inferences should be drawn from the defendant's failure to present witnesses, and the judge so charged. He asked the judge to charge that there was no negligence unless the defendant should have known that the package contained fireworks, and the judge declined. He asked the judge to charge that the act of assisting the passenger onto the train thereby knocking over the package was not "the proximate cause" of the plaintiff's injuries, and the judge declined. He asked the judge to set aside the verdict, and the judge refused. McNamara's performance was that of a workmanlike lawyer earning his salary with an economy of motion. He spent part of an afternoon and a morning trying the case and had given, perhaps, half a day to preparing it. If his salary, which would not have been above $6,000 a year, is prorated to this time, the railroad had spent no more than $16 in defending itself.

Opposing him was Matthew W. Wood, a solo practitioner who had an office in the tallest building then in New York, the Woolworth Building on lower Broadway. He was from Middleburgh, a small town in upstate New York. A bachelor of science from the University of Pennsylvania, he had studied law at New York Law School but had graduated from Yale Law School. He had been admitted to the bar when he was twenty-eight, and he had been in practice twenty-one years when he took Mrs. Palsgraf as a client. His biography gives the outline of a boy from the country, making with diligence a modest legal career. Only his longevity and endurance are remarkable: until his death in 1972 at the age of ninety-seven, he was listed in the standard lawyers' directory as in practice at the Woolworth Building.

Operating by himself, he was in the least prosperous category of urban practitioners and had to resort to stratagems to dig up business. The Canons of the American Bar Association prohibited "advertising" by lawyers as unethical, but they did not prevent members of the bar from announcing their specialties in Hubbell's *Directory*. In the 1920's Wood's "professional card" in Hubbell's stated that he had "a commercial department" and handled "bankruptcy matters"; he pressed up to if not beyond the limits of propriety with the insinuating claim, "Special Attention Given to the Interests of Non-Resident Heirs." How he and Mrs. Palsgraf had come to each other's attention and why she thought he would be a good torts lawyer are not evident. He became her lawyer two months after the accident.

Wood's preparation of the case was not elaborate. He presented the plaintiff; her two daughters, Elizabeth and Lilian; her local doctor, Karl Parshall; an engraver and his wife, the Gerhardts, who had been on the platform too; and a neurologist, Graeme M. Hammond, for thirty years professor of nervous and mental diseases and chief of clinic at the Post Graduate, with a war service record of examining 68,000 soldiers, close to eighty years old at the time of the trial and still specializing in mental diseases on West Fifty-fifth Street in Manhattan. On the critical question of the plaintiff's injuries, Dr. Parshall, the local physician, thought they were permanent, but McNamara brought out on cross-examination that he had never treated a similar case; the jury could have taken his name as a significant pun. The testimony of the specialist, Dr. Hammond, that his patient was suffering from "traumatic hysteria" was vital. Hammond's services were obtained the day before the trial. Wood's case, like Keany's, was an economical one, sparely presented and sparely financed.

Fees contingent on success were forbidden by earlier ethics on the basis that they were an incentive to unethical behavior. American practice had swept away the ethical objection on the practical basis that such arrangements were often the only method by which the victims of torts could acquire legal representation. Contingent fees had been normal in New York for almost eighty years. It was also not illegal in New York for a lawyer to pay the expenses of litigation if the purpose of the payment was not to induce the client to put the claim in his hands, but the state's Penal Code made it criminal for a lawyer to pay the expenses "as an inducement." The fine line between advancing expenses and advancing expenses as an inducement must have been invisible to most clients. Occasionally, however, and as recently as 1922, the Bar Association brought charges against a lawyer explicitly contracting to finance a client's case. Wood, no doubt, was familiar enough with what was tolerated to make his arrangements with Helen Palsgraf safe from the ineffectual prohibition of the Penal Code.

Filing costs and the clerk's fee in the lower court came to $142. Dr. Hammond charged $125. Mrs. Palsgraf made $416 a year. At the time of trial, she had not yet paid Dr. Parshall's bill of $70, now three years due. It is improbable to the point of implausibility that she would have had the cash on hand to pay the court and Dr. Hammond a total of $267. It is unequally implausible that she would have had the cash to pay Wood. It is not inconceivable that her relatives could have funded the case, but it seems more probable that Wood had a fee contingent on his success and that he financed the litigation. It would not have been unusual if his contingent interest was one half the recovery after a trial—one third if a settlement was made before trial. In the words of her own physician, the plaintiff was "very poor."

Wood asked for $50,000 in his complaint on her behalf. The discrepancy between this amount and any injuries he was able to show suggest strongly that he planned to bargain. As he did not get any expert medical opinion until the day before the trial, it may be inferred that Keany and McNamara were not interested in negotiating seriously short of what professional jargon denominates as "the courthouse steps." As McNamara's time was cheap, they may have offered only out-of-pocket expenses. Their offer was too low or Wood's expectations too high to produce a settlement at the last minute. Other negotiations, no doubt, must have gone on before the appellate division heard the appeal. The railroad would not have risked a written opinion holding it liable if it could have settled for a moderate amount. Wood made a serious misjudgment in not compromising after the jury verdict. His mistake was the necessary condition of Cardozo stating the rule.

Clients. "Plaintiff," "Palsgraf," "Mrs. Palsgraf" bore the Christian name of Helen. She was forty-three and the mother of three children, of whom the younger two, then fifteen and twelve, were with her at the time of the accident. She was married, but neither side judged it desirable to ask who her husband was or where he was. It may be inferred that they had separated. She testified that she paid the rent, that she had always worked, and that she was "all alone."

At the time of the accident Helen Palsgraf lived in a basement flat at 238 Irving Avenue in Ridgewood, performing janitorial work in the apartment building, for which she was allowed ten dollars a month on her rent. She did day work outside the apartment, earning two dollars a day or about eight dollars a week. She spoke English intelligibly but not with complete grammatical correctness.

The day of the accident was a hot Sunday in August. She was taking Elizabeth and Lilian to the beach. It was ten o'clock. She carried a valise. She bought their tickets and walked onto the station platform, which was crowded. Lilian went for the Sunday paper. As a train started to pull out, there was the noise of an explosion. Then, "Flying glass—a ball of fire came, and we were choked in smoke, and I says 'Elizabeth turn your back,' and with that the scale blew and hit me on the side."

Fire engines and ambulances arrived. She was trembling. A policeman led her into the waiting room. A doctor from an ambulance gave her something to drink. She took a taxi home. On Monday a doctor from the Long Island Railroad Company visited her and asked her about what had happened. Tuesday she called her own doctor, Karl Parshall. He visited her several times at the house over the next two weeks, and she came about twenty times to his office in the next two months.

Helen Palsgraf had been hit by the scales on the arm, hip, and thigh. The chief perceptible effect of the accident, according to the doctors, was a stammer. Dr. Parshall said that she began to stutter and stammer about a week after the event. Dr. Hammond declared that "it was with difficulty that she could talk at all." Oral incapacitation was not reflected in the transcript of the trial, but the stenographer may have decided not to try to reproduce the stammer. The neurologist took the position that the stammer was symptomatic of a deeper trauma, associated with the litigation itself: "While her mind is disturbed by litigation she will not recover, but after litigation—I don't mean by that her getting any verdict but as soon as the worry of the trial is over and she knows she doesn't have to go here on the witness stand and undergo cross-examination she should make a fairly good recovery in about three years." On cross-examination, McNamara asked him "[M]ight this condition have been corrected before this time by medical treatment?" and he answered, "Not while litigation is pending. It has been my experience that it never is benefitted or relieved or cured until the source of worry disappears by the conclusion of the trial." Dr. Hammond's answers were capable of a cynical interpretation. As a clinical description of a trauma and its possible resolution by reparation for the injury, his responses attributed no malingering motive to his patient. The jury did not understand him cynically. The only way it could have estimated how much Helen Palsgraf should receive was by translating Dr. Hammond's statements about her hysteria, which had lasted three years and which he thought would last three years after the verdict, into a cash equivalent.

The two most important facts of the case from Helen Palsgraf's perspective must have been the time it took to be heard and the size of the verdict she won. The accident took place August 24, 1924. The summons beginning her suit was served on October 2, 1924. The trial took place on May 25 and 26, 1927. For anyone who has been injured and is awaiting compensation, two years and nine months is a very long time to wait. The testimony of Dr. Hammond that this wait contributed to the continuation of Helen Palsgraf's hysteria was undisputed. When the trial was finally held, she won a verdict fourteen times her annual income. Even if she could keep only half for herself, she had a fortune in prospect. She was able to enjoy the thought of disposing of it for a whole year before the Court of Appeals took it from her, and she could nurse a faint hope for another five months until, on October 9, 1928, the Court of Appeals denied Wood's motion for reargument.

The defendant operated 366 miles of track in New York State, including the Rockaway Beach Division, running from Glendale Junction to Rockaway Park, and carried annually over 80 million passengers. Since 1900 it had been a subsidiary of the Pennsylvania Railroad, which owned 99.2 percent of its stock. Its president was Samuel Rea, president of the Pennsylvania. Its first vice-president was Henry Tatnall, Vice-President in Charge of Finance of the Pennsylvania. Its second vice-president was A. J. County, Vice-President in Charge of Accounting and Corporate Work of the Pennsylvania. Its third vice-president, George Le Boutillier, was a railroad manager, based in New York City. The majority of its directors were officers of the Pennsylvania or the Long Island. The minority of "outside" directors were headed by August Belmont, the financier of the New York subways.

In 1924 the Long Island's total assets were valued at $114 million of which $98 million was the valuation set on track and equipment. Net income from railroad operations was just over $4 million, reflecting a return just over the 4 percent that was usual for railroads of the period to show. Over 60 percent of the operating income was from passenger traffic. The parent Pennsylvania had a net income of $48 million and assets of $1.7 billion, of which almost one half billion represented capital stock and surplus; taking into account its revenues from the entire system it controlled, valued at $2.2 billion, the parent made 4 percent.

For reasons originally connected with its state at the time of the Pennsylvania's takeover, and latterly either for reasons connected with its imminent insolvency (to believe Vice-President Le Boutillier) or for reasons connected with the obtaining of fare increases (to believe counsel for the Associated Commuters of Long Island), the Long Island had paid no dividends. It had a surplus in 1923, 1925, 1926, and 1927, and in May 1928 paid its first dividend in twenty-eight years, from a surplus of $3,839,646.

In 1924 the railroads of the United States killed 6,617 persons and injured 143,739 persons. A substantial number of those killed and injured were the railroads' own employees and another large fraction were classified as "trespassers," those who had no business on railroad property. Helen Palsgraf fell in the classification neither of employees nor of trespassers but of passengers, of whom 204 were killed and 6,822 were injured in 1924. The global figures suggested that the maiming and killing of passengers was a necessary by-product of the running of railroads.

If Helen Palsgraf's accident was analyzed as a "non-train accident"—that is, one not caused by the movement or operation of a train but by such acts as "collapse, fall, etc., of objects" or by "explosives, and inflammable, hot, or corrosive substances," she fell within a subcategory where the railroads, as a whole, had killed only 4 passengers and injured 669. From this perspective, it was arguable that death or injury to passengers was such a rarity in "non-train" situations that maiming and killing in this way should not be looked upon as necessary to the running of railroads. The precise number of passengers the Long Island had injured in this way was not set out in the annual reports of the Interstate Commerce Commission, but the grand total in 1924 was 5 killed, 492 injured in non-train accidents on the Long Island. If the Long Island was like other roads, a tiny percentage of these casualties were passengers. On the other hand, every year there were some passengers killed and wounded in non-train accidents, so that to suppose that such injuries were totally avoidable by the railway system would be an illusion.

More probably Helen Palsgraf's accident fell within the classification of a "train service" accident, that is, it was one "arising in connection with the operation or movement of trains," for the man would not have been pushed aboard if the train had been stationary. The railroads in "train service" accidents in 1924 had killed 108 passengers and injured 3,229, and the Long Island in particular had killed 4 and injured 88. The number of "train service" injuries to passengers, even more than the number of "non-train" accidents to passengers, suggested that these injuries were necessarily incident to the operation of a railroad.

Jury and Judges. Burt Jay Humphrey presided. A country boy like Matthew Wood, from near Berkshire in Tioga County, he had read law in a judge's office and then gone west to Seattle for six years before returning to Jamaica, Long Island, to practice. He had been nominated in 1902 as county judge—a joke by the Democratic organization, which intended his Republican opponent to win; but he had campaigned so hard that he won the office in which he remained twenty-two years. He had eventually been elected to the Supreme Court for Kings County with its higher salary of $6,000 per year. For most of his judicial career his income from the state was no larger, but he left an estate of $200,000. When he conducted the *Palsgraf* trial, he was sixty-four; he had been on the bench twenty-five years and a judge of the New York Supreme Court for three.

Judge Humphrey's charge to the jury was balanced. He emphasized that the defendant had no duty to examine the packages of passengers. If every package was inspected, "none of us would be able to get anywhere. The purpose of railroad travel is that we can get some place." He said that if "the trainmen of the defendant" omitted to do the things which prudent and careful trainmen do for the safety of those who are boarding their trains, as well as for the safety of those who are "standing upon the platform waiting for other trains," and "the failure resulted in the plaintiff's injury," then the defendant would be liable. He described the harm done to Mrs. Palsgraf as "a nervousness which still persists and which, according to her claim, will persist for some time in the future."

The jury was drawn from Brooklyn, where Mrs. Palsgraf lived, where the accident had occurred, and where the trial took place. It would be too much to say that they were Mrs. Palsgraf's neighbors, but it may be guessed from the result that they were persons used to traveling on the Long Island and not overly sympathetic to railroads. They retired at 11:55 a.m. and returned with their verdict at 2:30 p.m.—time enough to eat lunch at the expense of the state of New York and to discuss liability and damages for at least an hour, and perhaps longer.

The case went from Judge Humphrey's court to the appellate division in Brooklyn, where two formal opinions were given by Judge Seeger and Judge Lazansky. Albert H. F. Seeger, born in Stuttgart, Germany, came to the United States as an infant, graduated from the Newburgh Free Academy, read law, and was elected to the Supreme Court of New York in 1917. Governor Al Smith had appointed him at the age of sixty-seven to the appellate division, and he was now enjoying the second year of this delayed promotion, one year short of retirement. Edward Lazansky had only that year been designated by Governor Smith as the presiding justice of the appellate division in Brooklyn, a post he was to hold for fifteen years. Of the judges below the Court of Appeals who considered the case, he had the most formal education, possessing both a B.A. and an LL.B. from Columbia. The son of Czech immigrants, he had been a Brooklyn lawyer, active in Jewish philanthropy and Democratic politics, and the Democrats' successful candidate for Secretary of State in 1911. He had been elected to the state Supreme Court in 1917, when he was forty-four, and became the presiding judge when he was fifty-five.

Seeger, joined by William F. Hagarty and William B. Carswell, decided in favor of Mrs. Palsgraf. He emphasized that the accident had been caused by the efforts of the railroad's employees to assist someone onto a moving train, an act which "caused the bundle to be thrown under the train and explode." He pointed out that businesses permitted to transport the general public—"common carriers"—had always been held to high standards of safety for those transported. "It must be remembered," Seeger wrote, "that the plaintiff was a passenger of the defendant, and entitled to have the defendant exercise the highest degree of care required of common carriers." Lazansky, joined by J. Addison Young, dissented. The negligence of the passenger carrying the package of explosives had "intervened," Lazansky said, between the negligence of the defendant and the injuries of the plaintiff. Hence "the negligence of defendant was not a proximate cause of the injuries to plaintiff."

The Court of Appeals to which Keany and McNamara then took the railroad's case had been composed with that attention to religious affiliation (Protestant, Jewish, Catholic) and regional origin (upstate, metropolis) which often has exhausted political wisdom in New York. Its members were exclusively white, male, and over fifty. It consisted of Benjamin N. Cardozo of New York City, Chief Judge; William S. Andrews of Syracuse; Cuthbert W. Pound of Lockport; Frederick E. Crane of Brooklyn; Henry T. Kellogg of Plattsburgh; John F. O'Brien of New York City; and Irving Lehman of New York City. In age they ranged from Andrews, seventy, to Crane and O'Brien, fifty-four; Cardozo, Lehman, and Kellogg were in the later fifties, Pound in his middle sixties. Two had not gone to a regular day law school—O'Brien had gone nights to New York Law School, while holding a job in the office of the Corporation Counsel of New York City; Pound had read law with his father in Lockport. Cardozo was technically a dropout, having studied only two years at Columbia Law School at a time when three years had just become the requirement. Andrews, Crane, and Lehman were all actual law graduates of Columbia, as was Kellogg of Harvard.

The court was an elected body, to which no one radically outside the orbit of the Democratic-Republican norm could aspire, but an institution where electoral competition was often blunted by governors designating able men for vacancies and by the two parties agreeing, as in Cardozo's run for Chief Judge, on the same candidate. Crane, Lehman, and O'Brien had been identified as Democrats; Andrews, Pound, and Kellogg were Republicans. Cardozo had begun as an independent Democrat on a Fusion ticket and had been advanced by both a Democratic and a Republican governor.

All were members of the upper middle class, the sons of prosperous fathers, although Cardozo's father after his resignation had had to struggle; three were the sons of judges— O'Brien's father had been for eighteen years a judge of the Court of Appeals himself; Kellogg's and Cardozo's fathers had been judges of the New York Supreme Court. All, save O'Brien, had been in private practice. All, save O'Brien, had been first elected to the Supreme Court before promotion to the higher level. All now received a salary of $22,000 ($500 more for the Chief Judge) and $3,000 in lieu of expenses. The richest was Lehman, the son of Mayer Lehman, founding partner of the investment bankers, Lehman Brothers. He had inherited $400,000 on his father's death in 1897. His father-in-law, the New York merchant Nathan Straus, had contributed between $25,000 and $50,000 to the Democratic party in the year he was appointed to the New York Supreme Court. Irving Lehman considered the contribution to be causally related to his appointment, and Frederick Crane thought the relationship between a contribution and appointment not unusual.

Cardozo was a trustee of Columbia, Pound of Cornell. Neither university had in their portfolio of investments any stock in the Pennsylvania Railroad. All of the judges must, on at least a few occasions, have ridden the Long Island Railroad, but only one person on the Court of Appeals was intimate with the locale of the case—Crane, who had grown up in Brooklyn, been an assistant district attorney in Kings County, and then lived in Garden City. To him the courts of Kings and the trains of the Long Island must have been as familiar as the law reports.

An observer detached from the system might have dared to predict the outcome on the basis of class interest, but the court was so closely split that such a prediction would have been temerarious. As for the Holmesian view that law is prediction, how would one have ventured to state the law at all—so mixed were the precedents, so divided was the mind of the court? The judge who wrote the opinion had to win and keep the votes of at least three other vigorous and experienced men—to do so required a skill distinct from judging yet indispensable. At such orchestration Cardozo excelled. "I wish," Irving Lehman later wrote, "that I could enable others to see and hear Judge Cardozo at these conferences as I have seen and heard him; then they would understand, I think, why the Court of Appeals was a really great court while Judge Cardozo sat there, and why Judge Cardozo's influence there was so great." What "saint" is in the religious vocabulary, "great" is in the judicial; and when a judge calls his court great, he has bestowed a canonical honor. In the final result, in *Palsgraf,* although every vote counted, what swayed Cardozo was decisive. He was joined by Pound, Kellogg, and Lehman.

THE INGREDIENTS OF THE OPINION

"[T]o determine to be loyal to precedents," Cardozo had written in *The Nature of the Judicial Process,* "and to the principles back of precedents, does not carry us far upon the road. Principles are complex bundles. It is well enough to say that we shall be consistent, but consistent with what? Shall it be consistency with the origin of the rule, the course and tendency of development? Shall it be consistency with logic or philosophy or the fundamental conceptions of justice? All these loyalties are possible." When, he continued, "the social needs demand one settlement rather than another, there are times when we must bend symmetry, ignore history, and sacrifice custom in the pursuit of other and larger ends . . . The final cause of law is the welfare of society."

The first, though not the final, loyalty was to precedents. Cardozo marshaled two dozen opinions—from his own court, the Supreme Court of the United States, the courts of Kansas, Maryland, Michigan, New Hampshire, North Carolina, and Great Britain—pointing toward the result he reached. American and English treatises on torts—Beven, Cooley, Jaggard, Pollock, Salmond, Shearman and Redfield, Street, and Wharton—he wove into the same coherent pattern. Leading law-review articles by Leon Green, Warren A. Seavey, and Jeremiah Smith he brought into the same seamless web.

No negligence, he declared, in *Palsgraf,* existed "in the air"—the defendant must have caused a risk to a person he should have known to exist within the range of his act. Confirmation of this view, he wrote, was to be found "in the history and development of action on the case"—that is, in the story told by legal historians of the procedural form, "case," or "action on the case," in which damages for negligence became recoverable in England. Cardozo cited John Wigmore in *Essays in Anglo-American Legal History* and, more heavily, the eighth volume of William Holdsworth's *History of English Law,* a history in the classic pattern of Holmes's *The Common Law*.

Very much as in Holmes, the history of the tort of negligence in Holdsworth was the account of the evolution of a "medieval" rule of strict accountability to a "modern" rule, where the true doctrine was that one was liable only for the harm caused if one ought to have foreseen it; biographical data on the judges who had shaped the rule was set out in a separate volume unrelated to the narrative of doctrinal development, the true history of "The Principles of Liability." His account depended as much on the interpretations offered by modern analysis such as Pollock and Wigmore as on the precedents he cited. What Cardozo meant by "history" was the story of evolution from "a very primitive basis," as Holdsworth put it, to modern orthodoxy.

Satisfied as he was that he was being loyal to precedent and "the course and tendency of development," did Cardozo consider other factors? "Affront to the personality," he wrote, "is still the keynote of the wrong." But by "personality" he meant "body." Not even mentioning Mrs. Palsgraf's physical injuries, he said nothing of the effect on her spirit of being kept suspended by the process for almost four years. What she had suffered was affront to the personality—traumatized, she had a sense of unrequited injury; but Cardozo used the phrase in a sense which put this problem out of his sight.

What place did "fundamental conceptions of justice" have? In Aristotle's classic analysis, commutative justice is equality of exchange between two parts, distributive justice is proportionate distribution from whole to part; a judge deciding between two litigants appears to be determining what is commutatively just, what is an equal exchange. When the transaction between the two parties has been involuntary, however, as it is in the case of an accident, it is not self-evident that commutative justice requires the party causing the loss to restore equality by making the victim whole—who would agree that if by chance he stepped on a firecracker igniting a blaze which destroyed the neighborhood, he should be liable for all the loss? To determine what is fair requires more than establishing who caused the injury. This intuition is clearly dominant with Cardozo. To make *A* pay *B* for causing a freak accident when *A* could have foreseen neither the accident nor its effect on *B* seems actually unfair—an inappropriate spreading to *A* of what is simply *B*'s misfortune.

If one is in a business which unavoidably produces certain types of injury, however, it seems more consistent with the Aristotelian canon to conclude that compensation for them should be a cost of the business. Who ultimately bears the cost—the stockholders, the customers, or the taxpayer—is an economic question subordinate to the larger question of fairness, of making one who voluntarily engages in an activity for his profit make restitution for injuries which are his activity's inevitable by-product. This line of argument was not considered by Cardozo, who thought in terms of *P* and *D*, not in terms of a business and its necessary accompaniments. Still less was he attentive to where the Augustinian definition of justice—"love serving only the one loved"—might have pointed.

But the final cause of law, Cardozo had said, is "the welfare of society." What was socially desirable—that railroads not have the added burden of compensating passengers for all train-service accidents, or at least not have the burden where the accident was improbable, or that the loss of an innocent victim of the line be relieved? Did the economics of railroads in the 1920's show that such a burden would be absorbed as an extra cost diminishing the stockholders' return, or passed on to all the passengers, or be so substantial as to drive the railroads to bankruptcy and public ownership? However this question was resolved, was it socially preferable to have loss incurred by the user of a necessary public service confined to that user, or passed on to a going enterprise with the capacity to distribute the loss to a larger number? Was it good to stimulate the railroads to higher standards of safety by the extension of liability or better not to discourage their zeal by the imposition of rules which did not discriminate between the probable and the improbable? Was a form of transportation which was known to kill several thousand persons a year and to injure many thousands more to be treated as responsible for the injuries it generated only when its employees could reasonably have foreseen the particular persons they might injure? Doing no more by safety legislation than to reduce the killing, Congress had, in effect, decided that railway transportation was worth six thousand lives a year, provided each killing was reported. The courts still had the option of deciding whether the social good was served if the railroads went without absolute liability, or if they should pay for all the

lives they took and all the injuries they unintentionally in-
flicted.

The social interests to be weighed were affected by the
process by which they were presented to a court. A rule of
absolute liability for injury to passengers might encourage
claims against railroads by hungry tort lawyers. It might discourage delay and appeals by the railroad protracting the victim's trauma and intensifying it. If one looked at the lawyers
actually before the court, circumstantial evidence, visible in
the record, suggested that Matthew Wood had violated the
penal code of the state, that he should not be permitted to
practice as a lawyer. Should he be rewarded with a handsome
fee, perhaps half of what Mrs. Palsgraf would receive, as
much as half the salary of a judge of the state supreme
court? Was there not a social interest in rebuking such a
stirrer-up of litigation, such a harasser of corporate enterprise? On the other hand, it might also be suspected from
the record that in this close case, where the railroad had
caused an injury to a passenger, the railroad's lawyers had
offered no reasonable settlement. Was it socially desirable
that, to establish her claim to compensation, a woman earning $416 a year had to hire a lawyer on a contingency basis
and wait four years, while the defendant, with assets of over
$100 million, if taken by itself, or assets of over $1 billion, if
more realistically regarded as a subdivision of its parent,
prolonged the contest, using more experienced counsel employed at a lower cost? Granted that judgment should be
even-handed between the rich and the poor, that the judge
should not automatically favor David over Goliath, should
not the judge take into account Goliath's advantages and
frame a rule to make the contest even? If, under the present
system, the rules as they actually were used by lawyers in the
process favored the large corporate defendant, did not the
social welfare require consideration of the process as well as
consideration of the principles?

None of these social needs or interests, none of these components of the social welfare was discussed by Cardozo.

None of these questions was asked. Neither the economics of railroading nor the course of the judicial process as it affected the values at stake was mentioned. To have done any one of these things would have required looking at the litigants and their lawyers.

At the climax of his opinion, where he enunciated the central conclusion, "The risk reasonably to be perceived defines the duty to be obeyed," Cardozo cited the latest article of Warren Seavey in the *Harvard Law Review,* "Negligence—Subjective or Objective?" a masterful analysis of the mixed (subjective and objective) components of the Prudent Man, who was the standard by whom liability for tort was measured. Seavey's presentation was, in a Holmesian vein, so avowedly neutral that he concluded that it would do no violence to his analysis to return to the medieval rule of absolute liability and, with a certain unpleasantness, indicated that was likely to be the preference of a modern society with "a mechanistic philosophy of human motives and a socialistic philosophy of the state." If Cardozo had sought a reading of modern aspirations, he had it there. He did not use Seavey for this grudging insight but for what Seavey's article really focused on—the most general and therefore the most abstract considerations of fairness in framing a rule on negligence. Seavey's "personification of a standard person" was an individual, identified with no industry, capable of existing in any environment, variously described as *"A"* or "the actor." By what was fair to this anonymous fiction Cardozo discovered the welfare of society.

THE EYES OF THE ORACLE

In the harmonious whole presented by his opinion, Cardozo acknowledged no divergence between history, the welfare of society, and his sense of fairness. In *The Nature of the Judicial Process* he had observed that they were not the same: "At first we have no trouble with the paths; they follow the same lines. Then they begin to diverge, and we must make a choice between them. History or custom or social utility or some compelling sentiment of justice, or sometimes perhaps a semi-intuitive apprehension of the pervading spirit of our law, must come to the rescue of the anxious judge, and tell him where to go.''

What Seavey later was to declare refuted by ''the entire record'' of Cardozo's decisions was acknowledged by Cardozo himself as sometimes determinative in difficult cases—a ''compelling sense of justice'' which could not be further explicated, ''a semi-intuitive [why semi?] apprehension of the spirit of our law.'' Cardozo personified the sentiment or intuition—they were outside the judge. Like history, custom, or social utility, they came as objective inspirations. Learned Hand in his memorial to Cardozo observed of a judge, ''He must pose as a kind of oracle, voicing the dictates of a vague divinity.'' In *The Nature of the Judicial Process* Cardozo dropped the oracular pose and spoke of what came from within him as a human being:

> More subtle are the forces so far beneath the surface that they cannot reasonably be classified as other than subconscious. It is often through these subconscious forces that judges are kept consistent with themselves, and inconsistent with one another. We are reminded by William James in a telling page of his lectures on Pragmatism that every one of us has in truth an underlying philosophy of life, even those of us to whom the names and the notions of philosophy are unknown or anathema. There is in each of us a stream of tendency, whether you choose to call it philosophy or not, which gives coherence and direction to thought and action. Judges cannot escape that current any more than other mortals. All their lives, forces which they do not recognize and cannot name, have been tugging at them—inherited instincts, traditional beliefs, acquired convictions; and the resultant is an outlook on life, a conception of social needs, a sense in James' phrase of ''the total push and pressure of the cosmos,'' which, when reasons are nicely balanced, must determine where choice shall fall. In this mental background every problem

finds its setting. We may try to see things as objectively as we please. None the less, we can never see them with any eyes except our own. To that test they are all brought—a form of pleading or an act of parliament, the wrongs of paupers or the rights of princes, a village ordinance or a nation's charter.

Who decided? The person who was the judge. The detachment, the self-effacement, the freedom from one's past that Hand celebrated in his praise of Cardozo was repudiated by him in advance. The insistence of Seavey that the judge knew only precedents and weighed only interests in producing rules was denied in anticipation. If the judge were a computer, he could have conformed to Seavey's idealization. Cardozo, writing autobiography, spoke differently. The more conscious a judge was, the more creative a judge's labor, the more was he personally involved. The judge's eyes might be on God or on the rule, but it was the judge who saw things: "we can never see them with any eyes except our own." The decision depended on his vision and his perspective. If Cardozo was taken as a guide, the creation of a rule could not be fully understood apart from its creator.

Why are Helen Palsgraf's children relevant to the judgment any more than the color of her hat? Holmes or an analyst of the school of Seavey may ask. If they are not relevant to the judgment, why are they relevant to the history of the case? But such impatient questions assume that the historian will agree with Cardozo. As Fuller observes, as he defends the "skeletonizing" of cases, reduction of the facts "is a delicate business, and necessarily anticipates the analysis which will be applied to the simplified situation." Facts which cannot be shown to be crucial to the disposition of a case are important in grasping how person affected person; Mrs. Palsgraf's children, Cardozo's preeminence, and others I have stated are among them. Even details which are purely extrinsic to any participant in the process have an effect on the understanding of the case. The day of the accident was "hot"—a detail of consummate irrelevance in terms of any legal principles but suggestive of the circumstances in which urban users of public transportation need to travel, a reminder of the innocence of Helen Palsgraf's seaside excursion. How such a fact should affect the outcome is nondemonstrable, yet it will play a part in the process by which judgment is reached. What is true of each additional fact is equally true of a philosophical perspective different from that enjoyed by Cardozo: it cannot be demonstrated that a shift to a less rule-focused jurisprudence would require a different judgment—it cannot be demonstrated, but having had the experience of making such a shift, I can say that my conclusion would not be Cardozo's.

The easiest way of misinterpreting such a shift is to frame a rule that persons injured on hot days should always win or that very poor persons should always win. Speculating in terms of such rules, a law professor would ask, "Suppose the day had been mild and overcast, suppose the passenger had been Mrs. Cornelius Vanderbilt, would the judgment be the same?" Such questioning is intended to force us back to the blank faces of P and D. To resort to the hypothetical, escaping the actual facts, is the mark of the mind oriented to rules. But when, in writing the history of *Palsgraf,* I call attention to the facts known to the judge and not considered relevant by him, my purpose is not to offer a new rule but to increase our understanding of the legal process. My concern is what a legal historian should record, what a legal philosopher should explain, what a law professor should teach. Only indirectly do these matters suggest how a judge should judge.

As evidence that consideration of actual persons makes a difference, I mention my modest experiment in the rewriting of *Palsgraf.* If a judge could look at all these facts available either in the record of the trial (as far as Mrs. Palsgraf is concerned) or in standard reference works (as far as the railroad is concerned) and still hold that the railroad had no liability, one could not show that he was wrong by pointing to the atmosphere of the day or the income of Mrs. Palsgraf. If, however, a judge, as he pondered these facts, was uncomfortable with reaching a result of no liability, then the enlargement of his focus would mean, perhaps, that he would select a different rule. At no point could the judge act without using a rule. Exercising his option to select a rule, the option commonly present in contested litigation, he would act less blindly the more conscious he was that he was acting as a person, using his "own eyes," and affecting other persons.

Cardozo as a person was involved in deciding *Palsgraf* v. *Long Island Railroad*. An account of all the influences upon him must await the conclusion of the biographical labors of Andrew L. Kaufman, now in progress. Three public facts stand out. First, Cardozo never married and never had any children. He lacked the experience of conjugality and the experience of fatherhood. These lacks are not disqualifications for shaping social conduct. The judgment of the unmarried has sometimes been the finer for freedom from domestic involvement—that of St. Paul, for example, on charity, or of Tomás Sanchez on marriage. Childless, Holmes, Brandeis, and Frankfurter prescribed for generations of Americans yet to come. Personal experience is scarcely necessary to judge the quality of an act or relationship. Empathy suffices. The way accidents are perceived, the way sharing of risks is visualized, the way responsibility for a mess is understood, will be affected by the experience of marriage and fatherhood. The childless and *a fortiori* the unmarried will have an approach to a chain of calamities like *Palsgraf* different in outlook and emotional context from that of the reflective spouse and parent.

Second, Cardozo was the son of a Supreme Court judge, Albert Cardozo, who was a sachem of Tammany Hall when Tammany was ruled by Boss Tweed, and who as a judge was believed to have done the bidding of Jay Gould in the fight with Vanderbilt for the control of the Erie Railroad; he resigned from office after a committee of the legislature had recommended his impeachment for corruption. No further distance could exist between father and son in the universe of justice than that which seemed to exist between this father and son. No further distance could be put between himself and his father than for Benjamin Cardozo to take no interest in the identity of the contestants before him. In his court was to be only *A* or *B*. The wonderfully abstract world of the opinion in *Palsgraf* was created in a well-established judicial style, but that Cardozo should create it was not the mechanical following of tradition. Contrary to Hand's contention, Cardozo was affected by his past. He wrote as the son of Sisamnes.

Severe impartiality led in *Palsgraf* to the aspect of the decision which seemed least humane: the imposition by Cardozo of "costs in all courts" upon Helen Palsgraf. Under the New York rules of practice, costs were, in general, discretionary with the court. An old rule, laid down in 1828, was that when the question was "a doubtful one and fairly raised, no costs will be allowed." In practice, the Court of Appeals tended to award costs mechanically to the party successful on the appeal. Costs here amounted to $142.45 in the trial court and $100.28 in the appellate division. When the bill of the Court of Appeals was added, it is probable that costs in all courts amounted to $350, not quite a year's income for Helen Palsgraf. She had had a case which a majority of the judges who heard it—Humphrey, Seeger, Andrews, Crane, and O'Brien—thought to constitute a cause of action. By a margin of one, her case had been pronounced unreasonable. If Cardozo thought Matthew Wood's behavior had been unethical, a judgment against Helen Palsgraf would not reach him. The effect of the judgment was to leave the plaintiff, four years after her case had begun, the debtor of her doctor, who was still unpaid; her lawyer, who must have advanced her the trial court fees at least; and her adversary, who was now owed reimbursement for expenditures in the courts on appeal. Under the New York statute the Long Island could make execution of the judgment by seizing her personalty. Only a judge who did not see who was before him could have decreed such a result.

Third, Hand again to the contrary, Cardozo had ambitions, although they were of the most exalted character. He wanted to be a reader, as he put it, of "signs and symbols given from without," a judge who would objectify not only his own "aspirations and convictions and philosophies, but the aspirations and convictions and philosophies of the men and women of my age." In this spirit, he had been in 1922 one of four reporters of a committee formed for the "Establishment of a Permanent Organization for the Improvement of the Law" and in 1923 became a member of the council, a member of the executive committee, and vice-president of the American Law Institute, which became the "Permanent Organization." The intention of the Institute, according to the organizing committee, was to remedy the principal defects in American law, and in that perspective "the most important task that the bar can undertake is to reduce the amount of the uncertainty and complexity of the law." To that task the A.L.I. and Cardozo were devoted.

There were those in America who believed that the great failing of American law was to give effective access to the courts to people of small means. In a famous study *Justice and the Poor,* sponsored by the Carnegie Corporation in 1919, Reginald Heber Smith concluded that "the administration of justice is not impartial"—it discriminated against the needy. Delay in deciding cases, court costs, counsel fees—these three were the chief defects of the system. They were all defects which "weigh heavily upon the poor."

Henry W. Taft, with Cardozo one of the founders of the American Law Institute, dismissed Smith's work, now "being used by radicals to aid them in their attacks upon our institutions," as based on "a few striking, though hardly typical instances of delay and expense." Elihu Root wrote an introduction to Smith's report, but his sympathies were with his old friend Taft. As far back as 1904, when he was counsel for Speyer and Company, Root had celebrated the faith of the people in "the supreme value of the great impersonal rules of right." To preserve that faith, he told the graduating seniors of Yale Law School in June 1904, was "the highest and ever-present duty of the American lawyer." He took a principal place in the formation of the A.L.I. In an address inaugurating the new society, Root observed that, in a five-year period, 62,000 decisions of courts of last resort had been printed. It was apparent, he said, that "whatever authority might be found for one view of the law upon any topic, authorities could be found for a different view upon the same topic." It was evident, he declared, "that the time would presently come, unless something were done, when courts would be forced to decide cases not upon authority but upon the impression of the moment, and that we should ultimately come to the law of the Turkish Kadi, where a good man decides under good impulses and a bad man decides under bad impulses, as the case may be; and that our law, as a system, would have sunk below the horizon, and the basis of our institutions would have disappeared." The preeminence of rules, the stability of rules, the meaning of rules were threatened—everything would depend on the person choosing the applicable rule. To prevent this debacle, to turn back, as it were, the waves, the American Law Institute would make "a restatement of the law." In place of conflicting authorities there would be the Restatement saying what the right rule was. The Restatement—authoritative because of the men who prepared and approved it—would identify the true principle, the better rule, the wider generality.

The idea of a Restatement was to be scoffed at by the realists who became articulate in the decade following its launching. An article by a psychologist, Edward S. Robinson, in the *Yale Law Journal* struck two persistent themes of realist criticism: the enterprise reflected the unwillingness to face the fact that the law was "full of normal conflicts"; to decree the true principle by committee vote was not unlike the Council of Nicea defining the true nature of God by majority action of the council. Objections of this character did not trouble Cardozo, nor did the distance between the Restatement and a realist's reading of Holmes's teaching: Cardozo took the teaching of Holmes as Holmes had lived it—law lay in the law reports. To be sure, in *The Nature of the Judicial Process* he gently derided the view of law as prophecy—"Law never *is*, but is always about to be"—without mentioning that this was Holmes's definition. But his evasion of direct criticism was consistent with his general evaluation of Holmes—"the greatest of our age in the domain of jurisprudence, and one of the greatest of the ages." In a sense he was as much Holmes's pupil as Thomas Jefferson was George Wythe's: in each case a strong man learning from a strong man, in each case the pupil not being comprehensible without the teacher. When Cardozo acknowledged his own yearning "for consistency, for certainty, for uniformity of plan and structure," when he spoke of "the constant striving of the mind for a larger and more inclusive unity, in which differences will be reconciled, and abnormalities will vanish," when he sought this unity in the universe of law, he spoke for himself, he expressed desires which were personal and religious, but he was fortified by Holmes's example of satisfaction. Like the master, in "the remoter and more general aspects of the law," he sought "an echo of the infinite, a glimpse of its unfathomable process." That Holmes could inhabit the legal universe as its "overlord" was a sign and promise to Cardozo that pursuit of rules would produce such a resonance, that the comprehensive generality would yield such a vision.

In the formation of the American Law Institute, Cardozo was a leader, and to the work of restatement of the rules he gave his devoted support. The "task of legal science," he told another Yale audience in 1923, in words almost identical with the A.L.I.'s program, is to "bring certainty and order out of the wilderness of precedent." The need, "deeply felt and widely acknowledged"—he repeated himself and Root—would be met by the Institute. As adviser to the *Restatement of Torts,* Cardozo participated in "a very considerable number of the conferences" in which the restated rules were given shape. In this capacity, he attended a meeting on Section 165 of the *Restatement of Torts* while *Palsgraf* v. *Long Island Railroad* was being appealed to his court.

The case had been twice decided in Mrs. Palsgraf's favor,

by the trial court and the intermediate court, when it came to the attention of the reporter for the *Restatement of Torts,* Francis H. Bohlen, professor of law at Pennsylvania University Law School, then working on what the *Restatement* should say on duty to "an unforeseeable plaintiff." *Palsgraf* was "a perfect illustration" of the problem. He presented the case to his advisers on the *Restatement,* along with the draft of a text contrary to the position adopted by the lower courts which had heard the case.

By convention embedded in the view of law as rules, the facts of a case are distinct from the law governing a case. It would be improper for a judge about to decide a case to hear new versions of the facts out of the presence of the lawyers responsible for the cause. It is not considered improper for a judge to hear argument about the governing law outside of the interested lawyers' presence, for in hearing others debate the rule applicable in a real case the judge is supposed to be looking at principles larger than particular litigants. It has, for example, not been uncommon for judges to hear issues argued by students in a moot court in fact situations not much different from the real case they must decide. The propriety, of course, depends on keeping firm the distinction between the rules and the process in which they are applied, or supposing that "the facts" are frozen and that the judge is only seeking counsel about their proper categorization; that facts and categorization reciprocally affect each other is not acknowledged. Bohlen invited Cardozo to attend a meeting of "an eminent and entirely impartial group" of his advisers— lawyers, law professors, and judges—who would consider what the correct law in the *Palsgraf* type of situation should be. Cardozo came.

A "long and lively debate" ensued. The kind of argument advanced by those denying liability may be inferred from Seavey's article "Negligence—Subjective or Objective?"—it had originally been written precisely for use by the Restatement group. Cardozo listened. He did not vote. By a margin of a single person the group recommended a rule of no liability.

The incident was not publicly reported until 1953, when Prosser gave his Cooley lecture "Palsgraf Revisited." He then recounted it on the basis of information provided by his collaborator, Young B. Smith, who was present at the meeting of the reporter and his advisers.

The way this story was received was revealing of the values of law teachers. They were uncomfortable with the anecdote and, on the whole, did not care to discuss it in print. Prosser himself did not bring it into the casebook jointly edited with Smith. In 1959, Harry Kalven of the University of Chicago Law School and Charles O. Gregory of the University of Virginia Law School referred to it in this fashion in their casebook: "Dean Prosser reports some scuttlebutt that is interesting if true." Why the skepticism as to what a witness of the scene, a disinterested professor of law, had reported to another? Why the derogatory characterization "scuttlebutt"? Kalven and Gregory made manifest the hostility of the orthodox teacher of doctrine to information about the play of persons in the process.

Prosser himself described Cardozo's presence, when he mentioned it in his lecture, as "one of those accidents which shape the course of the law"—a strong characterization of the importance of the incident but one he did not choose to develop. In 1962, Smith no longer alive, he brought the story into the references in the casebook itself. He now described it as "the process by which Cardozo's opinion and section 281 of the *Restatement of Torts* elevated one another by their own bootstraps." In other words, in the view of the most knowledgeable academic authority on *Palsgraf,* the work of the Restatement and the opinion in *Palsgraf* were vitally interdependent.

The problem of determining the cause of a rule is not unlike determining the proximate cause of an injury. Was the nomination of Burt Jay Humphrey in 1902 as a joke the cause of the *Palsgraf* case, because but for it a different judge would have sat in the Supreme Court in Kings County? Was Matthew Wood's determination or self-interest, or Keany and McNamara's stinginess in their settlement offer, the real reason why the rule was formulated? Was Helen Palsgraf's poverty and inability to present an overwhelming case, or the court's identification of the Long Island with the needs of a mobile society the decisive factor? Were Cardozo's celibacy, paternity, and idealism important to the result? No cause acts alone, and the chain of causation is endless. There is no reason, however, to limit the causes of a rule so narrowly that one looks only at the books the opinion writer cites.

Out of a sequence of events as improbable as a Rube Goldberg cartoon, reconstructed by lawyers seeking partisan advantage, on a factual basis that was probably inaccurate, above the pain of Helen Palsgraf and the plodding of Matthew Wood and the calculation of the Long Island, Cardozo fashioned a statement of clarity, symmetry, simplicity. Presented with that pervasive problem of sociology, government, and law, the "unintended consequences" of a social action, he imposed order and aesthetic design and generality.

"Many a common law suit can be lifted from meanness up to dignity," so Cardozo wrote of Holmes, "if the great judge is by to see what is within." As "a system of case law develops," so Cardozo declared at Yale, "the sordid controversies of the litigants are the stuff out of which great and shining truths will ultimately be shaped." The particular facts which interlocked were not all the circumstances of the case but the construction of events he made as he molded his opinion to lift the case up to dignity, to create a great and shining truth.

When Section 165 of the *Restatement of Torts* was presented at the May 1929 meeting of the members of the American Law Institute, Cardozo's opinion in *Palsgraf* appeared in this form as an Illustration of Clause b of the rule:

> A, a passenger of the X and Y Railway Company, is attempting to board a train while encumbered with a number of

obviously fragile parcels. B, a trainman of the company, in assisting A does so in such a manner as to make it probable that A will drop one or more of the parcels. A drops a parcel which contains fireworks, although nothing in its appearance indicates this. The fireworks explode, injuring A's eyes. The railway company is not liable to A.

Matthew Wood, Joseph Keany, and William McNamara, adventitious figures, had disappeared. The judges no longer disputed. Helen Palsgraf had become the injured A and the Long Island Railroad the X and Y.

It was not only the eyes of A which had been blinded.

5

The Alliance of Law and History

LAW FORMED on the judicial paradigm is an incurably historical enterprise. Rights and remedies are assumed to exist anterior to the judge's decision. He makes his decision after ascertaining what happened. He understands what the rights and remedies are by reading the statutes and the precedents. It is generally accepted, however, that lawyers and judges are poor historians.

The facts presented by lawyers and "found" by judges are events arranged within a small number of preexisting categories. The statutes and precedents are read to produce practical guidance. The habits of mind engendered carry over when lawyers self-consciously appeal to history. English history has been studied ex professo for little more than a hundred years. Milsom sums up the experience of his two most distinguished predecessors as follows: "Like Maitland before him, Plucknett believed that just as the history which emerges from legal history is apt to be bad history, so the law which relies on historical justification is apt to be bad law. It is," Milsom adds for himself, "a good working principle." In this conclusion, endorsed by three generations of English legal historians, is fair warning that history and law must go different ways.

The split between law and history emerges because lawyers, judges, and lawmakers must employ past decisions, which are the proper domain of history, but they may employ them only by interpreting them. Interpretation alters the historical meaning of what is interpreted. The most acceptable way to save appearances as this alteration occurs is to appeal to metaphor. Doctrine is not changing but evolving. Growth, not random succession, is what is happening. The process is organic. Interpretation is the unfolding of what was always present.

Are these metaphors anything more than reassurances murmured in the face of change, incantations muttered so that the unbearable break with the past is not fully felt? In our experience we are familiar with several kinds of growth—our own as we change from infants into adults, where by introspection we are aware of some continuity and some development; that of other men and animals, where by observation we can follow processes that begin in small chromosomal packages and can detect not only beginnings but tendencies and fruition; and that of crops and plants, where we can observe seeds become flowers or food. Are we justified in transferring the notion of growth from these kinds of experience and discerning an analogous process in ideas?

In the nineteenth century, in the first era of belief in general evolution, it was easy to believe that thought did evolve, and the most important philosophical system of the century consisted in a high Germanic explication of this evolution. Even within a more concrete English context, Newman could proclaim the development of theological doctrine as the key to ecumenical reunion. In our own legal tradition, such a cautious and skeptical mind as Holmes's was not skeptical about the process. Cases, he maintained, contain "the germ of some wider theory." The Puritans, he wrote, "planted a congregational church, from which grew a democratic state." In the history of the law, he declared, is "the history of the moral development of our race."

Taken for granted in all of these metaphors of growth is

the continuity and directedness of doctrinal change. When William Holdsworth spoke of the American historians of the common law, he said, approvingly, that all had had "an eye on the end of the story." This has been the classic Anglo-American approach. Without belief in continuity, directedness, teleology, the Anglo-American historian of evolving rules could not function. He intends not merely to reproduce the past verbatim but to add to the line of thought. Like a judge, he assumes that what he does is not the arbitrary chalking up of a new sum upon a blackboard from which he has erased the old addition. Mere sequence of decisions does not warrant his reference to development. If he is to bind his work significantly to that of his predecessors, he must resort to the horticultural imagery which suggests that what he does has roots and that what he adds is flower or fruit.

Appealing as the vernal associations of these figures of speech are, there are difficulties with them. The metaphors taken from the processes of the earth suggest cycles, not uninterrupted growth. The metaphors based on human development point to old age and to death. In physical existence there is no development without decline and fall. Yet no philosopher or historian or judge is willing to see his ideas as the decrepitude or senescence of once-vigorous thought.

With ideas, moreover, no physical continuity is found of the kind observable in the processes from which the imagery is derived. In what sense can it be said that one thought is the organic extension of another? A Hegelian may explain by positing a comprehensive Idea that absorbs into its own substance each state of thought, but for those who do not share a Hegelian faith, how may propositions evolve? No more than the paper on which they were written do the terms of a proposition change. Once a new idea is formed, one may see its structural relation to the old, one may even speak of its entailment by the old, but the observable relationship is not the equivalent of the process of birth. If a second proposition appears pointing to the first as its source, it is because a human person has added a new thought; and as the new thought was not contained in the first proposition, as it was not compelled to issue from it, it seems an abuse of language to say that it grew from it. Development appears as yet another mask. Under this figure a living lawyer, judge, or legal historian speaks modern thoughts disguised as an ancestor.

The problem of the meaning of development runs through all branches of the law where a document must be newly deciphered. Legislation must be applied to cases never contemplated by the legislators, a will must speak in a situation never imagined by the testator, a contract must be enforced after a risk not specified by the parties has endangered performance. Standard technique calls for the court to find the intention of the legislator, testator, parties; and standard commentary notes that this process involves an interaction between the language and circumstances of the document and the court's conception of social values, so that the intention found is generally the intention of a hypothetical reasonable legislator, testator, or contractor, endowed with the values of the court. In this unequal contest between inert language and the living power of the present interpreters, it cannot be supposed that the language of the document will offer any substantial constraint. "Implicit" in the document may always be found the directions necessary to resolve ambiguity and conflict.

This subjection of past words to present social needs appears on first inspection as an affront to history. The historian is interested in precisely what was said, what happened, what was intended, not in what analysis may imply from the data. There seem to be two truths—the legal and the historical; and the problem does not appear confined to law but to flourish in any branch of retroactive knowledge desiring to claim the authority of the past. A great historian of medieval philosophy, Étienne Gilson, writes as follows: "The age of commentators, as some are pleased to call it, was above all an age of commentator-philosophers. Therefore, they are not to be blamed for having at once the name of Aristotle constantly on their lips, and for constantly making him say what he did not say. They would philosophize, not play the historian, and, unless it should be demanded, which God forbid, that philosophy should be exclusively a field for historians of philosophy, not even history itself can find any fault with them.'' Gilson is a fierce opponent of the heresy of Averroës that there is one thing true in theology and another in philosophy—he will not permit the unity of truth to be so shattered. But here, with equanimity, he accepts the idea of a double standard for truth in history—''constantly making Aristotle say what he did not say'' is an acceptable way for commentators to philosophize. So courts and lawyers must constantly make their authorities, from constitutions to contracts, say what they did not say, unless they are to surrender their work to historians.

The misery of historians is their powerlessness to supplant the modern interpretation with a reconstruction of the reality. At least history cannot supplant interpretation in the realm of practical affairs, of morals, politics, theology, and law. Social interests will always make current constructions more pleasing than exact reconstructions. In his weakness the historian's work will be levied upon to support the prevailing myths. At the worst his own work will take their form, imbibe their substance. He may become, like many sociologists, a foreteller of the future. At best, if he is aware of his modest role and scrupulously observes it, he will stick to recounting what actually was thought, while, like Gilson, wistfully congratulating the writers of bad history for their creative development of past ideas.

But will the scrupulous historian speak of development at all? Bent on capturing a past act, will he not in fidelity to his task deny himself the license of the lawyers and the judges who so readily perceive in their predecessors' actions the substance of their own? Will he not engage in identifications of this kind only to the extent that, forsaking his own task, he becomes involved in contemporary issues whose solution must be sanctioned by the past?

These questions suppose two conclusions: one, that there

are true historical accounts to be contrasted with the history often made by lawyers and judges; and two, that the metaphor of development is misleading self-deception. To accept the first conclusion and to reject the second is to see the possibility of collaboration between law and history, or, to speak accurately, the possibility of lawyers using good historical knowledge. The possibility exists because there is true history and because development may be related to it.

True history in the realm of ideas—of ideals, morals, and law—must be, as Collingwood has described it, a rethinking of a past thought, a reenactment of a past response. In Aristotelian terms, it is drama, the probable re-acting of a significant action. In American idiom, it is a stepping into the shoes of another, perceiving his problem, assessing the means he had at his disposal to meet it, grasping the purpose he had at his disposal to meet it, grasping the purpose he had in mind in the solution he proposed. The difficulty of reconstructing the exact situation faced, the difficulty of total identification with the subjectivity of another will be partially but never fully overcome by research and empathetic immersion in an era or tradition or life. Closer approximations of what was intended may always be essayed. Yet, given the assumption that human problems and human psychology have not altered radically in several thousand years, approximations of what was thought and of what was intended will be possible and true.

Doctrinal development stands in this relation to that process: If it is possible to approximate a past thought, to rethink a purposeful solution, to identify a dominant purpose, it is also possible to articulate that purpose in a new situation challenging its fulfillment. That articulation is not a rethinking of an old thought; it is a fresh response to new data. Yet it is made with conscious reference to the past idea. The person now acting will not stop with history; but he may start there.

Development does not take place in the air, it is not a mere spinning of theory as seems good to the spinner: it is necessarily grounded in the past. History cannot compel the modern answer. It may always compel rethinking of the answer by objecting that the initial data were wrongly read. If the history is merely imagined, then, as Bickel has shown, the decision remains vulnerable to historical challenge. The better the history, the more the person acting now will be able to gauge the past purpose and maintain it in his own action.

Development is not the unfolding of principles as though they were so many yards of cloth being unwound, or even as though they were so many seeds waiting to germinate. It is the response of men in a new environment faithful to purposes they perceive informing past actions. The new acts cannot be the same as the old. Not only is the situation new; the presence of the past itself adds complexity and the past itself is beyond exact reproduction.

It is not in the old idea that growth can occur. Growth occurs only in the thought of the person now thinking, combining an old thought with his present thought. His action will be organically continuous, he will achieve development, if he takes account of past purposes and attempts to give them place in his present response.

Where the issue is the interpretation of a single private document such as a will, it may be relatively easy to isolate the purposes which its author held. But when the analogous process of development occurs in a theological, philosophical, or legal tradition, detectable purposes of the past are multiple. The synthetic developmental act must shake out some, pronounce others basic, and combine anew. Every vital work in a tradition must be, like Gratian's, a harmony of unharmonious canons, in which it is determined which purposes shall survive.

This act, the determination of the purposes to be recognized as dominant, is crucial. It appears to be entirely contemporary and creative, ungoverned by history, dictated by present needs. Yet the pressure of history will be felt if this last and crucial decision is made by persons who have such a conception of their predecessors that they seek to be faithful to them even as they respond to questions unasked and unanswered in the past.

Why, however, should this kind of fidelity be valued or encouraged, why should the dead affect the living in this way? "We must beware," says Holmes, "of the pitfall of antiquarianism, and must remember that for our purposes our only interest in the past is for the light it throws upon the present." In this view the past has no claims in its own right. We seek to know it for the sake of present action as we shape the future. In Jefferson's classic formulation, "The earth belongs in usufruct to the living." We reach then the true misery of history—not its subordination to development, for in development its part is critical—but its impotence to shape the future.

Perceiving this impotence we are driven to ask if law should not cut itself loose from the shackles which history imposes. History binds law to past purposes. It is powerless to predict the future, it is unable to give society a new direction, it is good for nothing but to preserve the memory of the dead. Would not law enter on a new era if development were not controlled by history, was in fact no longer development but conscious experimentation and creation?

Lévi-Strauss sets out the Neolithic Paradox in the history of science as follows: For ten thousand years man knew the great arts of civilization—agriculture, animal husbandry, pottery, and weaving. These arts were not the product of chance but of bold hypotheses, repeated experimentation, careful observation. Possessing the essence of the scientific method, man did not, however, advance scientifically; only in the last four centuries has scientific method been put to work methodically. There is a seeming contradiction in the long possession of the method and the long inability to use it.

The explanation of the paradox does not lie in a difference in capacity to think abstractly. For millennia before the scientific revolution, man was good at making categories and at tirelessly imposing order on phenomena by categorizing them. Despite the prevalence of magic, earlier man did not lack a concept of causality. Magic, like early medicine, was carried on not in defiance of the laws of causality but with an imperfect ability to measure the effects produced. If anything, magic too readily assumed that a rigid determinism existed so that the manipulation of selected homologues could affect their living counterparts. Neither abstractive capacity nor scientific method was lacking. Yet earlier man was in Lévi-Strauss's phrase a *"bricoleur,"* an assembler of the material at hand, capable at best of putting the physically observable together within coherent forms, able to structure events but not create them. The scientific revolution began to occur when man not only abstracted quantity from the other properties of objects but began to manipulate it, when he began to make plans not dependent on the bric-a-brac in sight but realizable by the production of new forms, when he began to use quantitative models to bring about new realities, when he moved from being a *bricoleur* to being an engineer.

Might not it be said that law is in the process of a similar evolution? Legal method, the specification of social behavior by rules, has been known for several thousand years. The same abstractive genius visible in primitive man's botany and pharmacology has been shown in the development of law by definition and classification. There have been similarities in legal procedure to magic—in the insistence on the exact formula, in the faith that human procedures may evoke the cooperation of the universe, even in the trust that subjecting A to a procedure such as a criminal trial will affect A's human homologues, B, C, and D. A sense of causality has not been lacking. The constant effort has been to make laws which are not mere verbal pronunciamentos but which efficaciously alter behavior. Like the magician, however, the lawmaker has been handicapped by the lack of means to measure the effects of his words. Limited in his ability to experiment, he has been compelled to rely on the cultural equivalent of the *bricoleur's* material at hand, the images tossed up by the culture. Unable to work with smooth quantities, he has been the prisoner of past purposes.

May it not be only in the period since 1776 that a legal

revolution, parallel to the scientific revolution, has begun with the articulation of the view that law should shape society? With Holmes's explicit declaration that the quantitative measurement of social desire is the path of perfection for the law, with Pound's encapsulation of the whole enterprise in the phrase "social engineering," have not lawyers moved with a new self-consciousness of creative power? Is not the new era testified to by the proliferation of the American law school and not only its proliferation but its empowerment as a social force?

If a revolution so relatively recent in its launching is to be carried forward to a triumphant conclusion, must not law be purged of all that clings to it from an earlier day, which associates it with magic, with religion, with history? As long as law has to make do with past images and take into account the thoughts of the dead, will it not be *bricolage?* "Only in such disciplines as theology and law," writes a modern historian of religion, "is there a self-conscious effort to determine truth in the light of the value decisions made by one's past religious or social community." Holmes supposed that the study of history might liberate law from this servitude. From a practical point of view, he said, such study was "mainly negative and skeptical." History "sets us free and enables us to make up our mind dispassionately whether the survival which we are enforcing serves any new purpose when it has ceased to answer the old." Unchallengable as this conclusion is in itself, the necessity of the resort to history may be questioned. If a rule cannot establish its rationality by an appeal to present conditions, why not declare it obsolete forthwith without a tedious investigation of its origins? Why should a presumptive rightness attach to ancient doctrine which can be dispelled only by resort to antiquaries? Well enough, it might be said, for a religious institution which bases its claims upon its foundation to be sensitive about consistency, but why should this be the rule of more secular legal enterprises? Is not history necessary to liberate only those who have subjugated themselves to history?

Close study of past practice, it may be added, can only inhibit innovation and lead to repetition of the sorry schemes that have passed for social structure. True engineering requires the building of new channels. History, looking backward, ascribes responsibility judgmentally. But if conflicts do arise, they must be dealt with without fixation on past status and past rights. Treatment should be flexible, pragmatic, therapeutic. The evolution of marriage law could be taken as a portent and a model: from the most sacred of contracts, marriage has become in a state such as California less than any contract, terminable without penalty at the option of one party to the bargain. So, in general, from a concern with past commitments, law moves to a focus on the future.

"Cognitive science," writes a contemporary anthropologist, Weston LaBarre, "is essentially anti-historical; it seeks ahistorical validities on grounds of present testing, not of traditional authority or of sacral past revelation." By this criterion, how can law tolerate any admixture of history? In terms of this requirement, general predictions, tested as hypotheses by quantitative means, alone deserve the name of knowledge. History fails to qualify. It puts forward few, if any, general propositions. It does not predict. If it uses quantitative measurement, it is not reducible to quantitative judgments. It may not be verified experimentally. The privileged moments it preserves from the great flow of phenomena share the characteristics of myth. They are moments of experience dramatically isolated from the flux as being more real than the unrecorded forgotten past, as significant—the very term suggests their function of pointing. Whether they are part of an explicit religious tradition or part of the apparently secular, they partake of the numina of past revelation and must be banished if law is to be scientific.

To this sustained challenge, answer may be given. To begin with, the model of human knowledge that, in preempting the field, banishes history is still open to challenge for its credentials. Few, perhaps, would today champion its exclusive authority as vigorously as the anthropologist just quoted. The methodology of classical physics is seen to be neither self-sufficient nor exclusive. Personal knowledge, even in matters of physical science, is perceived as the crucial component of progress. What is disparagingly labeled myth by narrowly rationalist criteria turns out to be an ordering of experience which is the vital precondition of the entire rationalist enterprise.

If history falls on the side of knowledge that may be classified as myth, it is a species distinguished from poetry by the attempt of historians to approximate the actual acts of actual persons. To treat law as separable from history is to suppose that law can be made apart from a knowledge of those acts, apart from experience vicariously apprehended. Ahistorical law of that kind would be the putting together of dead abstractions.

Assault on history in the name of more scientific law has the character of an apocalypse, in which previous ages are put down as preparation for the age dawning or about to dawn. Visions of this kind, whether they are Joachim of Fiore's famous triad of the Age of the Father, the Age of the Son, and the present Age of the Spirit of Love; or Auguste Comte's progression from the Age of Theology to the Age of Metaphysics to the present Age of Positive Science; or Charles Reich's contemporary triad culminating in the greening of America—such visions have the common characteristic of appealing to historical data to establish the inevitability of the evolution they describe, while professing to make history irrelevant by the new and absolute character of the revolutionary era entered. To establish the progression they flatten history, omitting data inconsistent with their linear presentation. So here the view of legal creativity as just beginning with American experience ignores a wealth of earlier legal creations, from the structure of marriage to the modes of representative government, creations which could only have been fashioned by men possessed of some consciousness of their power to mold action by legal form. The scientific revolution itself is no argument for quantitative methodology driving out its predecessor. As Lévi-Strauss himself puts it, "It is important not to make the mistake of thinking that there are two stages or phases in the evolution of knowledge. Both approaches are equally valid." Eschatological attack on history, however, demands an evolutionary climax. The spurious excitement which it generates depends on its insensitivity to the historical process which it at once appeals to and ignores.

That process cannot be abolished by the revolutionary's fiat. We are bound to the past, that is, to the past participants. Within the context of the community they have made we are in dialogue with them; and law is a form of the dialogue.

Human desires may be quantified by psychological devices, and human beings may be considered in their quantitative aspect as is commonly done in demography. It is difficult to persuade any individual human being that such abstractions are commensurate with himself or herself. The complex rationality of individuals escapes reduction. As long as it does, the rational rules which speak to them must address them as persons—that is, the rules must be more than stimuli reaching a single locus in the brain, causing fear or inducing pleasure; they must be capable of internalization as standards of conduct and as directions to the achievement of human goods. They must teach much more than coerce. But who can speak to persons?

To minds attuned to a biblical tradition, Jewish or Christian, there is a persuasive power in a fundamental written document which may make the search for extrinsic validation seem unnecessary. Secularized, such minds replace the Bible with the Constitution and bring to constitutional interpretation an ingenuity and zeal formerly reserved for Holy Writ. But to stop at a document smacks of bibliolatry.

For others, not the document or documents, but the reasons expressed, appear to carry authority—in the case of the Constitution the reasons of the judges expounding it, in the case of the common law generally, the reasons of the judges elaborating it. But the reasons which the judges give are not often the reasons the judges have—*American Banana* and *Palsgraf* illustrate the common divergence; the commentators and the law professors, always possessing greater leisure and sometimes more expertise, find better reasons than the judges to explain their actions. It is difficult to believe that many persons do, in fact, respond to the particular reasons recited by the lawgivers or judges.

Rules and reasons detached from their authors do not speak at all. Perceived as the edict of some leviathan, some military-industrial complex, rules do offer bait for compliance, punishment for non-compliance, but where there is response to them, it is to the letter, to obtain the bait or avoid the sanction. Perceived as the logical implication of a single concept, reasons do coerce as long as that concept is focused on, but in determining moral action there is often more than one concept to start from; the choice of premises is crucial. Rules abstracted from those enunciating them may be analyzed academically and arranged into imposing schemes; or they may be manipulated to serve the interest of the manipulator. Reasons set out in the air have no weight; one reason can always be countered by another. Notations on paper, rules and reasons afford no resistance to their academic or practical masters. Rules and reasons speak persuasively to persons only as the purposeful acts of other persons.

To reach this determination is to return to the relation between the development of doctrine and history; for it is to say that all persons when they do not merely comply with a regulation but respond to its purpose become interpreters of the purpose of its author. Applying the rule now in a living situation, every citizen must attempt to understand the past purpose as it was enunciated. For each of them history provides the point of departure and the point of reference. Without it communication is not possible between those who speak through the rules and those who interact with them.

Rational community structure of any kind, therefore, invites at least a limited dependence on history, on the ascertainment of past purpose, but two principal questions are left open: First, how far back shall the dependence go? Second, how shall the good purposes of the past be discriminated from the bad? As to the first, there seems nothing inconsistent with the notion of a structured community to say that only the past purposes of persons still alive shall count, or to declare a Rule Against Perpetuities making a purpose obsolete and invalid after so many lives in being have elapsed. Without commitment to the past participants, Burke has observed, we have no commitment to the future participants. But must we follow Burke in accepting community with the dead? To let their purposes count may always seem a ghost dance in which the ancestors are invoked in a pathetic ritual to draw down aid which the dead are powerless to give. Yet the characteristics of human reason which enable it to transcend time and place to understand the purposes of the past make the fact of whether a person is our contemporary or not immaterial when the focus is on his thought. In the communal symposium in which the development of law takes place, George Wythe and Thomas Jefferson, Oliver Wendell Holmes, Jr., and Benjamin N. Cardozo speak with as much force as— It is difficult to complete the sentence. What present lawyer, law professor, or judge is as influential in determining our purposes?

''Our dead brothers still live for us,'' Holmes declared in the famous Memorial Day address that paid tribute to the Puritan and to New England, ''mother of a race of conquerors.'' Explaining what he meant, however, he made it clear that the heroes of the Civil War lived only by example and in memory, showing us how finely men might do their duty. This way of perpetuating the past involves a response to those who have gone before. It leaves the content of duty empty, to be defined. It is not enough. Response in the legal process to the ancestors must also be a response to their aspirations.

The earth belongs to the living, but those persons to whom we respond are not inert. No greater difficulty exists in divining the purposes of the persons who shaped our community in 1785 or 1900 than in understanding the communications of those who write as our contemporaries. Illusions and fictional manipulations are doubtless possible. But the ability to distinguish between persons and masks is the ability on which history depends. The human beings to whom we respond are not ghosts, not masks. The invocation of the past participants is neither denial nor concealment of our own humanity. It is an affirmation at once personal and communal, binding us to the future as it unites us with our predecessors.

No doubt the ancestors had bad purposes as well as good. The historian—here the mere historian—may not enter judgment on them; but human beings must discriminate between those purposes which are worth being kept alive and those which must be interred. Who would wish to maintain Wythe and Jefferson's purpose in enforcing slavery? Who would wish with Holmes to uphold the extension of an American monopoly by corruption and armed force abroad or with Cardozo to tax the penniless plaintiff with costs? An ahistorical present appears to assert itself as alone real, the purposes of past great men being raw material along with contemporary data, all of equal value in deciding the good purposes of the future. The notion of fidelity to past persons disappears.

Against the logic of this conclusion the historian must protest: these good purposes do not exist abstractly in some Platonic realm; they exist now in living human persons recapturing the thought of past living persons. These purposes, and with it their vitality, their toughness, arise out of the lives of past persons; they speak to us out of those lives. Whether they are moral ideals or judicial opinions, they must be understood in the multiple contexts which enfold each individual's experience. The act of understanding enhances our power to discriminate between what was fundamental to, say, a Wythe, a Jefferson, a Holmes, or a Cardozo and what was, even within their own framework, weakness or misapprehension or contingent solution. The community of rational discourse is rooted in the history of human beings. Persons speak to persons, heart unmasked to heart.

Notes and
References

Notes and
References

FOREWORD

For a view of the moral education achieved by Seavey's teaching, written two years after experiencing it, see my "Value References in the Teaching of Negligence," *Journal of Legal Education* (1955), 8, 150 at 159, 169.

On the moral responsibility of lawyers, see my "From Social Engineering to Creative Charity," *Knowledge and the Future of Man,* ed. Walter J. Ong (1968), 179–98.

1 THE MASKS OF THE PARTICIPANTS

"The life of the law . . .": Oliver Wendell Holmes, Jr., *The Common Law* (1881), 1.

"by the very necessity of its nature": *Ibid.,* 38.

"the personification of inanimate nature . . .": *Ibid.,* 11.

"The vessel acts and speaks . . .": Marshall, quoted by Story, *The Makel Adhel,* 2 *Howard's Reports* 210, 233 (1844), cited by Holmes, 29.

"personifying language": *Ibid.,* 30.

A general criticism of combining active verbs with abstract nouns in the fashion of Holmes and other jurisprudents is made in Dorothy Emmet, *Rules, Roles, and Relations* (1966), 28.

THE DOMINANCE OF RULES IN LEGAL STUDY

Edward H. Levi, *An Introduction to Judicial Reasoning* (1949), 2.

"When will it be just . . .": "the principal agencies of law": J. Willard

Hurst, *The Growth of American Law: The Law Makers, vi.* In Hurst's most original work, *Law and Economic Growth: The Legal History of the Lumber Industry in Wisconsin, 1836–1915* (1964), a detailed and massive study of economic regulations, lawyers are rarely mentioned, and judges and litigants do not have a prominent place. Roujet Marshall, Chief Justice of Wisconsin, is noted in connection with his remarkable opinion holding invalid an amendment of the state constitution which provided new limits on private lumbering; Hurst has already observed that Marshall had been the lawyer for Frederick Weyerhaeuser, the leader of the lumber industry. The connection between Marshall's opinion and his earlier experience in practice is, perhaps, obvious, but it is not developed; nor is there any exploration of the relation of Frederick Weyerhaeuser to other lawyers and to the legislators and governors of Wisconsin. As an example of work continuing in the Hurst tradition, see Lawrence M. Friedman, *Contract Law in America: A Social and Economic Case Study* (1965). Friedman's book, also devoted to Wisconsin, does refer to Roujet Marshall with interest (211–13), criticizing the abstractness of his judicial style. Writing not as a professed legal historian, but as a law professor sensitive to psychology and sociology, Walter O. Weyrauch has examined "the interrelations between the perspectives of lawyers and legal practices as a whole," Weyrauch, *The Personality of Lawyers* (1964), 5. Significantly, Weyrauch had been educated in continental Europe and took as his subjects German lawyers.

"I shall use the history of our law . . .": Holmes, *The Common Law*, 2.

"politic": *Ibid.*, 89; "a great judge": *Ibid.*, 106.

"a story . . . an instructive example of the mode": *Ibid.*, 5.

"to discover . . .": *Ibid.*, 77.

Milsom's method: S. H. C. Milsom, *Historical Foundations of the Common Law* (1969). From a different perspective than mine, the self-containment of most legal historical writing has been sharply criticized, see Barbara J. Shapiro, "Law and Science in Seventeenth Century England," *Stanford Law Review* (1969), 21, 728. See also the earlier complaint of Daniel J. Boorstin, "Tradition and Method in Legal History," *Harvard Law Review* (1941), 54, 424.

THE DOMINANCE OF RULES IN JURISPRUDENCE

The jurisprudential equivalents of the railroad experts are, in order of the speakers, John Austin, *The Province of Jurisprudence Determined,* Lecture I; Oliver Wendell Holmes, Jr., "The Path of the Law," *Harvard Law Review* (1897), 10:457 at 458; Hans Kelsen, *The Pure Theory of Law,* trans. Max Knight (1967), esp. 195–202; Roscoe Pound, "An Engineering Interpretation," *Interpretations of Legal History* (1932), 152–65; H. L. A. Hart, "Definition and Theory in Jurisprudence," *Law Quarterly Review* (1954), 70, 37 at 53–4.

For emphasis on persons from two distinct perspectives, see Jerome Frank, "Are Judges Human? The Effect on Legal Thinking of the Assumption That Judges Behave Like Human Beings," *University of Pennsylvania*

Law Review, 80, 1731 (1931), and Lon L. Fuller, "Human Interaction and the Law," *American Journal of Jurisprudence* (1969), 12, 1–36.

Chase as attempted rape: *Lewis* v. *The State,* 35 Ala. 380 (1860); cited by Holmes, *The Common Law,* 68.

"The status of a slave . . .": Hart, "Definition and Theory in Jurisprudence," at 54, n.21.

"in slaveowning societies . . .": H. L. A. Hart, *The Concept of Law* (1961), 196; "painful facts of human history": *Idem;* "a profound study . . .": *Ibid.,* 254. The conversation quoted is in Mark Twain, *Huckleberry Finn* (1964 ed.), 287; the irony of Jim already being free occurs at the book's climax, 369.

"the science of law": Austin, Lecture I, *The Province of Jurisprudence Determined,* ed. H. L. A. Hart, 13.

"the key to the science of jurisprudence": Hart, *The Concept of Law,* 79.

"command of ideas": Holmes, "The Path of the Law," at 478.

Grundnorm: Kelsen, "The Pure Theory of Law," trans. Charles H. Wilson, *Law Quarterly Review* (1935) 51, 517 at 518.

"the remote and the more general . . .": Holmes, "The Path of the Law" at 478.

"game": Thomas Hobbes, *Leviathan* (Cambridge Classics ed., 1904), 252; Hart, *The Concept of Law,* 99, 140–1.

THE INDISPENSABILITY OF IMPERSONALITY

"regardeth not persons": Deuteronomy 10.17; "no acceptance of persons," Colossians 3.25; "shall not accept persons": Deuteronomy 16.19; "if you show respect . . .": James 2.9.

"respect of persons": Thomas Aquinas, *Summa theologica,* II–II, 63.4; Condemnation of the innocent defended, Thomas Aquinàs, *Summa theologica,* II–II, 64, 6, obj. 3 and ad 3. That the judge should judge according to what was alleged, not according to conscience, was a legal maxim stated and debated by twelfth- and thirteenth-century Romanists and canonists. The history of early controversy on this question is given by Krut Wolfgang Norr, *Zur Stellung des Richters im gelehrten Prozess der Frühzeit: Iudex secundum allegata non secundum conscientiam iudicat* (1968). Max Radin illustrates discussion of the problem at English common law beginning in the fourteenth century, Radin, "The Conscience of the Court," *Law Quarterly Review,* (1932) 48, 506. Radin cites instances where the case has actually arisen that the judge knows from knowledge gained outside of court that the man he is about to condemn is innocent, but he expresses some doubt as to the authenticity of the accounts.

"Put aside fear and favor . . .": Innocent III, "Qualiter et quando," *Decretales Gregorii IX,* ed. E. Friedberg (1881), 5.1.17.

"Relieve the judges of the rigor . . .": Thomas Jefferson to Philip Mazzei, November 1785, *Writings,* ed. Paul Leicester Ford (1894), IV, 114–16.

THE COMPLEMENTARITY OF RULES AND PERSONS

"as wholly made up of rules": Roscoe Pound, "Juristic Science and Law," *Harvard Law Review* (1918), 21, 1047 at 1060; "standards": 1061; "principles," "significant legal institutions," "a living part . . .": 1062.

Dworkin on rules and principles: Ronald M. Dworkin, "The Model of Rules," *University of Chicago Law Review* (1967), 35, 14 at 22–4. In his most recent article, Dworkin has developed and refined "The Model of Rules" by emphasis on the institutional context of judicial decision making; his judge of "superhuman skill," symbolically named Hercules, appears as a magnified personification of the belief that principles decide cases, see Dworkin, "Hard Cases," *Harvard Law Review*, 85 (1975), 1,057 at 1,059, 1,083. Dworkin at 1,094 remarks on "the magnitude of this enterprise," an implicit concession, I suppose, that Hercules' work of constructing "a scheme of abstract and concrete principles," etc., is never accomplished. But why should this imaginary construct be used to explain the actions of real judges? It is strange to talk of Hercules when your starting point is Harry Blackmun.

The position of the Kadishes, Mortimer R. Kadish and Sanford H. Kadish, *Discretion to Disobey. A Study of Lawful Departures from Legal Rules* (1973), 29–31, 217–18.

For an approach analogous to mine, see I. A. Richards, *Beyond* (1974), 162, transplanting to the humanities the principle of complementarity set out by Niels Bohr for modern physics.

"Justice—love serving only the loved one": *iustitia—amor soli amato serviens,* Augustine, *De moribus ecclesiae catholicae et de moribus Manichaeorum,* 1.15, 125, *Patrologia latina,* ed. J. P. Migne, 32, 1322. I am indebted to Stephan Kuttner for this reference as well as for the opportunity to read his remarkable essay "A Neglected Definition of Justice," in which the notion of justice as "a silent compact of nature in aid of the many" is traced back to St. Martin of Braga and Calcidius' Latin commentary on the *Timaeus.* Professor Kuttner's essay will soon appear in *Mélanges au honneur de Gérard Fransen,* edited by A. M. Stickler as a volume in *Studia Gratiana.*

"The intense desire . . .": Pound, "Juristic Science and Law" at 1059.

"(Goya) shows one aspect . . .": Kenneth Clark, *The Romantic Rebellion* (1973), 81–8.

MASKS DEFINED AND DISTINGUISHED FROM ROLES

"As those who knew him . . .": Warren A. Seavey, "Mr. Justice Cardozo and the Law of Torts," *Harvard Law Review,* 52, 372, *Yale Law Journal,* 48, 390, *Columbia Law Review,* 39, 20 (1939).

Socrates on physicians whose purpose is to make money: Plato, *The Republic,* trans. Francis M. Cornford (1945), Book I, 341–2.

For the relation of persons to roles, and the analogy of clothes: Paul Tournier, *The Meaning of Person,* trans. Edwin Hudson (1957), 73–83.

MASKS SUBJECTIVELY AND OBJECTIVELY CONSIDERED

For a study of children's invisible companions: Humberto Nagera, "The Imaginary Companion: Its Significance for Ego Development and Conflict Solution," *The Psychoanalytic Study of the Child*, XXIV (1960), 165–96; "second stage of development": Jean Piaget, *The Moral Judgment of the Child*, trans. Margaret Gabain (1948), 84–95.

"Many a common law suit . . .": Benjamin N. Cardozo, "Mr. Justice Holmes," *Harvard Law Review* (1933), 44, 682, 685. The analysis of law as literature has been made in particular by James B. White, *The Legal Imagination* (1973), a book addressed to law students. A case and materials book of a new genre, White's pioneering work is rich in jurisprudential implications.

"the interest of the stronger": Plato, *The Republic*, I, 338; Socrates' answer, I, 351. The effect on the lawmakers of the Southern law on slavery was noted by contemporaries from George Mason to Alexis de Tocqueville, see Charles S. Sydnor, "The Southerner and the Laws," *Journal of Southern History* (1940) 6, 3 at 9.

"violence": Thomas Aquinas (on unjust law), *Summa theologica* I–II, 96, 4.

"Observing that words . . .": Soedjatmoko, "The Javanese Past," in *An Introduction to Indonesian Historiography*, ed. by Soedjatmoko, Mohammad Ali, C. J. Resink, and G. M. Kahin (1965), 89.

THE REMOVABILITY OF MASKS

"pervasive": Lon L. Fuller, *Legal Fictions* (1967), p. ix; on the function of legal fictions: *Ibid.*, 49–92, 124–37.

particular flesh and blood and consciousness: cf. Thomas Aquinas, *Summa Theologica* I, 29, 4: person signifies "these pieces of flesh, these bones, and this soul": A. J. Ayer, *The Concept of a Person* (1963), 126: "it is essential that a person be identified at any given time by reference to some body." This view of the person implies an ontology. I accept that proposed by Maritain, distinguishing between "the person" with his or her end transcending the temporal good, and "the individual," that is, the person considered as a material substance whose welfare is centered in the communal good. Cf. Jacques Maritain, *The Person and the Common Good*, trans. John F. Fitzgerald (1947), 31–46, 76–89.

"human self-alienation": "The immediate task of philosophy, which is in the service of history, is to unmask human self-alienation in its secular form, now that it has been unmasked in its sacred form. Thus, the criticism of heaven is transformed into the criticism of earth, the criticism of religion into the criticism of law . . ." Karl Marx, *Zur Kritik der Hegelschen Rechtsphilosophie Einleitung.*, trans. T. B. Bottomore, in Marx, *Early Writings* (1963), 44; cf. *Karl Marx's Economic and Philosophic Manuscripts of 1894, Marx-Engels Werke,* supplement I, 304–5, and the interpretation of this passage by István Mészáros, *Marx's Theory of Alienation* (1970), 184–5. "Consequently," Mészáros writes, "if the other person is merely a cook, a maid, and a whore for man, their relation only satisfies his dehumanized animal needs."

"Among the Bali . . .": Clifford Geertz, *Person, Time and Conduct in Bali* (1966); cited in Amelie Oksenberg Rorty, "Persons, Policies, and Bodies," *International Philosophical Quarterly* (1973), 13, 72. For a general comparison of law to magic, see Walter O. Weyrauch, "Taboo and Magic in the Law," 25 *Stanford Law Review* (1973), at 797–800. While I differ from Weyrauch on the extent to which law is magical, as my discussion of the relation of persons to rules has made clear, I see the force of his analogy when black letter formulae dominate and suppress the person.

"The concept of physical (natural) person. . .": Kelsen, *General Theory of Law and State*, trans. Anders Wedberg (1949), 95.

"the most perfect": Thomas Aquinas, *Summa theologica*, I, 29, 3. For an overview of all the development, see Marcel Mauss, "Une Categorie de l'Esprit Humain: La Notion de Personne, Celle de Moi," *Journal of the Royal Anthropological Institute* (1938), 68, 263–82.

"nightmare": James Joyce, *Ulysses* (1961 ed.) I, 34; "terror of history": Mircea Eliade, *Cosmos and History*, trans. Willard R. Trask (1959), 141–62; "History! Read it and weep": Kurt Vonnegut, *Cat's Cradle* (1963), 168.

2 VIRGINIAN LIBERATORS

"faithful and beloved Mentor," "most affectionate friend . . .": Jefferson, *Autobiography*, in *Works*, ed. Paul L. Ford (1904), I, 6.

"Law and Police": Thomas Jefferson, *Notes on the State of Virginia*, ed. William Peden (1955), 151.

"I know of no place in the world . . .": Jefferson to Ralph Izzard, quoted in Julian P. Boyd, "The Murder of George Wythe," *William and Mary Quarterly*, 3rd Series, 12 (1955), 515.

"I give my books and small philosophical apparatus . . .": George Wythe, First Codicil to his Last Will and Testament, January 19, 1806, printed in B. B. Minor, "Memoir of the Author," *Virginia Reports Annotated* 2 (Wythe), 95.

"one of the most virtuous . . .": Jefferson to Richard Price, August 7, 1785, Jefferson, *Writings*, ed. Paul L. Ford (1894) 4, 83.

"a more disinterested person never lived": Jefferson, "Notes for the Biography of George Wythe," enclosed with a letter to John Sanderson, August 31, 1820, Jefferson Papers, Library of Congress MS, volume 218, 38934; excerpted in *Virginia Reports Annotated* II (Wythe), 93; "the purest kind . . .", *Idem.* "judgements were all as between A and B . . .": John Randolph, quoted in B. B. Minor, "Memoir of the Author," *Virginia Reports Annotated* II, 91.

"the honor of his own and the model of future times": Jefferson, "Notes for the Biography of George Wythe," *supra.*

"do equal right . . .": An act for establishing a High Court of Chancery, Acts of October, 1777, chapter XV, *The Statutes at Large*, being a

Collection of all the Laws of Virginia, ed. William Waller Hening (1824) (hereafter Hening), IX, 389. For the royal judges' oath, see Acts of November, 1753, chapter 1, Hening, VI, 326.

The story of Sisamnes: Herodotus, *History* (trans. George Rawlinson, 1922) Book 5, p. 273; West's suggestion of the story for the seal: Wythe, note to *Page v. Pendleton and Lyons, Administrators, Virginia Reports Annotated* 2 (Wythe), 221.

"legislative omnipotence": *Page* v. *Pendleton and Lyons, Administrators, Virginia Reports Annotated* 2 (Wythe), at 222; "As Antigone says to Creon . . .": *Idem.*

Wythe's enmity with Pendleton: David John Mays, *Edmund Pendleton* (1952), II, 291–6; Wythe's reversals: *Ibid.,* II, 290. Pendleton and Wythe contrasted: *Ibid.,* II, 290–302; on Pendleton and the Robinson Estate: *Ibid.,* I, 178–208. Compare *Deutsche Bank Filiale Nurnberg v. Humphrey* 272 U.S. 517 (1926) where, for a court divided 5–4 (and to the enrichment of the Alien Property Custodian) Holmes gave a very different decision on the legality of paying off a debtor on the basis of an inflated currency. Walter O. Weyrauch brought this case to my attention.

THE UNEQUIVOCAL EMANCIPATORS

Wythe's part in the seal of Virginia: Wythe to Jefferson, November 18, 1776, Jefferson Papers, Library of Congress MS, volume 2, 312.

"a warm opponent . . .": Lyon Gardiner Tyler, "George Wythe," *Great American Lawyers,* (ed. William Draper Lewis, 1907), I, 89. "With other eminent Virginians . . .": Theodore S. Cox, "George Wythe," *Dictionary of American Biography* (1943), 20, 588; "Among the eminent Virginians . . .": Robert McColley, *Slavery and Jeffersonian Virginia* (1964), 136.

"unequivocal": Jefferson to Price, August 7, 1785, Jefferson, *Writings,* IV, 83.

"the courage . . .": *Ibid.,* 82; "in conflict . . . one of the most virtuous . . .": *Ibid.,* 83.

The first Emancipation Proclamation: Mays, *Edmund Pendleton,* II, 57.

"For if a slave . . .": Jefferson, "Query XVIII, Manners," *Notes on the State of Virginia,* 162–3. "Boisterous," the key word in this passage carried in the eighteenth century the meanings "abounding in rough but good-natured activity bordering upon excess" and "full of rough violence," Murray's *New English Dictionary on Historical Principles* (1888).

"all persons . . . free": Jefferson, "Draught of a Fundamental Constitution for the Commonwealth of Virginia," Appendix 2, *Notes on the State of Virginia,* 214.

THE LEGAL STRUCTURE OF PRE-REVOLUTIONARY SLAVERY

The statutes on the conduct of slaves: Acts of October, 1705, chapter 49, Hening III, 459–61; Acts of October, 1748, chapter 38, Hening, VI, 102 (the law on medicine); Acts of November, 1769, chapter 19, Hening, VIII, 38 (on attempted rape).

Prescription to read statutes aloud: Acts of October, 1705, chapter 49, Hening, III, 461.

Death sentence of Cupid: Mays, *Edmund Pendleton,* I, 43.

"to make what just defense . . .": Acts of October, 1705, chapter 2, Hening, III, 270; castration, owner's option, Acts of October, 1748, chapter 38, Hening, VI, 111; Genovese points to the discretionary enforcement of other statutes, Eugene D. Genovese, *Roll, Jordan, Roll* (1974), 41.

"every such offender . . .": Acts of May, 1723, chapter 4, Hening, IV, 127.

"Without force . . .": Robert Williams Fogel and Stanley L. Engerman, *Time on the Cross. The Economics of American Negro Slavery* (1974), I, 237.

"Slaves, see Negroes,": Index, Hening, I, 593. For magisterial analysis of the ways in which the European colonists distinguished the Negro, see Winthrop Jordan, *White over Black: American Attitudes toward the Negro, 1550–1812* (1968).

"For the better settling and preservation . . .": Acts of October, 1705, chapter 23, Hening, III, 333; "to the heirs and widows . . .": *Idem.;* "very inconvenient . . . owner . . . humane consideration" *Spicer v. Pope, Virginia Reports Annotated* I (Jefferson), 27 at 29 (General Court, October 1736).

Inconsistency between the control and property statutes: see also, Arnold A. Sio, "Interpretations of Slavery: The Slave Status in America," *Comparative Studies in Society and History* (1965) 8, 289 at 299, 305; Genovese, *Roll, Jordan, Roll,* 28–29.

THE LEGAL STRUCTURE AND REALITY

The anti-miscegenation statute: Acts of April, 1691, chapter 16, Hening, III, 87.

The incest statute: Acts of May, 1730, chapter 2, Hening, IV, 245.

"must lock up the faculties . . .": Jefferson, Query XVIII, *Notes on the State of Virginia,* 162.

"overstocked": "The Humble Address and Representation of the Council and Burgesses . . . April 15, 1772," Hening, V, 441.

Slaves to be personalty with certain exceptions: Acts of February, 1727, chapter 11, Hening, IV, 226.

"had never been made": Acts of October, 1748, chapter 2, Hening, V, 440, 442; approval refused by the Crown: *Ibid.,* 432.

"Slaves are in their nature personal . . .": "The Humble Address of the Council and Burgesses . . . April 15, 1752": Hening, V, 440.

"for first he is not a manor . . . : *Blackwell v. Wilkinson, Virginia Reports Annotated* I (Jefferson), 41 at 45 (General Court, October 1768). On the entailment law of Virginia, see Acts of October, 1705, chapter 21, Hening, III, 320, and also C. Ray Keim, "Primogeniture and Entail in Colonial Virginia," *William and Mary Quarterly,* 3rd Series, 25 (1968), 545–86.

"our property . . .": Jefferson, Preface to Reports, *Virginia Reports Annotated* I, 5; "arising under . . .": *Idem.*

"we are all born free": *Howell* v. *Netherland, Virginia Reports Annotated* I (Jefferson), 49 at 52. (General Court, April 1770); "wicked enough": *Idem.*

"that our whole code must be reviewed . . .": Jefferson, *Autobiography, Works,* I, 66–7.

"all men . . . inherent and inalienable": Jefferson, Draft of the Declaration of Independence, *Autobiography,* 66–7.

"Natural persons are such . . .": William Blackstone, *Commentaries on the Laws of England* (1765), Book I, chapter 1, 118; persons formed in the womb: *Ibid.,* 125–6.

"in the enjoyment of those absolute rights . . .": *Ibid.,* 120.

"War itself is justifiable . . . Much less . . . slavery within this nation": *Ibid.,* Book I, Chapter 14, 411–12.

"American master": *Ibid.,* Book I, Chapter 14, p. 425 (1770 ed.).

"Il est impossible . . .": Charles de Secondat, Baron de Montesquieu, *L'Esprit des lois,* 15, 5 *Oeuvres complètes* (1843), 309.

"tolerable only when they relieve . . .": John Rawls, *A Theory of Justice* (1971) 248; "enslavement is better . . .": *Idem.* Elsewhere, Rawls suggests that his approach is superior to utilitarianism (pp. 158–159) and to Nietzsche's perfectionism (p. 325) by not justifying slavery. But all any defenders of slavery need is a "transition case" defense.

Somerset's release: *Somerset* v. *Stewart* (1772), Lofft, *English Reports,* 98, 499; on the case and its influence, William M. Wiecek, "Somerset: Lord Mansfield and the Legitimacy of Slavery in the Anglo-American World," *University of Chicago Law Review* (1974), 42, 84–146. On Blackstone's hedging and Mansfield's qualifications, David Brion Davis, *The Problem of Slavery in the Age of Revolution 1770–1823* (1975), 485–6, 496, 500.

On the influence in America of Blackstone's view of slavery: Robert M. Cover, *Justice Accused: Antislavery and the Judicial Process* (1975), 15–19; Blackstone's modern reputation, see Daniel J. Boorstin, *The Mysterious Science of the Law* (1941), 166–80.

"to abolish the whole existing system . . .": Jefferson, *Autobiography,* 67; "take Blackstone for that text . . .": Jefferson to John Tyler, June 17, 1812, *The Letters and Times of the Tylers* (1884), ed. Lyon G. Tyler, I, 265–6; "model": Jefferson, *Autobiography,* 67.

THE CONTROL STRUCTURE OF THE REVOLUTIONARIES

"systematical": Jefferson, *Autobiography, Works* I, 68; "would become a subject of question . . . render property uncertain": *Idem.*

"they must have restored slavery . . .": John Quincy Adams, *Memoirs,* ed. Charles Francis Adams (1877), VIII, 284.

Jefferson's work on the control laws: Jefferson, Bill No. 51, *The Papers of Thomas Jefferson,* ed. Julian P. Boyd (1950), II, 470–473.

"riots, routs . . .": the new control laws, Acts of October, 1785, chapter 77, Hening, XII, 132.

"Be it enacted . . . the females of them": *Idem.*

"No person hereafter . . .": Jefferson, "A Bill for new-modelling . . ." June 1776, Jefferson Papers, Library of Congress MS, vol. 2.

Julian Boyd, an authority on Jefferson, notes that no text of an emancipation bill has been found but argues that what the committee intended was "a definite proposal for a system of gradual emancipation, the anticipated decline being brought about by failure to replenish the stock through importation and by manumission on the part of individual owners," Boyd, *The Papers of Thomas Jefferson,* II, 672–73. Boyd's reading of Bill No. 51, Jefferson's draft, is too optimistic. Why should he or the others have supposed there would be "failure to replenish the stock"?

"the government of a family . . . a principal means . . .": Burke to Henry Dundas, one His Majesty's Secretaries of State, Easter Monday, 1792, *The Writings and Speeches of the Right Honorable Edmund Burke* (1901 ed.), VI, 263. The date for Burke's draft is supplied by Robert H. Murray, *Edmund Burke* (1931), 248.

Jefferson's account of the bill to emancipate, educate, and transport: Jefferson, "Query XIV, Laws," *Notes on the State of Virginia,* 140; "emancipation" and "deportation": Jefferson, *Autobiography, Works* I, 77; "It was thought better . . . at this day": *Ibid.,* 76–7.

"imposing upon our fellow men . . .", St. George Tucker, "On the State of Slavery in Virginia", Blackstone's *Commentaries with Notes of Reference* (1803) I, Appendix, 31. The plan of emancipation follows at 77–78. On Tucker, see Armistead M. Dobie, "Tucker, St. George", *Dictionary of American Biography* 19, 38–39.

Jefferson and Wythe responsible: for an exposition of the meaning of responsibility, criticizing the "rule-oriented" theory on this subject of H. L. A. Hart, see John R. Silber, "Being and Doing: A Study of Status Responsibility and Voluntary Responsibility," *University of Chicago Law Review* (1968), 35, 47–91.

THE VIRGINIA PARADOX

"Property in Slaves," George Mason, "Plan Settled by the Committee of Revisors, in Fredericksburg, January 1777," in Kate Mason Rowland, *The Life of George Mason, 1725–1792* (1842), I, 276.

"to make slaves distributable among the next of kin, as other moveables": Jefferson, "Query XIV, Laws," *Notes on the State of Virginia,* 137; "the most remarkable alterations": *Idem.*

"absurd and repugnant," "ordinarily thought . . ." "the principles of law and reason": *Turpin* v. *Turpin, Virginia Reports Annotated* II (Wythe), 162 at 165 (Chancery, October and November 1791); "As the law is now . . .": *Ibid.,* 164.

"The property of slaves . . .": *Fowler* v. *Saunders, Virginia Reports Annotated,* II (Wythe), 284 at 287 (Chancery, 1798).

"the birthright of every human being . . . in slavery . . . perfectly white": Wythe in *Wrights* v. *Hudgins* (Chancery, 1806), quoted by St.

George Tucker in *Hudgins* v. *Wrights, Virginia Reports Annotated,* XI (Hening and Mumford), 134 (Court of Appeals, 1806).

Jefferson's "uncertain commitment": Davis, *The Problem of Slavery in the Age of Revolution 1770–1823,* 169–83; on judges enforcing the rules of slavery as Creons, and the responsibility-shifting techniques used by them, see Cover, *Justice Accused,* 1–8, 236–8.

"Compassion ought not to influence . . .": Wythe, "Commentary" on *Field* v. *Harrison,* etc., *Virginia Reports Annotated,* II (Wythe), 283.

master Roman law: compare John Adams in Braintree, Massachusetts: "I am resolved to translate Justinian and his Commentators Notes by day light and read Gilberts Tenures by night till I am master of both," Adams, Diary, October 5, 1758, *John Adams: A Biography in His Own Words,* ed. James Bishop Peabody (1973) 44.

"impossible" things: the horse, a priest; the past wiped out, see David Daube, "Greek and Roman Reflections on Impossible Laws": *Natural Law Forum* (1967) 12, 1 at 6, 74–84; compare Genovese's comments, in his study of Southern slavery, on "the degree of autonomy law creates for itself," Genovese, *Roll, Jordan, Roll,* 25. Genovese with equal penetration points to the "educative" function of the law, *ibid.,* 27.

"Relieve the judges . . .": Jefferson to Philip Mazzei, November 1785; *Writings,* IV, 114–16.

"clothes for Sally": quoted by Fawn Brodie, *Thomas Jefferson. An Intimate History* (1974), 239.

WYTHE'S MURDER

The murder of Wythe by Swinney: Julian P. Boyd, "The Murder of George Wythe," *William and Mary Quarterly,* 3rd Series 12 (1955) 530–41; W. Edwin Hemphill, "Examinations of George Wythe Swinney for Forgery and Murder; A Documentary Essay," *William and Mary Quarterly,* 3rd Series, 12 (1955), 544–68.

IMPERSONATIONS DISTINGUISHED

"confessed to be enormous": *Hinde* v. *Pendleton and Lyons, Administrators, Virginia Reports Annotated,* II (Wythe), 299; "not unlawful or exceptionable . . .": *Idem.;* "a dolus malus . . . [T]he by-bidder . . . : *Ibid.,* at 300; "manifested a tender affection . . . : *Ibid.,* 299; "to gratify . . .": *Ibid.,* at 300.

3 THE OVERLORD OF AMERICAN LAW AND THE SOVEREIGN OF COSTA RICA

"Only let the material interests . . .": Joseph Conrad, *Nostromo* (1960 ed.), 80–1.

Payment to persuade Central American President: *The Wall Street Journal* (April 9, 1975), 1.

HOLMES'S PLACE IN LEGAL HISTORY

"the great overlord," Benjamin N. Cardozo, "Mr. Justice Holmes," *Harvard Law Review* (1933) 44, 682 at 691.

"non-Euclidean legal thinking": Jerome Frank, "Mr. Justice Holmes and Non-Euclidean Legal Thinking," *Cornell Law Quarterly* (1931), 17, 569–603. "completely to undermine . . . ": *Ibid.,* at 571. Holmes a Machiavelli: *Ibid.,* at 570; Holmes a Vesalius and a Galileo: Frank, "What Courts Do in Fact," *Illinois Law Review* (1932), 26, 772–3.

"The object of your study . . . The prophecies . . .": Oliver Wendell Holmes, Jr., "The Path of the Law," *Harvard Law Review* (1897), 10, 457.

"we all derive": Karl Llewellyn, *The Bramble Bush. Some Lectures on Law and Its Study* (1930), IX.; on the links between the legal realists and American pragmatism as a philosophical movement, see Note, "Legal Theory and Legal Education," *Yale Law Journal* (1970), 79, 1153, 1157–78.

"At Ball's Bluff . . .": Oliver Wendell Holmes, Jr., "Wound at Ball's Bluff," in Mark DeWolfe Howe, Jr., *Justice Oliver Wendell Holmes, Jr.: The Shaping Years* (1957), 102–8. For another judgment, from the point of view of Holmes's greatest admirer, that the war experience was critical, see Felix Frankfurter, "Holmes, Oliver Wendell," *Dictionary of American Biography,* XXI (Supplement One, 1944), 418: "For the Civil War probably cut more deeply than any other influence in his life."

"Wounded in breast . . .": *Who's Who in America 1901–1902,* 551.

"objections to treating a man like a thing . . . If a man lives in society, he is liable . . .": Holmes, *The Common Law,* 44.

"We have seen more than once . . .": *Buck* v. *Bell* (1927), 274 U.S., 200 at 207.

"It seems clear to me . . .": *The Common Law,* 44.

"the general principle . . .": *Ibid.,* 94.

"the relative worth of our different social ends": Holmes, "Law in Science and Science in Law," *Harvard Law Review* (1899), 12, 462.

"If you want to know . . .": Holmes, "The Path of the Law," 457 at 459.

"a body of reports . . .": "The Path of the Law," 457.

"Good and universal (or *general law*) . . .": Holmes, "Wound at Ball's Bluff," 106.

"the remoter and more general aspects . . . a hint of the universal law": Holmes, "The Path of the Law," 478.

"is scarcely a dialectical problem . . .": Thurman Arnold, "Apologia for Jurisprudence," *Yale Law Journal* (1935), 44, 729, 745.

"perhaps the greatest living legal theologian": Anon., "Book Notices," *American Law Review* (1880), 14, 233. (Anon. = Holmes, see Mark DeWolfe Howe, *Justice Oliver Wendell Holmes: The Proving Years,* [1963] 155).

Holmes's veneration of the law: "The Path of the Law," 473.

"humbug": Holmes to Sir Frederick Pollock, July 23, 1916, *Holmes-Pollock Letters,* ed. Mark DeWolfe Howe (1941), I, 163.

Austin's sovereign: John Austin, *The Province of Jurisprudence Determined: Lectures on Jurisprudence* (3rd ed. 1869), Lecture VI, 224–348, esp. 295–7; personified as male, e.g., Lecture I, 97.

"It is admitted by everyone . . .": Holmes, "Book Notices," *American Law Review* (1872) 6, 723; "organizations of persons . . .": *Idem;* "a mere fiction": *Idem.*

FORMATION OF THE ANTAGONISTS

United Fruit's formation and growth: Stacy May and Galo Plaza, *The United Fruit Company in Latin America* (1958), 1–21; Charles David Kepner, Jr., and Jay Henry Soothill, *The Banana Empire* (1935), 33–53. Its income: United Fruit Company, *Annual Report for Year Ended August 31, 1900; Annual Report for Year Ending August 31, 1902; Annual Report for the Year Ending September 30, 1906; Annual Report for the Year Ending September 30, 1907.* Its share of the market: Moorfield Storey, Bradley W. Palmer, and Eugene Ong, *Reply of the United Fruit Company to the Statement Addressed to the Committee on Interstate Commerce of the United States Senate by Everett P. Wheeler and John W. Griffin of Counsel for the American Banana Company,* 5. (Both the *Reply* and the *Annual Reports* are available at the Harvard Business School Library.)

"the uncrowned king of Central America": May and Plaza, *The United Fruit Company in Latin America,* 8.

Palmer's position in the company: United Fruit Company, *Annual Reports, 1900–1911.*

Palmer's biography: Martindale-Hubbell, *Law Directory* (1933), I, 433.

McConnell's capital investment: Contract between Andrew W. Preston and Camors-McConnell Company attached as Exhibit D to the Answer in *American Banana Company* v. *United Fruit Company* (hereafter, Answer), printed as part of the record in that case, 213 U.S. 347 (1909), and now available in the records of the Supreme Court in the National Archives (hereafter, *Record*).

McConnell's agreement with United Fruit: *McConnell* v. *Camors-McConnell Co.,* 152 F. 321 at 328–9 (Fifth Cir. 1907). "this sudden accession of wealth . . .": B. W. [Bradley] Palmer, *The American Banana Company* (1907), 91; McConnell's income: *Ibid.,* 24.

On the arbitration between Colombia and Costa Rica: Gordon Ireland, *Boundaries, Possessions and Conflicts in Central and North America and the Caribbean* (1941), 31–3.

McConnell's plantation: *Complaint,* #21 in *Record.* $414,000 profits, $750,000 capital, *"Prospectus of the American Banana Company,"* printed in Palmer, *The American Banana Company,* 23–6; subscribers of stock, Certificate of Incorporation of the American Banana Company, *Ibid.,* 27. The Smiths' investment, Certificate of Incorporation of the American Banana Company, *Ibid.,* 27–9. Clients of the Smiths: Advertisement, *Hubbell's Legal Directory for Lawyers and Business Men,* ed. J. H. Hubbell (1906), Appendix 4.

"Parades, who is still *alcalde* . . .": Warren to McConnell, June 10, 1903, in Palmer, *The American Banana Company,* p. H; "I have just spoken . . .'': Warren to McConnell, June 19, 1903, *Ibid.,* p. J; ''The United Co. owns . . .'': Warren to McConnell, October 13, 1903, *Ibid.,* p. P.

BATTLE IN SAN JOSÉ AND WASHINGTON

''most reasonable'': McConnell to R. K. Warren, June 10, 1903, printed in Palmer, *The American Banana Company,* 1.

''Both Mr. Kyes and Mr. Leet'': Keith to McConnell, quoted by Storey, *United Fruit Company. Hearing before a Subcommittee on Interstate Commerce, United States Senate, on Resolution S. 139* (1908) [hereafter Hearing] 44.

Occupation of plantation: *Complaint,* #24.

McConnell's appeal: McConnell to Hay, September 24, 1903, *The American Banana Company,* 55; ''If facts are as represented . . .'': Hay to Merry, November 12, 1903, *Ibid.,* 58; Merry's action and Astua's answer: Merry to Hay, November 14, 1903, *Ibid.,* 58–9.

Claimants and assignees under the Astua Denouncements: ''Protocol No. 7, Translation of deed covering the cession of rights in Denouncements 425 and 427 of March 1, 1900, of Eleven Thousand Hectares of land located in the Sixaola and Estella Rivers,'' printed in *Ibid.,* 185–6; ''Certificate showing Acquisition of Astua Denouncements by John M. Keith and others, February 4, 1905,'' *Ibid.,* 187–8.

''the political interests'' of United Fruit: Merry to Francis B. Loomis, Acting Secretary of State, May 21, 1905, *Ibid.,* 112–13; Guardia's occupation: ''Protocol No. 7 . . .'': *Ibid.,* Hitchcock's occupation: ''Denouncement of Government Lands, April 30, 1906,'' *Ibid.,* 216–17; Astua's office: Astua to Merry, September 21, 1904, *Ibid.,* 63–5; Anderson's office, Anderson to the Chargé d'Affaires of the United States, May 26, 1906, *Ibid.,* 170–7.

''remember'': Wheeler, *Hearing,* 61.

Cromwell's lobbying for the New Panama Company: Arthur Dean, *William Nelson Cromwell* (1957), 137; Revolution in Panama: Dana G. Munro, *Intervention and Dollar Diplomacy in the Caribbean 1900–1921* (1964), 52–6.

''intervene in any part . . .'': Constitution of Panama, Article 136, translated and published in Committee on Foreign Relations, U.S. Senate, *Constitution of the Republic of Panama,* Sen. Doc. 208, 58th Cong., 2nd Sess. (1904), 22–3.

End of the Panamanian Army: Munro, *Intervention and Dollar Diplomacy,* 61.

McConnell's first memorial, December 21, 1904, by his counsel Macgrane Cox, *The American Banana Company,* 75; intervention of Congressman Taylor, 78.

''some satisfactory *modus vivendi*'': Hay to Merry, February 8, 1905, Palmer, *Ibid.,* 85–6; communication from United Fruit, James M. Beck to the Secretary of State, February 3, 1905, *Ibid.,* 143.

''of the benevolent attitude of the President'': Astua to McConnell, April

12, 1905, *Ibid.*, 98; "respecting, however the right of third parties": *Idem.*

"the business of the cultivation . . . .": Keith to the Minister of Public Works, May 18, 1905, *Ibid.*, 114; "probable . . . will not insist": *Idem.*

"with whom all our negotiations . . . ." *In the Matter of the American Banana Company . . . For Redress for Property Seized Near the Boundaries of Panama and Costa Rica,* filed with the Department of State, October 18, 1905, *Ibid.*, 132–4.

"the youngest and weakest . . .": *Ibid.*, 133.

"cede . . . to prejudice . . . .": Root to Merry, January 28, 1906, in Merry to Astua, January 29, 1906, *Ibid.*, 152–3.

"the axiom that the courts . . . .": Astua to Merry, March 3, 1906, *Ibid.*, 160.

"one of the best lawyers": Merry to Francis Loomis, Acting Secretary of State, April 23, 1905, Palmer, *Ibid.*, 100; Jiménez's former office: Joaquin Bernardo Calvo, *The Republic of Costa Rica* (1890), 286.

"It seems that it is the duty of the President . . . .": Jiménez to His Honor the Judge of Contentioso Administrativo, April 26, 1906, Palmer, *The American Banana Company,* 214.

THE CHOICE OF COUNSEL

"the new sort of firm . . . .": M. A. DeWolfe Howe, *Portrait of an Independent: Moorfield Storey 1845–1929* (1932), 186. Within this book are published excerpts from Storey's manuscript autobiography, giving the history of his firm (185–6). Storey "in charge of litigation," 185. Storey's work and salary on the *American Law Review,* 163; the dining club, 241; the growth of the Storey firm: compare Hubbell, *Legal Directory* (1900), 1147, and Hubbell (1905), 1201. On Thayer's move from Brandeis, Dunbar, and Nutter, William H. Dunbar, "Ezra Ripley Thayer," *Harvard Law Review* (1915), 29, 1.

"When beginners at the law . . . .": Storey to Holmes, August 12, 1900, Holmes Papers, Harvard Law School, Box 50, Folder 14.

"primarily business lawyers . . . acquired early . . . .": Howe, *Portrait of an Independent,* 139; "prosecuting state of mind . . . capacity for sharp distinctions . . . : *Ibid.*, 149; Howe as the model used by Marquand, see Helen Howe, *The Gentle Americans, 1864–1960* (1965), 321–2.

"was silent in the face of certain knowledge": Storey quoted in Phillip C. Jessup, *Elihu Root* (1938), I, 339. The pamphlet which Storey said made Roosevelt "very angry" (M. A. Howe, 230) was entitled "Secretary Root's Record: Marked Severities in Philippine Warfare, an Analysis of the Law and the Facts bearing on the Action and Utterances of President Roosevelt and Secretary Root" (1902). The attack on Taft was entitled "The Philippine Policy of Secretary Taft, Analyzed by Moorfield Storey" (1904).

"It is not safe . . . .": Storey, "The Recognition of Panama" (a speech delivered at the Massachusetts Reform Club, December 5, 1903, printed 1904), 18.

"the last of the Puritans": Howe, *Portrait of an Independent,* 174;

Forbes as the model used by Santayana, George Santayana to the author (April 1947).

"Ole Uncle S . . .": James Russell Lowell, "Jonathan to John," *The Biglow Papers, The Poetical Works* III, 144 (1904), applied by Storey to Roosevelt, Storey to William Ketchum, April 25, 1910, in Howe, 310; and applied by Storey to Root in *Problems of Today* (1920), 253. "We may feel that the United States . . .": *Idem.*

"I confess, however, that you . . .": Storey to Thayer, November 3, 1899, Howe, *Portrait of an Independent,* 224. Thayer's article is in 12 *Harvard Law Review,* 464–85 (1899), immediately after Holmes's "Law in Science and Science in Law."

"many of the most influential . . .": Roosevelt quoted in Storey, *The Reform of Legal Procedure* (1911), 17; "really telling their clients . . .": Storey, *idem.;* "the political religion of the nation" . . . : *Ibid.,* 1.

"did not undertake . . .": Storey, "Autobiography," in Howe, 185.

"a very busy business lawyer": Storey, "Autobiography," 185.

The biography of Strong and Cadwalader: Henry W. Taft, *A Century and a Half at the New York Bar, Being the Annals of a Law Firm and Sketches of its Members* (1938), 3–180.

Speyer a regular client: *Ibid.,* 192–3.

Autobiography of Henry W. Taft: *Ibid.,* 192, and Taft, *Legal Miscellanies* (1941), 1–16.

"corporation lawyer": Henry W. Taft, *Occasional Papers and Addresses of an American Lawyer* (1920), 14; "a relatively small portion . . .": *Ibid.,* 15; "constructive statesman": *Ibid.,* 19.

Taft as Special Assistant to the Attorney General: Taft, *Legal Miscellanies,* 116.

"the crowning service . . .": Taft to the State Bar Association of New York, *Occasional Papers,* 47.

"a great corporation lawyer": Theodore Roosevelt to Henry Cabot Lodge, July 21, 1899, *Selections from the Correspondence of Theodore Roosevelt and Henry Cabot Lodge, 1884–1918,* ed. Henry Cabot Lodge (1925), I, 415.

"I have had many lawyers . . .": attributed to either Ryan or Whitney, and discounted in Jessup, *Elihu Root,* I, 185.

"more and more friendly": Taft, *Legal Miscellanies,* 199; ". . . the tone of any discussion . . .": *Ibid.,* 200; "we conduct and try our cases . . .": Root to Brown, Jessup, *Elihu Root,* I, 434.

"The principles underlying . . .": Root, "Some Duties of American Lawyers to American Law," *Yale Law Journal* (1904) 14, 63 at 67.

The superiority of the legal system of the United States: Taft, *Occasional Papers,* 48.

"the leader of the bar . . .": Taft, *Legal Miscellanies,* 201.

"the best field for activity in the world": Jessup, *Elihu Root,* I, 431.

Root's representation of Speyer: *Ibid.,* I, 432.

Taft to Roosevelt on behalf of Speyer: September 5, 1906, *Ibid.,* I, 547–8.

Guthrie and Cravath as Speyer's counsel: Robert Swaine, *The Cravath Firm* (1948), I, 552; II, 119, 180–1.

Wheeler's biography: *Who's Who in America 1906–1907*.

THE DIRECTIVE OF ELIHU ROOT

"If a nation shows that it knows . . .": Roosevelt to Root, May 20, 1904, *The Letters of Theodore Roosevelt,* selected and edited by Elting T. Morrison (1951), IV, 801. For the letter's significance, see Munro, *Intervention and Dollar Diplomacy in the Caribbean 1900–1921,* 77. On Root's formulation of the letter, Jessup, *Elihu Root,* I, 469.

"the next door neighbor of Panama . . .": Root to John Hay, January 7, 1905, excerpted in Jessup, *Elihu Root,* I, 471.

"I have been and am now . . .": Roosevelt, quoted in Jessup, *Ibid.,* I, 198; "I don't see anything for it . . .": Choate to Root, quoted in Root to Jessup, July 26, 1934, Jessup, I, 199; "under well-settled and familiar law . . .": Root to Jessup, November 3, 1934, Jessup, I, 200; "I mixed my argument . . .": *Idem.*

"In the Department's conception . . .": Root to Magoon and Merry, April 16, 1906, printed in *Hearing,* 55.

THE INITIATIVE OF COUNSEL IN ALABAMA

Spencer's biography: Martindale-Hubbell, *Law Directory* (1933), I, 441; United Fruit's listing as Spencer's client: *Idem;* "Associate General Counsel," United Fruit Company, *Annual Report for the Year Ending August 31, 1901.*

"collateral": *Camors-McConnell Co.* v. *McConnell,* 140 F. 412 (S.D. Alabama, 1905), affirmed, *McConnell* v. *Camors-McConnell Co.,* 140 F. 987 (Fifth Cir., 1906).

Stockholder's suit against American Banana: Storey, Palmer, and Ong, *Reply to Statement . . . by Everett P. Wheeler . . .,* 55.

VICTORY IN NEW YORK

"a reasonable attorney's fee . . .": 26 Stat. 204 (1870), 15 *U.S. Code,* 15.

"The lawyer who stands . . .": Storey, *The Reform of Legal Procedure,* 40.

75 witnesses, Storey, Palmer, and Ong: *Reply to Statement . . . by Everett P. Wheeler . . . ,* 9; Esquivel examined: *Hearing,* 25.

Judge Lacombe's ruling: *American Co.* v. *United Fruit Co.,* 153 F. 943 (Cir. Ct. S.D. N.Y., 1907).

Lacombe's biography: *Who's Who in America 1906–1907,* 860.

Judge Lowell's ruling: Storey, Statement, *Hearing,* 14.

"is an ordeal which a man dislikes to face . . .": Storey, *The Reform of Legal Procedure* (1911), 43.

"There was but one tort . . . .": *American Banana Co.* v. *United Fruit Co.*, 160 F. 184, 188 (Cir. Ct. S.D. N.Y., March 4, 1908).

A JUDGE FROM BEYOND THE BRAZOS

Fifth Circuit panel in 1905: Palmer, *The American Banana Company*, 43.

"a very dishonest one": *McConnell* v. *Camors-McConnell Co.*, 152 F. 321 (5th Circuit, 1907).

Biography of McCormick: *Who's Who in America 1903–1905; The New York Times*, November 3, 1916, 12:5 (obituary).

Pascal's famous epigram: "Vérité au deçà des Pyrénées, erreur au delà." [Truth this side of the Pyrenees, error on the other.] Blaise Pascal, "La Justice et la Raison des Effets," *Pensées, Oeuvres*, ed. L. Brunschvig, 1921, 13, 216.

"these unnatural persons . . . grace from graceless and hurtful acts": *McConnell* v. *Camors-McConnell Co.*, 152 F. 321 at 332 (Fifth Cir., 1907).

Judge Toulmin's ruling: *Camors-McConnell Co.* v. *McConnell*, 163 F. 638 (S.D. Alabama, July 15, 1908).

THE CONGRESSIONAL ARENA

Senator Johnston's resolution: *Congressional Record* (1908), 42; 4149–4150; Commerce and Labor source of Consul's report, Wheeler, *Hearing*, 12.

"a mighty, unassailable position . . .": Consul of Germany in San José, Costa Rica, to the German government, "Bericht über Handel und Industrie," translated, *Congressional Record* (1908), 42, 4150.

"courted" an investigation: Wheeler, citing the *Boston Herald*, April 2, 1908, *Hearing* 10; the company seeks to block it: *Ibid.*, 47.

Biography of Senator Kean: *Who's Who in America 1908–1909*, 1025.

"I say they came over there . . .": Wheeler, *Hearing*, 5.

"little short of treason . . . absolutely regardless of law": *Ibid.*, 9.

"[T]hese are things . . . no law against it": Storey, *Hearing*, 32; "We do not owe this man . . .": *Ibid.*, 30.

"What do you expect . . .? . . . justice": *Ibid.*, 62.

APPEAL

Judge Noyes's biography: *Who's Who in America 1908–1909*, 1,402.

"The acts complained of . . .": *American Banana Co.* v. *United Fruit Co.*, 166 F. 261 (2nd Cir., December 15, 1908).

"I was shrewd enough . . .": Brief for the Appellant, 3, *Record;* "the tools": *Ibid.*, 41.

"there is and must be . . .": Blackstone, *Commentaries on the Laws of England*, (1765) I, sec. 2, p. 49.

"an absolute despotism . . . No human power": Argument for the Defendant in *Rafael* v. *Verelst*, 2 W. Blackstone 1055 (K.B. 1776) 96 *Eng. Rep.* 621; "contrary to his own inclination . . .": Blackstone in *Idem*.

The Nabob's case distinguished: *Brief for the Appellee*, 27, *Record;* Webb's *Pollock on Torts* cited: *Ibid.*, 13.

JUDGMENT BY HOLMES, J.

"about the U.S. Fruit Company": Holmes to Lewis Einstein, May 21, 1909, *The Holmes-Einstein Letters*, ed. James Bishop Peabody (1964), 46.

"If I had to bet . . .": Holmes to Einstein, August 1, 1908, *Ibid.* 38; "a humbug . . .": See note, *supra*, under Holmes's place in legal history.

"Law is a statement of the circumstances . . .": *American Banana Co.* v. *United Fruit Co.*, 213 U.S. 347 (1909) at 356; "The fundamental reason . . .": *Ibid.*, at 358. *Kawanakoa* v. *Polyblank*, 205 U.S. 349 (1909) had been Holmes's first occasion to expound the doctrine of sovereign immunity for the Court. At issue was whether the Territory of Hawaii, after signing a mortgage, could be sued in Hawaii to foreclose the mortgage. Holmes held the Territory immune from suit. In Hawaii, he noted, the Territory was "the fountain from which rights ordinarily flow." Its immunity, he said, was both "logical and practical." He did not observe that there could scarcely be any practical difficulty in a federal court enforcing a mortgage against a Territory of the United States. He did not say if a "Territory" could not be sued, the persons who signed the mortgage for the Territory could be. Logic put the sovereign beyond suit— he would not say more.

"Yes, but very hard . . .": Fuller to Holmes, undated, on back of draft Holmes opinion in *American Banana Co.* v. *United Fruit Co.*, Holmes's Bound Opinions, Holmes Papers. Harvard Law School.

SOVEREIGNTY AS A MASK

Holmes's assets: "Property of O. W. Holmes and Fanny B. Holmes," January 1, 1909, Holmes's Ledger, Holmes MS, Harvard Law School.

"to avoid the great enterprises . . .": Holmes to Edward J. Holmes, December 27, 1905, Holmes MS, Box 20, Harvard Law School.

"The Puritan still lives . . .": Holmes, "Memorial Day," An Address Delivered May 30, 1884, at Keene, New Hampshire. In Mark DeWolfe Howe, *The Occasional Speeches of Justice Oliver Wendell Holmes* (1962), 10; "mother of a race of conquerors": *Idem*.

"a New England enterprise": Paine, Weber, Jackson, and Curtis, "New England Enterprises" (1913) (a stockbrokers' compendium of important New England businesses).

"In an hour . . .": Holmes to Lady Leslie Scott, April 24, 1911, Holmes MS, Harvard Law School, Box 35, Folder 21.

Rogat's analysis: Yosal Rogat, "The Judge as Spectator," *University of Chicago Law Review* (1964), 31, 213–56.

"the overlord of the law . . .": Benjamin N. Cardozo, "Mr. Justice

Holmes," *Harvard Law Review* (1930), 44, 682 at 691; "sceptic . . .": *Idem.*

"several rather startling propositions . . . surprising": 213 U.S. 347 at 355; "That could hardly be . . . the United Fruit Company": *Ibid.*, at 358–9.

"But then personality . . .": Holmes to Lewis Einstein, May 21, 1909, Peabody ed., 46.

"mere fiction": Holmes's earlier comment on Austin's sovereign, "Book Notices," *American Law Review* (1878), 6, 723; on the necessity of such a fiction for "the unity of law": Fuller, *Legal Fictions,* 128. Holmes's treatment of sovereignty as a fact may profitably be compared with the analysis of "fact" offered in L. J. Henderson, "An Approximate Definition of Fact," *University of California Publications in Philosophy* (1932), XIL, 179–99. I am indebted to Robert K. Merton for this reference.

"The common law is not a brooding omnipresence . . .": *Southern Pacific Company* v. *Jensen,* 244 U.S. 205 at 222 (dissenting opinion) (1917).

New England Calvinism as a logical system which had collapsed: Oliver Wendell Holmes, *The Deacon's Masterpiece or the Wonderful One-Hoss Shay* (1858).

Two years later, in a case involving the jurisdiction of Michigan over a defendant who had arranged a fraud on the state of Michigan in Chicago, Illinois, Holmes wrote: "Acts done outside a jurisdiction but intended to produce and producing detrimental effects within it, justify a state in punishing the cause of the harm as if he had been present at the effect if the State should succeed in getting him within its power." *Strassheim* v. *Dailey,* 221 U.S. 280 at 285 (1911). American Banana's complaint was precisely that United Fruit had intended to produce and had produced a monopoly in the import of bananas to the United States. United Fruit was within the power of the United States. Two generations later, Holmes's "Acts done outside a jurisdiction" was quoted by Judge Learned Hand in the *Alcoa* case, as he made the most celebrated application of the antitrust laws to activity outside the United States (*American Banana* was mentioned only to be ignored) *United States* v. *Aluminum Company of America,* 148 F.2d 416 at 443. Half a century after Holmes's ruling, in 1955, the United Fruit Company was sued in the Southern District of New York for acts done in Honduras to a rival, and its New York counsel, Davis, Polk, Sunderland, Wardwell and Kiendl, dusted off *American Banana* as a bar to suit. The trial judge, John F. X. McGohey, said, "The facts here alleged distinguish this complaint from that of the American Banana Company," but he did not find it necessary to say what the distinctions were, *Sanib Corp.* v. *United Fruit Company,* 135 F. Supp. 764 at 766 (S.D. N.Y., 1955).

Still, as late as 1958, Kingman Brewster, Jr., in *Antitrust and American Business Abroad,* could write on p. 75: "Given the doctrinal gap between *Banana* and *Alcoa,* it may be said that the counsellor can find little assurance." Discredited by Hand, untenable by Holmes's own test of jurisdiction, as doctrine the case still had power. But was it powerful if doctrinal analysis of its inadequacy was expanded by history?

4 THE PASSENGERS OF *PALSGRAF*

"the most discussed and debated,": William L. Prosser, *Torts* (1971 ed.), 254.

"Plaintiff was standing . . .": *Helen Palsgraf* v. *The Long Island Railroad Company,* 248 N.Y. 339, 340, 162 N.E. 99 (Court of Appeals, 1928); "The risk reasonably to be perceived . . .": 248 N.Y. at 344, 162 N.E. at 100; "his fellows": 248 N.Y. at 349, 162 N.E. at 102 (dissenting opinion); "we cannot trace the effect . . .": 248 N.Y. at 352, 162 N.E. at 103; "no such thing": *Idem;* "[P]ractical politics": *Idem;* "uncertain and wavering line": 248 N.Y. at 354, 162 N.E. at 104; "Assisting a passenger . . .": 248 N.Y. at 347, 162 N.E. at 101.

THE COMMENTATORS' HISTORY

Student Notes: *Michigan Law Review* (1928), 27:114; *Cornell Law Quarterly* (1928), 14:94; *Columbia Law Review* (1929), 29:53; see also *Boston University Law Review* (1928), 8:159; *Illinois Law Review* (1929), 24:325; *Minnesota Law Review* (1928), 13:397; *St. John's Law Review* (1928), 3:117.

Goodhart, Irving Lehman's nephew: Allan Nevins, *Herbert H. Lehman and His Era* (1963), p. 250.

Articles: Arthur L. Goodhart, "The Unforeseeable Consequences of a Negligent Act," *Yale Law Journal* (1930), 39, 449–67; Leon Green, "The Palsgraf Case," *Columbia Law Review* (1930), 30:789–801; W. W. Buckland, "The Duty to Take Care," *Law Quarterly Review* (1935), 51:637 at 647–8. William L. Prosser, "The Minnesota Court on Proximate Cause," *Minnesota Law Review* (1936), 21:19; at 31–33; Thomas A. Cowan, "The Riddle of the Palsgraf Case," *Minnesota Law Review* (1938) 23:46: Warren A. Seavey, "Mr. Justice Cardozo and the Law of Torts," *Columbia Law Review* (1939), 39:20 at 29–39, *Harvard Law Review* (1939), 52:372 at 381–391; *Yale Law Journal* (1939), 48:390 at 399–409; Anon., "Loss-Shifting and Quasi-Negligence: A New Interpretation of the *Palsgraf* Case," *University of Chicago Law Review* (1941), 8:729 (Anon = Albert A. Ehrenzweig, see Prosser, "Palsgraf Revisited," *Michigan Law Review* (1953), 52, 1 at 31. For further discussion of *Palsgraf,* see also Fowler Vincent Harper, "The Foreseeability Factor in the Law of Torts," *Notre Dame Lawyer* (1932), 7:468 at 472, 479; Richard V. Campbell, "Duty, Fault and Legal Cause," *1938 Wisconsin Law Review,* 402, 404; Charles O. Gregory, "Proximate Cause in Negligence—a Retreat from Rationalization," *University of Chicago Law Review* (1938), 6:36 at 44–7; Harland J. Scarborough, " 'The Unforeseeable Consequences of a Negligent Act' Reconsidered," *Rutgers Law Review* (1948), 2:196 at 197–8, 207, 212; Fleming James, Jr., "Scope of Duty in Negligence Cases," *Northwestern Law Review* (1952), 47:778 at 781–3.

Casebooks: Francis H. Bohlen, *Cases on the Law of Torts* (3rd ed., 1930), 144, 239; Walter H. Hamilton and Harry Shulman, *Materials from Torts* (materials prepared for the private and confidential use of the students in the course known as Torts given in the Yale University School of Law in the year 1931–1932); Leon Green, *The Judicial Process in Tort Cases* (1931); Edward S. Thruston and Warren A. Seavey, *Cases and Materials on the Law of Torts* (1939). Comparable treatment may be found in the fourth edition of Bohlen (1941), edited by Fowler V. Harper, 258, and in Harry Shulman and Fleming James, Jr., *Cases and Materials on the Law of Torts* (1942), 315.

Record: Austin Wakeman Scott and Sydney Post Simpson, Appendix A, *Cases and Other Materials on Civil Procedure* (1951), 891–940. (Hereafter *Record*.)

"The plaintiff was a Brooklyn janitress . . .": William L. Prosser, "Palsgraf Revisited," *Michigan Law Review* (1953), 52:1 at 2–3; "It has been, I think, always the formula . . .": *Ibid.*, at 32.

The record ignored: Fleming James, Jr., and Fowler Vincent Harper, *The Law of Torts* (2nd ed., 1956).

"The literature dealing with the *Palsgraf* case . . .": Leon Green, Willard T. Pedrick, James A. Rahl, E. Wayne Thode, Carl S. Hawkins, and Allen E. Smith, *Cases on the Law of Torts* (1968), 626.

"And Lilian began to cry . . .": Warren A. Seavey, Page Keeton, and Robert Keeton, *Cases and Materials on the Law of Torts* (1964 ed.), 355.

"Well, all I can remember is . . .": Helen Palsgraf, *Record,* ed. Scott and Simpson, 903.

"The Record in this case . . .": Prosser and Smith, *Cases and Materials on the Law of Torts* (3rd ed., 1962), 364. The 1952 edition had no reference to other facts. The 1957 edition merely cited Prosser's Cooley lecture by title.

"What the Palsgraf case actually did . . .": Prosser, *Torts* (1971 ed.), 254.

"the unwelcome task": Warren A. Seavey, "Mr. Justice Cardozo and the Law of Torts," *Columbia Law Review* (1939), 39:20 at 21; *Harvard Law Review* (1939), 52:372 at 373; *Yale Law Journal* (1939), 48:390 at 391; "In fact, in a majority of tort cases . . .": *Idem;* "entire record . . . from some interval . . .": *Idem;* "did his full part . . .": *Idem.*

"I am thinking of something . . .": Learned Hand, "Mr. Justice Cardozo," *Columbia Law Review* (1939), 39:at 10–11; *Harvard Law Review* (1939), 52:361 at 362–3; *Yale Law Journal* (1939), 48:379 at 380–1.

The Participants

COUNSEL

"Pennsylvania Station": *Record,* ed. Scott and Simpson, 892; "General Solicitor": Moody's *Manual of Railroads and Corporation Securities* (1924), 1,629; Heiserman, General Counsel: *Idem.*

McNamara's schooling: *The Martindale-Hubbell Law Directory* (1947), I, 1461.

McNamara's request for rulings: *Record,* ed. Scott and Simpson, 930–1.

Wood's schooling: *The Martindale-Hubbell Law Directory* (1934), I, 709; "Special Attention Given to the Interests . . .": *Hubbell's Legal Directory,* ed. Joseph A. Lynch (1926), appendix, 386.

Testimony of Helen Palsgraf: *Record,* 900–7; of Lilian: 922–4; of Elizabeth: 919–22; of Karl Parshall: 911–15; of Grace Gerhardt: 915–17; of Herbert Gerhardt: 908–11; of Graeme M. Hammond: 925–8.

Date of Hammond's examination of Palsgraf: Hammond, *Record,* 926.

Custom of contingent fees: Report of Committee on Contingent Fees, New York State Bar Association, *Proceedings of the Thirty-first Annual Meeting* (1908), 99; "as an inducement": Penal Code, Article 24, sec. 274, *Annotated Consolidated Laws of the State of New York,* eds. Clarence F. Birdseye, Robert C. Cumming, and Frank B. Gilbert (1918), I, 5637. Prosecution: *In re Tunnicliff,* 202 App. Div. 69 (1022). See also, "Discussion of Contingent Fees," New York State Bar Association, *Proceedings of the Fifty-first Annual Meeting* (1928), 168, 173.

Costs in lower court: Judgment, *Record,* 899; Dr. Hammond's charges: Hammond, Testimony, *Record,* 927; Helen Palsgraf's earnings: Palsgraf, 901; non-payment of Dr. Parshall: Palsgraf, 905.

CLIENTS

"very poor": Parshall, 914; $50,000: Wood, Complaint, *Record,* 897; biographical data on Helen Palsgraf: Palsgraf, 901, 905, 907; time of accident: Palsgraf, 901–2, Elizabeth Palsgraf: 920; weather: Palsgraf, 902; valise: Palsgraf, 906; crowd: Palsgraf, 906; Grace Gerhardt, 921; Lilian's errand: Lilian Palsgraf, 922; "Flying glass . . .": Helen Palsgraf, 902; fire engines and ambulance: Elizabeth Palsgraf, 921; trembling: Helen Palsgraf, 902; drink and taxi: Palsgraf, 904; visit by Long Island's doctor: *Idem;* call for Dr. Parshall: *Idem.;* visits to and by Dr. Parshall: Parshall, 912; where Helen Palsgraf was hit: Palsgraf, 903; stammer: Parshall, 912; "it was with difficulty . . .": Hammond, 926; "while her mind is disturbed . . .": Hammond, 927; "[M]ight this condition . . . ?": McNamara, 928; "Not while litigation is pending . . .": Hammond, 928; date claim filed: Statement under Rule 234, *Record,* 891, date of trial, *Record,* 900, 911.

Reargument denied: 249 N.Y. 511, 164 N.E. 564 (October 9, 1928).

Trackage of the Long Island: *Moody's Railroads and Corporation Securities* (1924), 1,618; officers of Long Island: *Ibid.,* 1,620; passengers: *Ibid.,* 1,623, assets: *Ibid.,* 1,622; operating income: *Idem.;* Pennsylvania's income: *Ibid.;* Pennsylvania's ownership of Long Island: *Ibid.,* 1,619, *The New York Times,* April 10, 1928, p. 40. Reasons for not paying dividends: *The New York Times,* April 10, 1928, p. 40; dividend announced: *Idem.*

Railroad-caused deaths and injuries: Interstate Commerce Commission, Bureau of Statistics, *Accident Bulletin* No. 93 (1925), 111; passenger deaths and injuries: *Ibid.,* 22; "collapse, fall, etc.": "explosives, inflammables . . .": *Ibid.,* 77; passenger casualties: *Idem.;* Long Island non-train casualties: 104; "arising in connection with operation . . .": *Ibid.,* 1; train service accidents to all passengers: *Ibid.,* 56; Long Island train service passenger casualties: *Ibid.,* 100.

JURY AND JUDGES

Humphrey biography: Obituary, *The New York Times,* December 12, 1940, p. 27; his estate: *Ibid.,* December 20, 1940.

"none of us would be able . . .": Humphrey, Charge, *Record,* 929; "The trainmen . . .": *Ibid.,* 930; "a nervousness which still persists . . .": *Ibid.,* 929.

Time of jury deliberations: *Record,* 931.

Seeger biography: Obituary, *The New York Times,* June 17, 1945, p. 26; Lazansky biography: Obituary, *The New York Times,* September 13, 1955, p. 31.

"caused the bundle . . .": *Palsgraf* v. *Long Island Railroad Company,* 222 App. Div. 166, 225 N.Y.S. 412 (1927); "It must be remembered . . .": 222 App. Div. at 167, 225 N.Y.S. at 413; "intervened . . ."; "the negligence of defendant . . .": *Idem.*

Biographical data on Andrews: *Who's Who in America 1922–1923,* 213; *Ibid.* (1928), 179; on Pound: *Who's Who in America 1922–1923,* 2,509; on Crane: Obituary, *The New York Times,* November 22, 1947, p. 15; on Kellogg: Obituary, *The New York Times,* September 7, 1942, p. 19; on O'Brien: Obituary, *The New York Times,* December 26, 1939, p. 19.

On Cardozo: Andrew L. Kaufman, "Benjamin Cardozo," *The Justices of the United States Supreme Court 1789–1969,* ed. Leon Friedman and Fred L. Israel (1969), III, 2,287–2,307. I am also indebted to Andrew Kaufman for information on Cardozo's father's later poverty and for the exact character of Cardozo's legal education.

On Lehman: Nevins, *Herbert H. Lehman and His Era,* 422 (inheritance); 46 (father-in-law's contribution and Crane's comment implying it was not unusual).

Salaries: *Judiciary Law,* Article 3, section 50, as amended in 1926, *Consolidated Laws of New York,* ed. William Edward Baldwin (1938); Non-ownership of Pennsylvania Railroad by Columbia and Cornell: 1974 communications to the author by their present treasurers.

"I wish that I could . . .": Irving Lehman, "Judge Cardozo in the Court of Appeals," *Harvard Law Review* (1939), 52, 364 at 369; *Columbia Law Review* (1939), 39, 17; *Yale Law Journal* (1939) 48, 387.

THE INGREDIENTS OF THE OPINION

"[T]o determine to be loyal. . .": Benjamin N. Cardozo, *The Nature of the Judicial Process* (1921), 64; "the social needs demand . . . the welfare of society": *Ibid.,* 65–6.

Holdsworth's account of the history of negligence: William S. Holdsworth, *A History of English Law* (1926), VIII, 446–59; "a very primitive basis": *Ibid.,* 447.

"Affront to the personality . . .": *Palsgraf* v. *Long Island Railroad Company,* 248 N.Y. 339 at 345, 162 N.E. 99 at 101; "in the history and development . . .": *Idem.*

Aristotle's analysis: Aristotle, *Nichomachean Ethics,* Book 5.

"a mechanistic philosophy . . .": Warren A. Seavey, "Negligence— Subjective or Objective?" *Harvard Law Review* (1927), 41, 1 at 28; "personification of a standard person": *Ibid.,* 9.

THE EYES OF THE ORACLE

"At first we have no trouble . . .": Cardozo, *The Nature of the Judicial Process,* 43.

"He must pose as a kind of oracle . . .": Hand, "Mr. Justice Cardozo," *Columbia Law Review* (1939), 39.9; *Harvard Law Review* (1939), 52:361; *Yale Law Journal* (1939), 48:379.

"More subtle are the forces . . .": Cardozo, *The Nature of the Judicial Process,* 11–13.

the color of her hat: Cf. Holmes, "The Path of the Law," *Harvard Law Review* 10, 457 at 458; "he [the lawyer] foresees that the public force will act in the same way whatever his client had upon his head."

"is a delicate business . . .": Lon L. Fuller, "American Legal Realism," *University of Pennsylvania Law Review* (1933), 82, 429 at 456.

On Cardozo and his father: See Cardozo's obituary, *The New York Times,* July 10, 1938, p. 30. On the basis of extensive research, Andrew Kaufman has concluded that the charges against Albert Cardozo in connection with the fight over the Erie are not substantiated by the available evidence; and I have modified my text to reflect this information received orally from him.

"a doubtful one . . .": *Patterson* v. *Hull,* 9 Cox 747 (N.Y., 1828).

Costs in the Appellate Division: Judgment of Affirmance, December 16, 1927, *Record,* 936.

Right to seize personalty for costs: Civil Practice Act, section 1520, *Consolidated Laws of New York.*

"signs and symbols . . . aspirations and convictions": Cardozo, *The Nature of the Judicial Process,* 173.

"The Establishment of a Permanent Organization . . .": "Report of the Committee on the Establishment . . . on February 23, 1923 at Washington, D.C."; The American Law Institute, *Proceedings* (1923), I, 1; Cardozo's offices: Statement by the Council to the Carnegie Corporation, *ibid.,* I, Appendix, 52 (Cardozo, a reporter); offices held in ALI, *ibid.,* I, inside cover page.

"the most important task that the bar . . .": *Report of the Committee on the Establishment of a Permanent Organization for the Improvement of the Law,* printed in The American Law Institute, *Proceedings* (1923), I, 3.

"the administration of justice is not impartial": Reginald Heber Smith, *Justice and the Poor* (1919), 8; "weigh . . .": *Ibid.,* 16; "a few striking, though hardly typical . . .": Henry W. Taft, *Occasional Papers and Addresses of an American Lawyer* (1920), 30; "being used by radicals . . .": *Idem.*

"the supreme value . . . the highest and ever-present duty": Elihu Root, "Some Duties of American Lawyers to American Law," *Yale Law Journal* (1904), 14, 63 at 68.

62,000 statutes, 65,000 decisions: Elihu Root, Address Presenting the Report of the Committee, American Law Institute, *An Account of the Proceedings at the Organization of the Institute in Washington, D.C., on February 23, 1923,* 49; "whatever authority . . .": *Ibid.,* 48; "that the time

would presently come . . .'': *Ibid.*, 49; "a restatement of the law . . .'':
Report of the Committee on the Establishment . . . American Law Institute, *Proceedings* (1923), I, 13.

"full of normal conflicts . . .'': Edward S. Robinson, "Law—an Unscientific Science," *Yale Law Journal* (1934), 44, 235 at 259, comparison to Council of Nicea, 261.

"Law never *is* . . .'': Cardozo, *The Nature of the Judicial Process,* 126.

"the greatest of our age . . .'': Cardozo, "Mr. Justice Holmes," *Harvard Law Review* (1931), 44, 681, 684. For a decision of Holmes comparable to that of Cardozo in *Palsgraf,* see *Spade* v. *Lynn and Boston Railroad* 172 Mass. 488, 52 N.E. 747 (1899) reversing a jury verdict for Margaret Spade, injured on a streetcar when the conductor removed a drunken passenger.

"for consistency, for certainty . . .'': Cardozo, *The Nature of the Judicial Process,* 50; "the constant striving . . .'': *Idem.*

"an echo of the infinite . . .'': Holmes, "The Path of the Law," *Harvard Law Review* (1897) 10, 478.

"overlord," Cardozo, "Mr. Justice Holmes," *Harvard Law Review* (1931) 44, 681, 691.

"task of legal science," "will bring certainty . . .'': Benjamin N. Cardozo, *The Growth of the Law* (1924), 1.

"a very considerable . . .'': William Draper Lewis, Introduction, *Restatement of Torts* (1934), xii–xiii.

"a perfect illustration": Prosser, "Palsgraf Revisited," *Michigan Law Review* (1953) 52:1ˀ, 4; "an eminent and entirely impartial group": *Idem.;* "long and lively": *Idem.* Preparation of Seavey's article for the Restatement: Seavey, "Negligence—Subjective or Objective?" *Harvard Law Review* (1927), 41, 1.

"Dean Prosser reports . . .'': Charles O. Gregory and Harry Kalven, *Cases and Materials on Torts* (1959), 337; "one of those accidents . . .'': Prosser, "Palsgraf Revisited," *Michigan Law Review* (1953) 52, 1, 4; "the process . . .'': Prosser, *Cases and Materials on Torts* (4th ed. 1962), 368. Eventually, section 165 became section 281.

"unintended consequences . . .'': See Robert K. Merton's seminal essay, "The Unanticipated Consequences of Purposive Social Action," *American Sociological Review* (1939), 1, 894–904.

"[M]any a common law suit . . .'': Cardozo, "Mr. Justice Holmes," *Harvard Law Review* 44:682, 685, quoted and applied to Cardozo in Andrew Kaufman, "Benjamin Cardozo," *op. cit.,* at 2,292; "a system of case law develops . . .'': Cardozo, *The Nature of the Judicial Process,* 35.

"A, a passenger of the X and Y . . .'': American Law Institute, *Restatement of the Law of Torts Preliminary Draft No. 20,* sec. 165, illustration under (f) (1928), *Restatement of the Law of Torts* (1934), sec. 281, illustration under (g).

For a comparable relation between a Cardozo opinion and the work of the Restatement, compare *Allegheny College* v. *National Chautauqua*

County Bank of Jamestown, 296 N.Y. 369, 159 N.E. 173 (1927), with American Law Institute, *Restatement of the Law of Contracts . . . containing New York annotations,* ed. Horace E. Whiteside (1933), sec. 90. I am indebted to Richard Danzig of Stanford Law School for drawing this analogy to my attention.

5 THE ALLIANCE OF LAW AND HISTORY

"Like Maitland before him . . .": S. F. C. Milsom, "Theodore Frank Thomas Plucknett 1897–1965," *Proceedings* of the British Academy (1965), 517. "That process by which old principles and old phrases are charged with a new content, is from the lawyer's point of view an evolution of the true intent and meaning of the old law; from the historian's point of view it is almost of necessity a process of perversion and misunderstanding." Frederick W. Maitland, "Why the History of English Law Is Not Written," *The Collected Papers of Frederick W. Maitland,* ed. H. A. L. Fisher (1911), 491. For a comparably pessimistic evaluation of the use of history by courts, see Charles E. Wyzanski, Jr., "History and Law," *University of Chicago Law Review* (1958), 26, 237.

The development of theological doctrine: John Henry Newman, *An Essay on the Development of Christian Doctrine,* ed. Charles Frederick Harrold (1949).

"the germ of some wider theory": Holmes, "The Path of the Law," 10 *Harvard Law Review* (1897) 475; "planted a congregational church . . .": *The Occasional Speeches of Justice Oliver Wendell Holmes,* compiled by Mark DeWolfe Howe (1962), 19–22; "the history of the moral . . .": Holmes, "The Path of the Law," 459. On Holmes's use of organic metaphors, see also James Willard Hurst, *Justice Holmes on Legal History* (1964), 23–5, 61–3. Hurst finds a greater awareness in Holmes of the limits of these metaphors than I can detect—even if Holmes did believe that "the mode in which the inevitable comes to pass is through effort," Holmes, "Ideals and Doubts," *Illinois Law Review* (1915), 10, 1, 2.

"an eye on the end of the story . . .": W. S. Holdsworth, *The Historians of Anglo-American Law* (1928), 116.

"Implicit" in the document: Holmes, "The Path of the Law," 466.

"The age of commentators . . .": Étienne Gilson, *The Spirit of Mediaeval Philosophy* (1936), 425.

Rethinking of a past thought: R. G. Collingwood, *The Idea of History* (1956), 282–302.

As Bickel has shown: the history of the Fourteenth Amendment was imagined by the majority in *Katzenbach* v. *Morgan,* 384 U.S. 641 (1966), see Alexander Bickel, *The Supreme Court and the Idea of Progress* (1970), 48.

"We must beware . . .": Holmes, "The Path of the Law," 474.

"The earth belongs": Thomas Jefferson to James Madison, September 6, 1789, Papers, ed. Boyd, 15, 392.

"The Neolithic Paradox": Claude Lévi-Strauss, *The Savage Mind* (1966), 13–16.

The scientific revolution and quantity: Lévi-Strauss, 16–20. On the shift to measurement in the scientific revolution, see e.g. Herbert Butterfield, *The Origins of Modern Science* (1956), 65–6.

since 1776: see Morton J. Horwitz, "The Emergence of an Instrumental Conception of American Law, 1780–1820," *Law in American History,* volume V of *Perspectives in American History,* eds. Donald Fleming and Bernard Bailyn (1971), 309–26.

measurement of social desire: Holmes, "Law in Science and Science in Law," *Harvard Law Review* (1899), 12, 456; "Social engineering": Roscoe Pound, "An Engineering Interpretation," *Collected Essays* (1923), p. 152.

"Only in such disciplines . . .": Frederick J. Streng, *Understanding Religious Man* (1969), 123.

"mainly negative and skeptical . . .": Holmes, "Law in Science and Science in Law," 452.

California marriage law: *California Civil Code,* secs. 4,500–4,503.

"Cognitive science . . .": Weston LaBarre, *The Ghost Dance* (1970), 598, n. 33.

Myth as a precondition: Robert Bellah, *Beyond Belief: Essays on Religion in a Post-Traditional World* (1970), 253–4; personal knowledge and physics: Michael Polanyi, *Personal Knowledge* (1964), xiv; for a review of new approaches in the understanding of biology breaking from a "physics-dominated metaphysics": Marjorie Grene, *Approaches to a Philosophical Biology* (1965).

"It is important not to make . . .": Lévi-Strauss, 22.

Community with the dead: Edmund Burke, *Reflections on the Revolution in France, and on the Proceedings in Certain Societies in London Relative to that Event,* Burke, *Works* (1869 ed.), III, 276. Burke's essay is a rebuke to the same Richard Price whom Jefferson addressed on Wythe's unequivocal opposition to slavery.

"Our dead brothers still live . . .": Holmes, "Memorial Day," 16. An Address Delivered May 30, 1884 at Keene, N.H. Before John Sedgwick Post No. 4, Grand Army of the Republic, in Howe, *The Occasional Speeches of Justice Oliver Wendell Holmes,* 16.

Index

Adams, Charles Francis, 82
Adams, Henry, 82, 105
Adams, John, 181
Adams, John Quincy, 40
aesthetics: of law, 23, 150
*Allegheny College v. National Chautau-
qua County Bank of Jamestown,* 197
American Banana Company, 75–6, 92–8,
100–4
*American Banana Company v. United
Fruit Company,* 94–6, 100–4
American Bar Association, 83, 123–4
American Law Institute, 145–51
Ames, James Barr, 117
analogy: in legal reasoning, 6
Anderson, Don Luis, 78
Andrews, William S., 112, 113, 132–3
Antigone, 31, 57
antinomies of law, 18
antitrust laws, 72, 86, 93–4, 102, 190
Aristotle: on history, 155; on justice, 136
Arnold, Thurmond, 71
Association of the Bar of the City of New
York, 125
Astua Aguilar, Don José, 77–80, 110
Augustine, St.: on justice, xii, 18, 137
Austin, John, 9–10, 12, 36
Averroës, 156
Ayer, A. J., 175

Beck, James M., 184
Bellah, Robert N., xiii, 198

Bible: provides model for judges, 15–16,
for incest laws, 43; present influence
of, 164
Bickel, Alexander, 197
Birdseye, Clarence F., 193
birth control, 43
Blackmun, Harry, 174
blacks, 39
Blackstone: on persons, 47; on slavery,
47–9; on sovereignty, 101; as model,
29, 49–50; criticized, 59
Blackwell v. Wilkinson, 45–6, 56
Boalt Hall, University of California,
Berkeley, 118
Bockenham's Will, 55
Bohlen, Francis, 116, 148
Bohr, Niels, 174
Bokonon, 27
Bologna, University of, ix
Boorstin, Daniel, 172
Boston University Law School, 67
Boyd, Julian P., 179, 180, 181
Brandeis, Dunbar, and Nutter, 185
Brandeis, Louis D., 143
Bregman, Leonard, 119
Brewster, Kingman, Jr., 190
Brodie, Fawn, 181
Brodnax, Lydia, 61–2
Brooks and Ball, 82
Brown, Michael, 30, 33, 61
Brown v. Kendall, 8
Buck v. Bell, 69

Buckland, W. W., 115
Burke, Edmund, 52–3, 166
Butterfield, Herbert, 198
Butterfield, Nan, 56

Cadwalader, John Lambert, 86
Calvinism, 107
carapace effect, 20–1
Cardozo, Albert, 143, 195
Cardozo, Benjamin N.: biography and
    personality of, 132–4, 143–51; view of
    Holmes, 23, 66, 105, 146–7, 150; of
    justice, 136–7; of judge, 140–1; of
    legal history, 135–6; of *Palsgraf* facts,
    111–12; present influence of, 166
Carswell, William B., 132
Castro, José Maria, 73
children: as slaves, 40, 45–6
Choate, Joseph, 91
Christianity: relation to law, 48, 164
Clark, Kenneth, 19
class interest: and law, 23, 30–1, 38–43,
    104, 133–4, 138, 142, 145
Clay, Henry, 32, 60
Collingwood, R. G., 157
Columbia Law School, 132–3
Columbia University, 133
communication systems: law as, 4–6, 14,
    24, 36
Comte, Auguste, 163
Conrad, Joseph, 65–6
conscription: as example of state power,
    69
Constable, Giles, viii
Cornell University, 133
corruption of public officials: as business
    method, 65, 76; as law school subject,
    70
Costa Rica, Republic of, 88–92, 95–6,
    101–4
costs: of legal process, 144–5
Cowan, Thomas A., 115
Cox, Macgrane, 184
Cox, Theodore S., 177
Coxe, Alfred C., 100
Crane, Frederick, 132–4
Creon, 31, 58
Cromwell, William Nelson, 78
Cupid (slave), 36
Curtis, Benjamin, 96

Danzig, Richard, 197
Darwinism: in legal history, 8, 70, 135–6

Daube, David, viii, 181
Davis, David Brion, 57, 179, 181
Davis, Natalie, xiii
Davis, Polk, Sunderland, Wardwell and
    Kiendl, 190
Dean, Arthur, 184
death: response of law to, 15, 39–40, 55
Dedalus, Stephen, 27
delay: in litigation, 127–8, 145
*Deutsche Bank Filiale Nurnberg v. Hum-
    phrey,* 177
development of doctrine, 153, 157–8
Dobie, Armistead M., 180
Dorsen, Norman, xiii
Dunbar, William H., 185
Dunmore, Lord, 34
Dworkin, Ronald, 17, 174

economic forces: and law, 7, 38–41,
    133–4, 138
Ehrenzweig, Albert A., 115–16
Einstein, Lewis, 102, 106
Eliade, Mircea, 27
Emancipation Proclamation of 1775, 34
Emmet, Dorothy, 171
Engerman, Stanley L., 39
entailment: of slaves, 43–5, 54
enterprise liability, 115–16, 137
equity, 59, 98
Esquivel, Ascensión, 95, 110
ethics, canons of, 123–4
evolution: and legal history, 4, 8,
    135–6, 153
experience: necessity of for law, 3, 163;
    types of, 143
eyes: as symbol of person, 139–41, 151

face: as symbol of person, 19–20
facts: affected by jurisprudence, 141–2;
    as frozen, 148; irrelevance to analysts,
    x, 119, 141; problem of defining, 190;
    "pure," 107; reduction of, 141; rela-
    tion to the law, 107–10
family, *see* marriage
fatherhood, xiii, 30, 43
fees: of lawyers, 94, 124–5
Feldman, Joe, xiii
fictions, 25–6, 27
fidelity: to beneficiary, 30, 83–4; to dead,
    159, 165–7; to institution, 15; to law,
    90; to promise, 97, 162
Fletcher, George, xiii
Fogel, Robert Williams, 38

Forbes, W. Cameron, 83
force: and law, 12, 24, 36, 38, 48, 69–73, 108
Fowler v. Saunders, 55–6
Frank, Jerome, 10, 66–7
Frankfurter, Felix, 143, 182
Friedman, Lawrence M., 172
Fuller, Lon L., 10, 25, 141, 190
Fuller, Melville W., 103–4
future: foretelling of, 156; orientation of law to, 161, 164

game: as model for law, 10–12, 14, 87
Geertz, Clifford, 26
Genovese, Eugene D., 178
Gerhardt, Grace, 124
Gerhardt, Herbert, 124
Gilson, Étienne, 155
God: and masks, 27; as foundation: of equality, 46; of liberty, 34, 47, 49; as model: for judge, 16, 31; for law, 31; for legislator, 51; for sovereign, 107–9; as person, 27
Goodhart, Arthur L., 114–15
Gould, Jay, 143
Goya, Francisco de, 19
Gratian, x–xii, 158
Green, Leon, 115, 121–2, 118, 135
Gregory, Charles O., 122, 149
Grene, Marjorie, 198
Grotius, Hugo, 47
Guthrie and Cravath, 88

Hagarty, William F., 132
Hamilton, Walter H., 116
Hammond, Graeme M., 124–7
Hand, Learned, 121, 144, 190
Harlan, John, 102
Harper, Fowler Vincent, 118
Hart, Herbert L. A., 9–12, 17, 180
Harvard College, 73, 107
Harvard Law School, 82, 86, 115, 117, 133
Hawkins, Carl S., 192
Hay, John, 77, 79, 89–90
Hegel, Georg Wilhelm Friedrich, 153–4
Heiserman, C. B., 122
Hemings, Sally, 60
Hemphill, W. Edwin, 101
Henderson, L. J., 190
Herodotus, 31
Hinde, Thomas, 62
Hinde v. Pendleton, 62–4

history: and economics, 7, 172; evolutionary model of, 8–9, 135–6, 154; misery of, 156, 159; relation to persons, vii, 6–9, 165–7; terror of, 27; truth of, 157; use of by judges and lawyers, 55, 135–6, 152–3; value of to law, 27, 165–7; in Holmes, 159; in Jefferson, 159
Hobbes, Thomas, 14
Holdsworth, William, 135, 154
Holmes, Oliver Wendell, 107
Holmes, Oliver Wendell, Jr.: alienation of, 105; assets of, 104; childlessness of, 143; experience of, 68–9, 83, 182; person of, xii; in *American Banana*, 65–6, 102–10; in *Deutsche Bank Filiale Nurnberg*, 177; evaluated, 22, 23, 27, 66–71, 146–7, 150; views of law: 3–4, 9–10, 13, 40, 67, 71–2, 95, 102–3, 141; of doctrinal development, 153; of legal history, 8, 59, 161; of negligence, 196; of slavery, 10; of sovereign, 72–3, 103–10; present influence of, 166
Holt, John, 8, 55
Horwitz, Morton J., 198
Hough, Charles, 96
Howe, Helen, 185
Howe, M. A. DeWolfe, 82, 185, 186
Howe, Mark DeWolfe, 182
Howe, Fenner, Spencer, and Cocke, 92
Howell, 45
Howell v. Netherland, 45–6, 56
Humphrey, Burt Jay, 130–1, 149
Hurst, James Willard, 7, 172, 197
hypotheticals: use of by law professors, ix–xi, 119

imperialism, economic, 73–81, 83–4, 88–92, 105
impersonality: in presentation of rules, ix–x, 106–10, 113, 150–1
Innocent III, 16
intention: of legislators, 155, 158; of parties to contract, 155; of testators, 55, 155, 158
Ireland, Gordon, 183

Jaffe, Louis, vii, xii
James, Fleming, Jr., 118
James, Henry, 82, 105
James, St., 16
James, William, 82

Jefferson, Thomas: as lawyer, 45–6; as legislator, 46, 49–54; as reporter, 45; evaluated, 22, 27, 32, 50–3, 59; relation of: to Michael Brown, 30, 61; to Sally Hemings, 60; to George Wythe, 29–30, 147; on Blackstone, 59; on equity, 16, 59; on history, 159; on slavery, 33–5, 43, 45–6, 50–3, 59–60; present influence of, 166

Jessup, Phillip C., 185, 187

Jesus, trial of, 6

Jiménez, Don Ricardo, 81, 99

Joachim of Fiore, 163

Johnston, Joseph, 98–9

Jordan, Winthrop, 178

Joyce, James, 176

judges: appointment of, 133; canonization of, 8, 134; consistency in, 134–5; egos of, 32; impartiality of, 15–16, 18, 21, 30–1, 57, 63–4, 97–8; influences upon, 67, 114, 121, 133, 148; invisible companion of, 22, 140; salaries of, 133; *see also* Andrews, Blackmun, Blackstone, Brandeis, Cardozo, A., Cardozo, B., Coxe, Crane, Curtis, Frank, Frankfurter, Fuller, M., Hagarty, Hand, Harlan, Holmes, Holt, Hough, Howe, Humphrey, Kellogg, Lacombe, Lazansky, Lehman, Lowell, F., McCormick, McGohey, Mansfield, Marshall, J., Marshall, R., Noyes, O'Brien, Pardee, Seeger, Shaw, Shelby, Story, Toulmin, Tucker, Wythe, Wyzanski, Young

jurisprudence: effect on perspective, 141–2; varieties of, 9–13, 70

justice: as virtue, xii; in Aristotle, 136; in Augustine, xii, 18; in Cardozo, 136–7; in Calcidius, 174; and class, 30–1, 138, 142, 145; paradigms of, 5–6, 15–16, 30–1; relation to process, 81, 99–100, 138–9

Justinian, 55

Kadish, Mortimer, 17

Kadish, Sanford H., 1, 17

Kalven, Harry, 122, 149

Kaufman, Andrew L., xiii, 143, 194–6

Kawanakoa v. Polybank, 189

Kean, John, 99

Keany, Joseph F., 113, 122, 125

Keeton, Page, 119

Keeton, Robert, 119

Keim, C. Ray, 178

Keith, John, 77, 80

Keith, Minor Cooper, 65, 73, 74, 77, 81, 110

Kellogg, Henry T., 132–4

Kelsen, Hans, 9–10, 13, 27

Kepner, Charles David, Jr., 183

Kreiger, Martin, xii

Kuttner, Stephen, 174

La Barre, Weston, 162

Lacombe, E. Henry, 95, 100

Langdell, Christopher Columbus, 71

law: as communication, 4–6, 14, 24, 35; as invisible companion, 22; as magic, 12, 24–25, 58, 159–60; 172, 177; as game, 10–12, 24, 87; as paper commands, 4–5, 84–5; as process, 4–5, 84–5; as science, 12, 17, 67, 147; as teaching, 12–13, 37–8, 41–2; as railroad system, 9–10; as religion, 13, 71–2, 84, 86, 134, 146–7, 161, 164; as social engineering, 9–10, 70, 161; as theater, 64; as war, 24; defining of, ix; existence in persons, 4; functions of, 12–13, 57–61; limits on, 31, 45–6, 57; personification of, 22; impossible laws, 53, 58; inconsistent laws, 42; monster sprung from law, 16–18, 26, 59

law firms, 81

law professors: in America, 28–9; as judges, 66; masks of, 21; methods of, ix, 49, 114–20, 149

law reviews, 7, 82, 114–15, 135

law students, 7, 114–15, 120–1

lawyers: advertising by, 124; fees of, 94, 124–5, 145; as historians, 152–3; as witness, 94–5; place in legal process, 4–6, 36; reputation of, 84, 86; *see also* Adams, C., Adams, J., Adams, J. Q., Ames, Andrews, Anderson, Arnold, Austin, Bickel, Blackstone, Bohlen, Brandeis, Bregman, Brewster, Cadwalader, Cardozo, A., Cardozo, B., Carswell, Choate, Clay, Cover, Cowan, Cox, M., Crane, Cromwell, Curtis, Danzig, Daube, Dean, Dorsen, Dunbar, Dworkin, Ehrenzweig, Feldman, Fletcher, Frank, Frankfurter, Friedman, Fuller, L., Fuller, M., Goodhart, Gratian, Green, Gregory, Grotius, Hagarty, Hand, Harlan,

Harper, Hart, Hawkins, Heiserman, Holdsworth, Holmes, Holt, Horwitz, Hough, Howe, Humphrey, Hurst, Jaffe, James, F., Jefferson, Jessup, Jiménez, Kadish, S., Kalven, Kaufman, Keany, Keeton, P., Keeton, R., Kellogg, Kelsen, Kuttner, Lacombe, Langdell, Lazansky, Leach, Lehman, I., Levi, Lewis, Lincoln, Llewellyn, Lowell, F., McCormick, McGohey, McNamara, Madison, Maitland, Mansfield, Marshall, J., Marshall, R., Mazor, Milsom, Mishkin, Monroe, Montesquieu, More, Nixon, Noonan, Noyes, O'Brien, O'Meara, Ong, E., Pacheco, Palmer, Pardee, Peabody, Pedrick, Pendleton, Plucknett, Pollock, Pound, C., Pound, R., Prosser, Pufendorf, Radin, Rahl, Randolph, Reich, Rodes, Root, Sacks, Scott, A., Seavey, Seeger, Shaw, Shelby, Shulman, Simpson, Smith, G., Smith, H., Smith, J., Smith, R., Smith, Y., Spencer, Storey, Story, Strong, G., Strong, G. W., Swaine, Taft, H., Taft, W., Thayer, E., Thayer, J., Thode, Thorndike, Thurston, Toulmin, Tucker, Weyrauch, Wheeler, White, Wiecek, Wirt, Wood, Wythe, Wyzanski, Young

Lazansky, Edward, 131–2
Leach, W. Barton, 61
Le Boutillier, George, 128–9
Lee, Thomas Ludwell, 50
legal education: ix–x, 6–7, 58, 70–1, 114–20, 132–3, 161
legal realists, 24, 66–8, 116
Lehman, Irving, 114, 132–4
Lehman, Mayer, 133
Levi, Edward H., 6
Lévi-Strauss, Claude, 159–60, 163–4
Lewis, William Draper, 177, 196
Lincoln, Abraham, 34, 84
litigants: part in legal process, see American Banana Company, Butterfield Nan, Cupid (slave), Hinde, Howell, Hudgins, Jesus, Long Island Railroad, More, Netherland, Palsgraf, H., Pendleton, Saunders, Socrates, Somerset, Spade, Swinney, Turpin, United Fruit Company
Llewellyn, Karl, 67
Locke, John, 41, 48

Long Island Railroad, 112, 122, 128–30, 144
Loomis, Francis, 185
love: relation to law, xii, 18, 84, 137, 167; to lawyers, ix; to roles, 21; to slavery, 48
Lowell, Francis Cabot, 95
Lowell, James Russell, 83

McColley, Robert, 177
McConnell, Herbert L., 75–81, 92–3
McCormick, A. P., 96–8
McGohey, John F. X., 190
McNamara, William, 113, 122–5
Madison, James, 41
magic: and law, 5, 24–5, 159–60, 172, 176
Maitland, Frederick, 152
Mansfield, Lord, 49, 59
Maritain, Jacques, 175
Mark Twain, 11–12
Marquand, John, 82
marriage: and recognition of persons, 43, 52, 69; experience of, 69, 143; creation of by law, 163; and fidelity, 162
Marshall, John, 3, 32, 60
Marshall, Roujet, 172
Martin of Braga, St., 171
Marx, Karl, 175
Marxism: and law, 23, 26, 175–6
mask: defined, 19–25; examples of, 20–1; as fiction, 26; and the dead, 155; removal of, 26–8, 167; used by Cardozo, 22, 27, 139, 144; used by Holmes, 66, 104–10; used by Jefferson, 27, 50–61; used by Wythe, 50–61; used by law professors, viii–ix, 21
Mason, George, 50, 175
Mauss, Marcel, 176
May, Stacy, 183
Mays, David John, 177, 178
Mazor, Lester J., xiii
measurement: of social desire, 70, 161
Merry, William Lawrence, 77, 79, 81
Merton, Robert K., xii, 190, 196
Mészáros, István, 175–6
metaphors: of law, 39–40, 44–5; for development, 153–4, 157–8
Milsom, S. H. C., 9, 152
Mishkin, Paul, xiii
Monroe, James, 32, 60, 62
Montesquieu: 47–9
More, Thomas, 6

Morrison, Elting T., 187
Moses, 16
Munro, Dana G., 184
Murray, Robert H., 180
myth: as foundation of discourse, 163

Nagera, Humberto, 175
nature: laws of, 31
negligence: legal analysis of, 70, 112–17, 134–9, 196
Nevins, Allan, 191, 194
Newman, John Henry, 153
New York Law School, 122
New York University Law School, 117, 122
Nietzsche, Friedrich, 179
Nixon, Richard M., 95
non-persons, 27
Noonan, John T., xiii
Nörr, Knut Wolfgang, 173
Northwestern University Law School, 115
Noyes, Walter C., 100

O'Brien, John F., 132–3
O'Meara, Joseph, Jr., xiii
Ong, Eugene, 183
Ong, Walter, S.J., xiii
options: in law enforcement, 36–7; in judging, 59, 140–1, 146

Pacheco, Don Ricardo, 78
Page v. Pendleton, 31
Palmer, Bradley W., 65, 73–5, 81, 85, 93–4, 109
Palsgraf: facts of, 111–12, 118–19; opinion in, 134–9
Palsgraf, Elizabeth, 124, 126
Palsgraf, Helen, xi, 111, 112–15, 124–8, 144
Palsgraf, Lilian, 119, 124, 126
paradigms: of law, 4–6, 15–18, 30–1, 152
Pardee, Don A., 97
Parshall, Karl, 12, 125–7
Pascal, Blaise, 97, 188
Paul, St., 16, 143
Peabody, James Bishop, 181, 189
Pedrick, Willard T., 192
Pendleton, Edmund, 31–2, 36, 45, 49, 50–3, 62–4, 87
Pennsylvania Railroad, 122, 128–9
person: defined, 27, 176; as body, 177; 136; as fiction, 27; like "gaslight at crossroads," 106; as property, 39–50; relation of to rules, 18; symbols of, 19–20, 139–41, 151
persona, 22, 27
personalty: as nature of slaves, 40, 44–5
personification: of prudent man, 139; of law, 3–4, 140; of principles, 18; in finding intention, 55, 155
Piaget, Jean, 22
Plato, 21, 23, 24
Plucknett, Theodore Frank Thomas, 152
Polanyi, Michael, 198
politics: and appointment of judges, 133
Pollock, Frederick, 102, 135
positivism: critique of, 17, 31
Pound, Cuthbert W., 132–4
Pound, Roscoe, 7, 9–10, 17, 18, 161
power: allocation of, 14–15; law as instrument of, 24; measurement of, 40; relation to love, xii; victims of, 19
precedents: place of in law, 71, 134–5
prediction: law as, 67, 73, 109, 147
Preston, Andrew W., 73–4, 93, 99, 110
Price, Richard, 33–4, 198
principles: personified, 17; related to rules, 18
property: as mask, 20–1, 39–50
Prosser, William, 111, 118, 122, 149
Prudent Man, xi, 139
Pufendorf, Samuel von, 47

Radin, Max, 173
Rafael v. Verelst, 101, 188–9
Rahl, James A., 192
Randolph, John, 30, 45
Rasselas, 13
Rawls, John, 48, 179
Rea, Samuel, 128
reason: use of in law, xi, 6, 55, 164–5
Reich, Charles, 163
reification, 23
religion: and law, 13, 71–2, 84, 86, 134, 146–7, 161, 164
responsibility: for participation in injustice, 53–4, 60–1
restatement of law, 146–51
revolutionary ideology: and slavery, 46, 50, 53
Richards, I. A., 174
ritual: and law, 5, 37
Robinson, Edward S., 146

Robinson, John, 31–2, 62
Rodes, Robert E., Jr., xiii
Rogat, Yosal, 105
roles: relation to masks, 19–21; to persons, 27; to service, 21
Roman law, 55, 58
Roosevelt, Theodore, 83, 87, 89–91
Root, Elihu, 66, 83, 87–92, 100, 107–9, 145–6
Rortz, Amelie Oksenberg, 26
rules: and law, 14–19, 66–7
Ryan, Thomas Fortune, 87

Sacks, Albert, xii
Sanchez, Tomás, 143
Sanib Corporation v. United Fruit Company, 190
Saunders, Lucy, 55–6
science: and law, 5, 8, 9–10, 12–13, 159–64
Scott, Austin, ix–xi, 117
Scott, Leslie, 189
Seavey, Warren A., x–xi, 115, 117, 119–21, 135, 139–41, 148, 171
Seeger, Albert H. F., 131–2
self: alienation of, 26, 175–6; disguises of, 22
Selznick, Philip, xiii
settlement: preferred to trial, 95–6; process in *Palsgraf*, 125–6
sexual crimes, 36, 43
Shapiro, Barbara J., 172
Shaw, Lemuel, 8
Shelby, David D., 97
Shulman, Harry, 116
Silber, John R., 180
Simpson, Sidney Post, 117
Sio, Arnold A., 178
Sisamnus, 31, 58, 144
slavery: dependence of on law, 60–1; in Blackstone, 47–9; in Hart, 11–12; in Holmes, 10; in Jefferson, 33–5; in Montesquieu, 47–8; in Rawls, 48; in Virginia, 35–43, 50–4; in Wythe, 33, 54–8
Smith, Al, 131
Smith, Gregory L., 76, 93
Smith, Harry T., 76, 93
Smith, Jeremiah, 135
Smith, Reginald Heber, 145
Smith, Young B., 119, 149
social contract: and slavery, 48
Socrates, 6, 21, 24, 62

sociology: compared to law, xi, 23; to history, 156
Soedjatmoko, 24–5
Somerset, 49
Somerset's Case, 49
Soothill, Jay Henry, 183
Southern Pacific Railroad Company v. Jensen, 190
sovereign: in Austin, 72; in Blackstone, 101; in Holmes, 72–3, 104–10; in Noyes, 100; in Root, 91–2
Spade, Margaret, 196
Spade v. Lynn and Boston Railroad, 196
Spencer, Walker B., 92, 94
Speyer and Company, 86, 88–9
Stendhal, 23
sterilization: by state, 69
Storey, Moorfield, 66, 81–5, 94–5, 99–101, 104–5, 109
Storey, Thorndike and Palmer, 81–2
Story, Joseph, 171
Strassheim v. Dailey, 190
Straus, Nathan, 133
Streng, Frederick J., 198
Strong, George Templeton, 86
Strong, George Washington, 85
Strong and Cadwalader, 85–6
Swaine, Robert, 187
Swinney, George Wythe, 61–2
Sydnor, Charles S., 175

Taft, Henry W., 85–9, 94–6, 101, 109, 145
Taft, William Howard, 83, 100
teaching: as function of law, 24, 37–8, 41–2, 51, 58, 66, 71–2
teleology: in legal history, 8–9, 139, 154
Thayer, Ezra Ripley, 82
Thayer, James Bradley, 84
theater: and law, 1, 64
Thode, E. Wayne, 192
Thomas Aquinas, St.: on acceptance of persons, 16; definition of person by, 27; on unjust law, 24
Thorndike, John L., 81
Thrasymachus, 21, 23
Thurston, Edward S., 117
Tillich, Paul, 13
time: effect on litigants, 127–8, 145; redemption from, 27
Tocqueville, Alexis de, 175
Toulmin, Harry T., 93, 98
Tournier, Paul, 174

transition cases, 48
trial: as ordeal, 95–6; as paradigm, 4–6
Tucker, St. George, 53
Turpin, Horatio, 54
Turpin v. Turpin, 54–6
Tweed, John Marcy (Boss), 143
Tyler, Lyon G., 177, 179

unborn, 40–1, 47
United Fruit Company, 65, 73–6, 92, 98–9, 101–3, 106–7
United States v. Aluminum Company of America, 190
unjust law, 24, 31

violence: relation to law, 24, 60–1
Virginia: slave laws of, 35–43, 44, 50–4
Virginia paradox, 57–8
virtues: and law, xii, 18; *see also* fidelity, justice, love
Vonnegut, Kurt, 176

war: and law, 24; impact of on Holmes, 68–9
war crimes, 83
Warren, R. K., 76
West, Benjamin, 31

Weyerhaeuser, Fredrick, 172
Weyrauch, Walter O., xiii, 172, 177
Wheeler, Everett Pepperell, 88–9, 94–5, 98–101, 106, 109
White, James B., 175
Whitney, William C., 87
Wiecek, William M., 174
Wigmore, John, 135
will: interpretation of, 55, 155, 158
William and Mary, College of, 29–30, 33–4, 53
Wilson, O. Meredith, xii
Wirt, William, 62
Wittgenstein, Ludwig, 11
Wood, Matthew W., 113, 123–6, 138, 144
Wrights v. Hudgins, 56, 180–1
Wythe, George: biography of, 29; murder of, 61–2; revision of laws by, 50–4; removes mask, 62–4; will of, 30, 61–2; as model, 29–32, 59–60; on judges, 54–61; on limits of law, 31, 46; on slavery, 33, 45, 54–61; present influence of, 166
Wyzanski, Charles E., Jr., 197

Yale Law School, 84, 116, 120, 145
Young, J. Addison, 132